William Lyon Mackenzie

Anthony W. Rasporich

Canadian History Through the Press Series

General Editors:
David P. Gagan, Anthony W. Rasporich

Holt, Rinehart and Winston of Canada, Limited
Toronto: Montreal
Distributed in the United States of America by Winston Press.

Copyright © 1972 by Holt, Rinehart and Winston of Canada, Limited

ISBN 0-03-925859-9

All Rights Reserved

Distributed in the United States of America by Winston Press, 25 Groveland Terrace, Minneapolis, Minnesota 55403.
It is illegal to reproduce any portion of this book except by special arrangement with the publishers. Reproduction of this material by any duplication process whatsoever is a violation of the copyright.

Printed in Canada

1 2 3 4 5   76 75 74 73 72

Anthony W. Rasporich, general editor of the *Canadian History Through the Press Series,* is currently Assistant Professor of History at the University of Calgary, Alberta.

David P. Gagan, general editor of the *Canadian History Through the Press Series,* is Assistant Professor of History at McMaster University, Hamilton, Ontario.

Editors' Preface

Newspapers are widely accepted by historians as useful vehicles of contemporary opinion. In a nation such as Canada, historically dependent on books and periodicals imported from Great Britain and the United States as the principal disseminators of informed opinion, the local daily or weekly newspaper has been almost the sole medium of information and attitudes. And the proliferation of Canadian newspapers since the early decades of the nineteenth century has created for students of Canadian history a vast reservoir of opinion reflecting the political, social, cultural, linguistic, religious and sectional diversity of our country. The *Canadian History Through the Press* series is an attempt to tap this reservoir by reproducing a cross section of journalistic opinion on major issues, events and problems of the Canadian past.

Using the press as a vehicle for the study of history has already been done with some success in the French series, *Kiosk,* which examines public issues and popular culture in volumes ranging from the Dreyfus affair to French cinéma. *Canadian History Through the Press* is not quite so ambitious a venture; but it does aim to introduce the student to events which were compelling subjects of discussion for Canadians through the medium in which public discussion most frequently took place. At its best, the Canadian press is a rich source of historical controversy, providing the historian with a sense of the excitement and contentiousness of contemporary issues. Newspaper editors like William Lyon Mackenzie, George Brown, Henri Bourassa and George McCullagh were themselves often at the centre of the political stage or were, like J. W. Dafoe of the Winnipeg *Free Press,* Joseph Atkinson of the Toronto *Star* and Gérard Pelletier of *La Presse* pundits whose voices were carefully heeded by national and local politicians. This is merely one example of the power of the press; but whatever the subject – Confederation, the Quiet Revolution, social reform, foreign policy or pollution – the press has operated (in Marshall McLuhan's words) as a "corporate or collective image [that] demands deep participation."

As editors of *Canadian History Through the Press* we are committed to the idea that students should be introduced to the study of Canadian history through contemporary documents from the very outset. The newspaper is a familiar, and therefore comfortable medium for the novice historian. We have chosen to use it exclusively, fully aware of the limitations of the press as an historical source. When a prominent Canadian politician observed recently that his colleagues spent much of their time "quoting yesterday's newspaper" he was acknowledging the power of the press not merely to reflect, but to dictate opinion. And Will Rogers' caricature of the man who "only knew what he read in the paper" is an equally cogent reminder that newspapers should not be used exclusively as a weathercock of opinion. The student, then, must and inevitably will come to grips with both the limitations and the advantages of newspapers as sources of history. In this respect, our series is also aimed at introducing the student to one of the historian's most crucial problems, that of discriminating between conflicting accounts and interpretations of historical events.

The volumes currently planned for the *Canadian History Through the Press* series embrace topics ranging from the War of 1812 to the Quiet Revolution of the 1960's, from economic history to religious issues. While it is not immediately possible, we hope that in time the series will eventually embrace an even wider spectrum of subjects which permit us to sample not merely the thrust, but the quality, of Canadian life.

David P. Gagan,
Anthony W. Rasporich,
May, 1972.

Author's Preface

It should be said at the outset that this book is not a definitive collection of documents on William Lyon Mackenzie. It is a partial selection of his editorial writings which range across a wide variety of subjects. Its main purpose is to let Mackenzie speak for himself without too much editorial interference. In a figurative sense he is on the historical analyst's couch expressing his attitudes and aspirations for and about himself and Canadian society. The danger of such an approach is that it might make him a one-dimensional figure, because only his perceptions and opinions are presented here. Because of limitations of space, it has been impossible to include editorial comment from other newspapers which either supported or opposed Mackenzie. Hopefully this one-sidedness has been resolved in this selection by a critical introduction, and by the balancing of flattering and unflattering documents throughout the text. A second difficulty of working with such a well-developed subject as Mackenzie is that a pre-existing frame of reference must be assumed. Historical controversy has swirled about Mackenzie ever since 1837, and the total body of that argument can only be touched on here. Students are therefore advised strongly to use the guide to further reading to broaden the limited dimensions of this study. Since no definitive treatment of Mackenzie yet exists, further exposure to the variety of historical opinion on him is almost mandatory.

Whatever contribution this volume makes to the study of Mackenzie, acknowledgement is due to a number of individuals who have helped it along. I am particularly indebted to my co-editor, David Gagan, who has been doing exactly what an editor should do, paring, pruning and sometimes performing necessary amputations. My colleagues in the Department of History at the University have been most helpful, either in making suggestions on the manuscript or on bibliography lying outside of the Canadian field. For deciphering my obscure microprints and even more obscure notations, I owe a great debt to Mrs. Marian Burke, who typed this manuscript with her usual efficiency. And finally, my thanks to the editors at Holt, Rinehart and Winston who have moved this project along at such a prompt rate.

A. W. Rasporich,
Calgary, 1972.

Contents

Preface v

Introduction *1*

Guide to Documents *16*

Section I   Newspapers and Biography *23*

Section II   Political Ideas *39*

Section III   Economic Ideas *89*

Section IV   Social Attitudes *111*

Guide to Mackenzie's Newspapers *147*

Selected Bibliography *151*

Introduction

The reader may well ask – why another study on William Lyon Mackenzie? Since the mid nineteen-fifties and the publication of William Kilbourn's *Firebrand*, Mackenzie has undergone a virtual resurrection. On the scholarly side, there have appeared at least ten articles in learned journals, an edition of his early writings, and a republication of the original Lindsey biography of 1862. A kit of Mackenziana has been assembled for classroom use, his colourful prose has been put into verse form by John Colombo, and films and radio scripts have been made about his life. And more yet will certainly be written on this apotheosis of English Canadian democracy. Professor F. H. Armstrong has recently predicted: "One fact appears to be certain: Mackenzie will remain the persistent hero; he and his rebellion are just too colourful to be shunted aside . . . and probably his remaining a hero is as it should be; our very constitutional, generally peaceful, somewhat alcoholic and quite sexless history needs some Mackenzies to keep it alive in the classrooms."[1]

Except for the final phase of his life after 1850, there is little that has not been discovered or told about Mackenzie. Yet despite this considerable body of biographical information, a hung jury has developed over the evidence he has left. On the one side there have been those who have cast Mackenzie in the role of a political and social theorist. For them, he was a man with a decided policy or policies which varied from Lockean constitutionalism to Bentham's utilitarianism and American Jacksonianism.[2] In contrast to these philosophical articles, there have been the debunkers of the Mackenzie legend. At the very least, he has been shown as an ineffective bog-jumper, running from clod to clod in search of temporary political victory.[3] At worst, he is seen as a "scandal-monger," and his role in the rebellion as "a cold comfort to the men and their families whose lives he had ruined and to the reform cause which he had greatly injured."[4] The difficulty with such conflicting interpretations is that the student is often left without enough evidence to make his or her own judgements. This void was partially filled by Margaret Fairley's edition of *The Selected Writings of William Lyon Mackenzie* which appeared in 1960. A fully documented reader containing Mackenzie's newspaper editorials and extracts from his major tracts and correspondence, it does however have some drawbacks. Since its chronological limit is 1837, it does not expose him to the indignities of exile and old age, and occasionally it overprotects even the young Mackenzie from the harsh winds of criticism. Leaning heavily as it does on his polemical addresses, broadsides, and manifestoes, it tends to place Mackenzie in the hagiographic mould of the popular tribune, martyred in the cause of democracy.

No selection of documents can fully escape the horns of negative and positive opinion. Controversy is the essence of Mackenzie. Hopefully it is sustained in this collection. But it should also be possible to avoid polemics and to seek a wider frame of reference. By extending the scope of analysis to include his social comment and his economic ideas, the student may be enabled to view Mackenzie as more than a good or bad politician. His newspapers were a mirror of a man and society in tension and transition. A significant segment of Upper Canadian society was ready for and demanded a colourful demagogue in the eighteen-twenties, a rebel in the eighteen-thirties, and found little use for either, except in a sentimental sense, in the eighteen-fifties. Central Canada had also moved steadily from an entirely agrarian region to a bustling commercial economy in the short span of Mackenzie's editorial life. Simply examined then in the light of changing circumstances, Mackenzie becomes a miniature or microcosm of Canadian historical development.

There are some difficulties inherent in the use of newspapers as the sole basis of discussion. Such an exercise necessarily precludes the use of private correspondence which might reveal more of Mackenzie's personal life and political motives. There is the added difficulty of not knowing absolutely whether Mackenzie wrote what he put into his editorial columns. The supposedly simple affair of attributing authorship to important statements of policy becomes especially difficult in the tangle of Reform organization just prior to the rebellion of 1837. More annoying was his casual treatment of private and public sources of information. Not only did he betray confidences, but he would also lift editorials without acknowledgement from the stacks of newspaper clippings which he had carefully numbered and classified for future use. Plagiarism notwithstanding, we cannot even be sure that he understood what he professed to have read, especially on such complex issues as banking policy. Operating at rapid speed to meet printing deadlines, he candidly apologized for his haste; but in his wake he left a tangle of misrepresentation, contradiction and jerry-built ideas. But whatever these limitations, and perhaps because of them, Mackenzie's newspapers made exciting reading and still do.

Considered as a journalist, Mackenzie belonged to an international fraternity of demagogues and disturbers of the peace. This colourful breed had been upsetting political applecarts all over Europe and America for nearly a half-century before Mackenzie entered the scene. John Wilkes had started it all in 1765 by scandalizing London with such grotesque pranks as releasing baboons dressed as satan into funeral services. He went further in his *North Briton* no. 45, which violently attacked King George III, and added a blasphemous *Essay on Woman* for good measure. Wilkes' libel charges, imprisonment, exile and constant re-election to the House of Commons provided future generations of journalists with a lively model to imitate in contesting the limits of free speech. In the revolutionary upheavals which then swept through western civilization, newspapermen were in the forefront of agitation. Propagandists like Tom Paine (*The Rights of Man*) and Jean-Paul Marat (*L'Ami du Peuple*) mobilized popular opinion behind the revolutions in both France and America. Even in England where the revolution failed, a colourful working-class press sprang up. Such titles as *Pig's Meat*, the *Black Dwarf*, *Gorgon*, and *Medusa* illustrated the sensationalism of the counterculture they represented. While the Tory repression killed off some of these underground newspapers after the Napoleonic Wars, the radical tradition was sustained, almost single-handedly, by William Cobbett through the eighteen-twenties. His epitaph might well have been written about Mackenzie – "Cobbett is a kind of fourth estate in the politics of the country, unquestionably the most powerful writer of the present day. The Reformers read him when he was a Tory, and the Tories read him now that he is a Reformer."[5] Then in the thirties, the Chartist press revived the corpse of working-class journalism. The new spirit of militancy was captured by the provocative motto of the *Poor Man's Guardian*, which boldly proclaimed that it was "Established contrary to Law, to try the Power of Might against Right."[6] In America, it was the age of Jacksonian democracy both in the eastern cities and on the frontier. Typical of the radical spirit which it generated among both labourers and farmers was William Leggett's *Plaindealer*, which thundered out the message of free trade against the chartered banks and privileged corporations of America.[7]

Of all the reform-minded journalists in British North America, Mackenzie was easily the most qualified for membership in this radical guild.

Other newspapers like Joseph Howe's *Nova Scotian*, D. B. Viger's *Le Spectateur*, and Étienne Parent's *Le Canadien* were either too parochial or too conservative to qualify. Mackenzie's uniqueness lay in his ability to cast his net far and wide in search of new and often eccentric ideas. Both personal association and intellectual affinity bound him to Jacksonian democracy and English radicalism. He regularly exchanged newspapers with George Evans of the *Workingman's Advocate*, and he subscribed for a time to William Leggett's ideas on free trade and direct taxation.[8] From England he appeared to borrow much in personal style and eye-catching invective from William Cobbett. While staying in England in 1832, he even visited with the grand old man of radical journalism whom he had often quoted in the pages of the *Advocate*.[9] Later in the thirties, Mackenzie became an ardent admirer of the Chartist press, particularly the Leeds *Northern Star*, edited by the Irish radical, Feargus O'Connor.[10] But the dispersion of Jacksonian democracy and Chartism in the eighteen-forties broke Mackenzie's faith in radical political ideas. Then he hitched his editorial car to the most popular social thinker in America – Horace Greeley of the New York *Tribune*. Once an employee of the *Tribune* and later its agent on returning to Canada, Mackenzie championed many of Greeley's favourite causes. Temperance, abolitionism, spiritualism, and homestead legislation were but a few of the social nostrums which Mackenzie transmitted to Canadians in the eighteen-fifties.[11]

Beyond the association of radical ideas, Mackenzie's newspapers reflected the bizarre character of this newspaper underworld. The diabolic and sensational were his stock in trade. He could conjure visions, and compared himself to the biblical prophets and romantic poets in possessing this divine gift. Ghastly images of his political enemies periodically wandered across the pages of his newspaper in the black robes of the damned. Grisly reports of every species of human misfortune gives Mackenzie's *Colonial Advocate* first claim to newspaper sensationalism in the Canadas. Axe-slayings of old women and children, and tales of human tragedy were all grist for his gothic mill.[12] Even his humour had a black quality. He delighted in ethnic dialect, often at the expense of the Jew or the Negro. His satire of the ruling class was much more direct and vicious, often aimed at the sexual foibles of tory nabobs, governors and clergymen. Typical of this kind of slander was his comment on Lady Colborne's and Mrs. Beverley Robinson's undue regard for a minor tory politician: "We are sometimes inclined gentle readers, to remember and apply the passage in Exodus, beginning 'and the Ass said unto Balaam, am I not thine Ass?' "[13]

Mackenzie's blackness is also an essential clue to his romanticism. He shared with the Romantics a common despair with the world as it was, against a common hope for the world as it ought to be. While he has been called by R. A. Mackay "a Puritan with a mission," he might also be considered a poet with a romantic social vision. In common with another Scot, Lord Byron, Mackenzie shared a Calvinist conviction in his own depravity as a youth. Similarly, Mackenzie's quest after an almost unattainable liberty resembles Byron's role in the Greek War of Independence. There are also strains of Robbie Burns in Mackenzie.[14] His Burns was an agrarian utopian who yearned for a world of democracy and brotherhood "when man to man the warld over, shall brithers be for a' that." Nostalgia for the rural past was yet another link which bound him to Burns, and to the Waverley novels of Sir Walter Scott. While their vision of pastoral simplicity was a gross distortion of the harsh realities of early Highland society, it was nevertheless a broadly accepted one which many Scottish emigrants carried with them into the colonies. For Mackenzie personally, that nostalgia was expressed in an arcadian view of his native Perthshire before the Jacobite Rebellion and the defeat of Bonnie Prince Charlie in 1745.[15]

Mackenzie also fits the anti-rational mould of romanticism. Some of its basic symptoms have been suggested in Isaiah Berlin's description of the romantic mind: – its concern with subjective or creative activity over and against the objective or real; a stress on the quality of vision, right attitudes of mind and heart rather than right answers provided by reason; and self-sacrifice as an ennobling ideal rather than worship of programmes in the abstract.[16] That Mackenzie himself deplored intellectual systems and dogma is reflected in a favourite passage from the French romantic, Robert de Lammenais: "There is nothing more pernicious than systems purely intellectual, especially if they exhibit a thoroughly uncompromising character . . . than economical or philosophical speculations which are not applicable at the moment."[17] Policies were temporary expedients honestly arrived at, and discarded if no longer applicable. Thus neither free trade, responsible government, nor elective institutions were ever metaphysical absolutes to him. Nor did he accept that victory was essential on any one principle, but instead believed that general human welfare and liberty might be advanced further by contesting a great number of issues with only partial success. If morally superior, lost causes were also preferable to victorious ones, and no one gloried more in old age than Mackenzie did in the personal sacrifices he had made for the "old Reform cause."[18]

A temperamental conservative, Mackenzie could never suppress a strongly felt prejudice, however much it ran against the grain of his liberal and rational beliefs. Thus Jews, Catholics, French Canadians and Negroes felt the butt of his satire and criticism, while Quakers and Indians remained curiously immune. Principles and institutions were in fact less important than the behaviour of men in determining Mackenzie's responses. As he said in the very first issue of the *Colonial Advocate*, "It is not the office which dignifies the possessor, but the man which renders honourable the office." Thus, institutions or forms were unimportant in themselves; rather more crucial were the particular uses to which good or evil men put them. To follow his political career then is not to pursue a rationally decided policy but to plot a zig-zag course of often contradictory moral judgements.

Accepting inconsistency as the norm in Mackenzie's political ideas is essential psychological preparation for entering the maze of contradictions they present. He began his career with the *Colonial Advocate* as a self-confessed whig. Such conservative beginnings were not unusual since most Scots politicians and journalists were either whigs or tories in the eighteen-twenties.[19] In this early phase, Mackenzie saluted all the whig symbols of social order and constitutional progress – the Glorious Revolution of 1688, the balanced constitution, and the landed English aristocracy. His political democracy at this stage was in fact confined to a narrow belief in John Locke's theory of popular sovereignty and the compact theory of government. Beyond that he paid some lip service to Jeremy Bentham's panglossian thesis that governments should govern in the interest of the greatest number.[20] But only in a limited sense did he express a conviction in social democracy for the farmers and mechanics of Upper Canada. If such a concern existed, the entire tone of the *Colonial Advocate* belied it. The farmers of the small backwoods colony must have rubbed their eyes in disbelief on encountering obscure literary references to the *Mysteries of Udolpho* and the *Castle of Otranto* in editorials devoted to political injustice in Upper Canada.[21] Even Mackenzie's political appeals to the people before 1830 were models of rationality and whiggish decorum, consisting usually of two closely printed pages which soberly argued the platforms of the reform party. In fact, it seemed at times that he was writing to impress the Family Compact, or what is morely likely, the aristocratic wing of the reform movement represented by Dr. W. W. Baldwin and his son Robert.

By 1830, Mackenzie had entered a radical phase of rising expectations which was to last until the mid-thirties. It appeared to be triggered by the cumulative effect of Andrew Jackson's presidential victory in 1828, the revolutions of 1830 in continental Europe, and the triumph of the Whigs with the Great Reform Bill in 1831. Shifting to accommodate these winds of political change abroad, Mackenzie adopted a radical posture at home. His wild temper was fully ventilated in the House of Assembly, resulting in repeated expulsions and angry recriminations against the dominant tory party. Failing to accomplish redress for his political grievances at home, he then visited England in 1832-33 and appeared to be on the verge of a major breakthrough in securing the support of the Colonial Office. But he returned to Canada only to find that the new Colonial Secretary had reversed the decisions of his predecessor. His anger and embarrassment then drove him to an irrational search for more radical solutions to Upper Canadian problems. But the nature of these reforms was still not clear in his mind. At times he claimed that it was the men who ran the government who had to be replaced, at others that the system itself had to be restructured along elective lines.[22] Nor does he appear to have abandoned hope in responsible government as a moderate solution to the Assembly's difficulties with the executive and the Colonial Office.

There is even less clarity to Mackenzie's revolutionary writings of 1836-37. A casual reading of his new journal, *The Constitution*, would suggest a strong attraction to American revolutionary thought and Jacksonian democracy. But there were anomalous strains of whiggism and utilitarianism in it as well. In some ways, Mackenzie's theory of rebellion can be interpreted as a conservative shift back to the whig theory of rebellion which he had articulated before 1830. He constantly argued that the British government had broken its Lockean compact with the people of Upper Canada, and that a bloodless revolution was possible to redress popular grievances. A further conservative feature was the pragmatic appeal that Mackenzie made to utility in reforming the political system in Upper Canada. He cautioned his readers in 1836 not to misinterpret his growing admiration for American institutions since he was not really concerned with institutions at all, but was "sincerely attached to that form of Government whatever its name, which can be proved to be best calculated to promote the innocent enjoyments, happiness and prosperity of the human race."[23]

On the eve of rebellion, there was also a wildly millenial and biblical flavour to Mackenzie's thought which placed it well outside of the mainstream of Jacksonian democracy. The uprising, as he saw it, would usher in the reign of the saints on earth, – "a government founded upon the heaven-born principle of Jesus Christ." It is in this messianic role that Mackenzie stepped far beyond the rationalist bounds of American republicanism into what Eric Hobsbawm has called the primitive rebel or social bandit, "the classical Robin Hood who was and is essentially a peasant rebelling against landlords, usurers, and other representatives of what Thomas More called the conspiracy of the rich." The Scottish prototype of this romantic revolt was, as William Kilbourn has pointed out, Bonnie Prince Charlie, "always away or in hiding, the incarnation of impossible loyalties, the secret hidden at the heart's core."[24] The rebellion Mackenzie led was less than a revolution, and more a mob action of rural protest. It expressed a vague desire to eliminate oppression, but followed neither a logically articulated plan of revolution nor a conscious military strategy. It led not so much to a brave new world, but to an old one where Christian justice reigned, where Mackenzie hoped "the lawgivers of Upper Canada will be found rejecting what is evil, and choosing what is good."[25]

This extreme puritanism and agrarianism was further hardened in the crucible of exile. By 1850, he was profoundly disenchanted with American politicians, whom he considered "idle, lazy, voluptuous," and for good measure, all politicians who were "the same selfish cold-blooded creatures, take 'em in gen'l everywhere."[26] After returning to Canada, he then settled into a mood of cranky agrarian sectionalism. By 1851, he was re-elected to the House as member for Haldimand in a bitterly fought election which pitted him against George Brown. But once elected and having established another newspaper, *Mackenzie's Weekly Message*, he became a glaring anachronism. He scarcely seemed to recognize the altered political structure of the Union and angrily called for its repeal. It was more apparent than ever that he had never understood the French Canadians, and his abstract sympathy for them wore thin under the pressures of Upper Canadian sectionalism. Worse still, he was losing his patience for his own constituents. He confessed bitterly to a friend that he had toiled for the people for "30 long years – with scarce a thank ye."[27] This misanthropy steadily worsened with old age. He retired from the Assembly in 1858 a tired and embittered old man. Then he closed down the *Weekly Message* in 1860, and withdrew into painful privacy until his death in August of 1861.

The tortuous character of Mackenzie's political ideas was given a further twist by his woolly economic policies. These had all of the bewildering charm and variety of Victorian patent medicines and purgatives.[28] They oscillated violently from protection to free trade, from state-controlled public improvements to complete free enterprise, and from a free banking system to none at all. The common root of these contradictory postures is difficult to locate, but there is an agrarian spirit which pervades them all. In common with many agrarian reactionaries of his age like the old Republicans of Virginia or William Cobbett, Mackenzie had formulated a haphazard economic and social philosophy based upon the emotional conviction that agriculture was the basis of a healthy, natural economy and a unified society. Such minds could not accept easily a theory of economic production based upon the profit motive, loose paper currency and convertible stock. The ultimate proof of agrarian superiority lay in the genetic waste which capitalism and urbanization created. To Cobbett's revulsion at the urban poor as "thin herrings, dragging their feet after them," we have Mackenzie's graphic query, – "Is the rickety and scrofulous little wretch that first sees the light in a workhouse or in a brothel, and who feels the effects of alcohol before the effects of vital air, equal in any respect to the ruddy offspring of the honest yeoman?"[29]

This agrarian conservatism made an odd couple with economic liberalism. In agreement with Adam Smith and the free traders, Mackenzie argued strongly for the elimination of monopoly and privilege as unnatural restraints on productivity. But he wanted at the same time to preserve an agrarian society and protect it if necessary with tariffs. A point that should be made here is that few exponents of free-trade in Great Britain had accepted by 1830 the idea of *laissez faire* as the self-regulating marketplace. As Karl Polanyi has shown in *The Great Transformation, laissez faire* usually meant freedom from monopolistic restraints against competitive *production* rather than free trade. It was not, he argued, until the 1840's that the Manchester School demanded the latter in their search for cheap bread and cheap labour.[30] Such cynicism was alien to Mackenzie. That he should propose protective tariffs at one time and a free trade area on the St. Lawrence at another

9

was a function of his fundamental lack of understanding or concern for the laws of commerce. His moral imperatives applied more to production of goods than to their distribution or consumption. This is especially evident in his radical constitutional demand in 1837 that there would be no incorporated trading companies or banks in his perfect state. Middlemen and the marketplace might even be eliminated entirely if they did not conform to the labour theory of value, the essentials of that age-old religious argument being that payment may properly be demanded by craftsmen who made goods and the merchant or forwarder who transported them, but not by the speculator who exploited public necessity for private gain.[31] While many economic liberals of the day would have endorsed Mackenzie's concern for free competition, few would ever have gone as far as he did towards throwing Upper Canada back into a medieval system of agricultural barter.

In spite of Mackenzie, the age of commercial revolution and free trade overtook Canada in the eighteen-forties. And, for a short time after his return to Canada, he was temporarily carried away by the gospel of free-enterprise and material progress. But as the decade wore on, he began to sour again. He started with his familiar enemies, the banks, and gradually widened his circle of criticism to include railways. As economic depression set in during the late 1850's, he reverted more often to the agrarianism which had been the bedrock of his economic faith. Unemployed labourers were advised to go into farming where they would be much less vulnerable to high-priced commodities. And more and more, he came to view the agricultural frontier in the United States as economic salvation for Canadians. That his competitor George Brown was promoting expansion to the Canadian Northwest, and his former mentor Horace Greeley of the New York *Tribune* was the prophet of American expansion, probably had much to do with Mackenzie's choice of the latter. It was not Brown but Greeley, the homespun social philosopher and promoter of the Homestead Bill, who kindled the agrarian imagination of Mackenzie for the last time.[32]

Agrarian conservatism also explains much about the unsystematic character of Mackenzie's social theory. If he had a social philosophy at all, it was a simple Calvinistic perception of good versus evil, their social personification being the humble poor versus the unholy rich. In his writings he made few acute distinctions as to social class which rested purely on economic function. He preferred to blur class lines by lumping commoners together whether they were farmers, labourers, or paupers; and aristocrats whether they were bureaucrats, rich merchants, or titled nobility. Ignoring in this way the potential tensions that could develop between farmers and town labourers, he papered over great cracks in the popular cause. It was evident that he himself favoured the farmer over the mechanic, and was only a fair-weather friend of trade unionism. There is good reason to suspect that the poor and the Negro slaves were less worthwhile than labourers because of their extreme economic dependence and greater social demoralization. As F. H. Armstrong has noted, Mackenzie, unlike many prominent reformers and even tories, was conspicuous by his absence from the patrons of the Mechanics' Institutes and anti-slavery societies. The same might be said of his championship of Toronto's poor. While he wrote delightful satire on the "soup kitchen" politics of prominent tories, there is little evidence to show that he himself did much towards the practical assistance of the poor.[33]

His attempts at social reform were equally haphazard and fundamentally conservative in their intent. Mackenzie was essentially a moral crusader, not a social reformer. His agitation against intemperance, prostitution, gambling and other social evils was designed to restore society to its pristine state before the advent of the city and the fall of man. His concern for mental health was in the same way little more than a wistful lament for bygone days of a happy rural life. In retrospect, his campaign against restrictive undergarments for women seems strange. Yet, it was probably a function of the same rebellion against the city that had driven William Cobbett to campaign against tea-drinking as a training ground for prostitution. On this issue at least Mackenzie was firmly on the side of British social conservatism, and against the radical tide of feminism which had swept the eastern seaboard of the United States. However much he admired Horace Greeley's moral crusades, feminism was not one cause which Mackenzie was prepared to import from New York, especially if it meant giving women equal pay for equal work. His sole concession to them would be to loosen their stays, but he would chain them more tightly than ever to their beds, stoves, and butter churns.

Only in the sphere of education did Mackenzie adopt a forward-looking programme of social reform. But even here he eventually receded into an agrarianism that denied his classical Scottish background. He had come to Canada with a rich inheritance of philosophy and classical education derived from the Scottish enlightenment of the eighteenth century. His *Catechism of Education*, despite its derivation from the English radical Joseph Hume, was heavily laced with references to Scottish philosophers like David Hume, Adam Smith, and Dugald Stewart. Mackenzie was also attracted to another Scot, Jeremy Bentham, and the utilitarian doctrine that education should always be in the interests of the greatest number. And in a practical way, he did much to promote the utilitarians' pursuit of Bacon's dictum that "knowledge is power." Before the rebellion, he actively participated in the formation of scientific societies, reading-rooms and libraries throughout Upper Canada. Even more central to his Scottish and utilitarian theory of education was his insistence on a greater role for the state in the promotion of public education and the creation of universities.[34]

This vision of a classical educational utopia for Upper Canada gradually faded during his exile to the United States. There he seemed to be caught up in the practical spirit of social democracy which swept the northeastern cities in the eighteen-forties. The two Horaces – Mann and Greeley – left an indelible mark on Mackenzie. Mann he admired for the magnificent overhaul he had accomplished on the public education of Massachusetts, and Greeley for his powerful social gospel of practical education and self-help.[35] Thereafter, an increasing note of anti-intellectualism is apparent in Mackenzie's writings. It was latent in his criticism of the academic colleges which sprouted throughout Canada in the early fifties, but undisguised in his later diatribes on Sir William Logan's Geological Survey. There was something incongruous if not ludicrous in Mackenzie's increasing waspishness, since Canada was finally in a position during the prosperous fifties to implement some of the reforms he had advocated twenty years before.

But that was the essential Mackenzie, the perpetual gadfly, always on the opposite side of actual progress, either too far ahead of it or too far behind. At a later point in time, he would have been a populist – a William Jennings Bryan or a John Diefenbaker. Always perplexing and paradoxical, such types characteristically defy rational definition. Their extraordinary capacity lies not in their ability to formulate policies, but to conjure visions that move men. And whether their projection be a negative one, like Bryan's "humanity crucified on a cross of gold," or a utopian one like Diefenbaker's vision of Canada's North, it ignites something basic in the human spirit. It is with these prophetic or charismatic individuals that Mackenzie should be judged. If verdicts are necessary, they should be based not so much on the particulars of policy, but on the qualities of his visions. Only such a willing suspension of rational disbelief can free one to get at the heart of Mackenzie's wild hopes for Canada, such hopes as he expressed on returning from the United States in 1850:

> I would like to live long enough to see Canada happy, and deservedly so – her sons united as one man to promote the common welfare, her lovely daughters rearing a young race of manly, mild, yet temperate freemen, and teaching them to hate every form of government through which the human mind is enslaved or enshrouded in mental or moral darkness, her hills and her valleys, her hospitable homesteads, towns and hamlets filled with tolerant, kindly citizens, each serving God as his conscience might dictate without fear or persecution or the hope of his recompense, and taking for his guide the Golden Rule. To this millenial state of things the worn out wanderer that now addresses you can scarcely hope to reach, but surely the child is born among you who will see it. We live fast in these times and the ball is rolling in the true direction.[36]

Notes to Introduction

1. F. H. Armstrong, "William Lyon Mackenzie: the persistent hero," *Journal of Canadian Studies* (August, 1971), 34.
2. In this category are articles noted in the bibliography at the back of this volume: Lillian Gates, "The Decided Policy of William Lyon Mackenzie"; R. A. Mackay, "The Political Ideas of William Lyon Mackenzie."
3. Most of F. H. Armstrong's articles on Mackenzie are of this iconoclastic type. See bibliography. Somewhere between the two poles of opinion is J. E. Rea's provocative article, "William Lyon Mackenzie – Jacksonian," *Mid-America* (July, 1968).
4. G. M. Craig, *Upper Canada, The Formative Years, 1784-1841* (Toronto: McClelland and Stewart, 1963), pp. 113, 249.
5. E. P. Thompson, *The Making of the English Working Class* (New York: A. Knopf, 1963), p. 627.
6. G. D. H. Cole, *Chartist Portraits* (London: Macmillan, 1965), p. 271.
7. E. Emery, H. L. Smith, *The Press and America* (New York: Prentice-Hall, 1954), pp. 192-212.
8. L. Gates, "The Decided Policy of William Lyon Mackenzie," *Canadian Historical Review*, XL (September, 1959), 201-202.
9. Charles Lindsey, *The Life and Times of William Lyon Mackenzie* (Toronto: P. Randall, 1862), I, 259-61.
10. M. Brook, "L. Pitkethly, D. V. Smyles and Canadian Revolutionaries in the United States, 1842," *Ontario History* (June, 1965), 82-83; *Mackenzie's Gazette*, June 8, 1839, December 23, 1840.
11. See, e.g., advertisement in *Mackenzie's Weekly Message*, November 17, 1853, seeking subscriptions for the New York *Tribune*.
12. Typical examples are "The Tragedy of Joseph Avery," *Mackenzie's Weekly Message*,

July 28, 1853; "Foul and Savage Murder," *Colonial Advocate*, December 2, 1830; "Plague of Fiery Serpents," *Mackenzie's Gazette*, July 28, 1838.

13. *Colonial Advocate*, March 8, 1832. For 'ethnic' humour see "A Few Ticklers ob de Panic by Jim Crow," *The Constitution*, August 23, 1837; "Lord Mansfield and a Jew," *Colonial Advocate*, October 5, 1833; "Jew Boy and Girl; Breach of Promise and Seduction," *Mackenzie's Weekly Message*, February 3, 1854.

14. "On Scottish Scongs," *Colonial Advocate*, October 7, 1824.

15. For more realistic accounts of Scottish life in the eighteenth century see John Prebble's works, *Culloden* (London: Secker and Warburg, 1961) and *The Highland Clearances* (London: Hillary, 1963).

16. Isaiah Berlin in an introduction to H. G. Schenk, *The Mind of the European Romantics* (London: Constable & Co., 1966), xvi-xvii.

17. *Mackenzie's Weekly Message*, December 1, 1855, a quotation from Lammenais' *Modern Slavery*.

18. M. H. Foley to W. L. Mackenzie, Simcoe, October 21, 1856, *Mackenzie-Lindsey Collection*, Public Archives of Ontario.

19. H. J. Hanham, *Scottish Nationalism* (Cambridge: Harvard University Press, 1969), pp. 70-71.

20. J. E. Rea, "William Lyon Mackenzie – Jacksonian," *Mid-America* (July, 1968), 228-29.

21. "The Late Trials," *Colonial Advocate*, April 29, 1828.

22. *Correspondent and Advocate*, July 2, 1835; W. L. Mackenzie to John Neilson, December 28, 1835, cited in M. Fairley (ed.), *The Writings of William Lyon Mackenzie* (Toronto: Oxford University Press, 1960), 345-46.

23. *The Constitution*, August 17, 1836.

24. E. Hobsbawm, *Primitive Rebels* (Manchester: University of Manchester Press, 1958), p. 4; W. Kilbourn, *The Firebrand* (Toronto: Clarke Irwin, 1963), p. 229.

25. *The Constitution*, August 17, 1836.

26. W. L. Mackenzie to A. N. Buell, Washington, D.C., March 15, 1850, *A. N. Buell Papers*, Public Archives of Ontario.

27. W. L. Mackenzie to William Carrol, Toronto, March 27, 1854, *Mackenzie-Lindsey Collection*, Public Archives of Ontario.

28. For a discussion of such panaceas as Henry George's single tax and other economic nostrums of the nineteenth century, see Robert Heilbroner, *The Worldly Philosophers* (New York: Simon and Schuster, 1968), chap. 7, "The Victorian World and the Underworld of Economic Ideas," pp. 154-91.

29. *Colonial Advocate*, April 26, 1827, "Open Letter to Lord Dalhousie"; J. W. Osborne, *William Cobbett* (New Brunswick, N.J.: Rutgers University Press, 1966), chap. 9, "Society on the Land," pp. 149-76.

30. Karl Polanyi, *The Great Transformation: The Political and Economic Origins of Our Time* (Boston: Beacon Press, 1968), p. 136.

31. R. H. Tawney, *Religion and the Rise of Capitalism* (New York: Mentor Books, 1958), p. 36.

32. For Mackenzie's disenchantment with the Canadian Northwest, see *Mackenzie's Weekly Message*, January 28, 1860, and for a description of Greeley's commitment to westward expansion, see F. L. Mott, *American Journalism: A History* (New York: Macmillan, 1966), pp. 271-78.

33. F. H. Armstrong, "William Lyon Mackenzie: the persistent hero," *op. cit.*, p. 26; "The Poor and the Tories," *The Constitution*, December 28, 1836; "The Relief of the Poor," *ibid.*, January 25, 1837.

34. For a discussion of utilitarian ideas on education see Elie Halévy, *The Growth of*

Philosophical Radicalism (Boston: Beacon Press, 1960), chap. 3, "Jeremy Bentham, James Mill, and the Benthamites"; no. 3, "The Education of the People," 282-96.

35. "Horace Greeley at the Indiana State Fair," *Mackenzie's Weekly Message*, November 17, 1853.

36. From J. E. Lesslie's *Toronto Examiner*, under Mackenzie's signature dated, Washington, 1850, cited in J. E. Middleton, *The Municipality of Toronto, A History* (Toronto: Dominion Publishing Co., 1923) I, 244.

Guide to Documents

SECTION I Newspapers and Biography

1. A Family History. *The Constitution*, February 8, 1837.
2. A Black Day in the Life of a Newspaper Editor. *The Colonial Advocate*, April 27, 1826.
3. The Necessity of Advertising. *The Colonial Advocate*, June 21, 1827.
4. Good and Bad Newspapers. *The Colonial Advocate*, September 16, 1830.
5. Mackenzie Embattled. *The Colonial Advocate*, July 8, 1830.
6. Tory Invective and Mackenzie's First Expulsion. *The Colonial Advocate*, December 29, 1831.
7. Tory Oppression and Re-expulsion. *The Colonial Advocate*, January 12, 1832.
8. Tory Newspapers and Postal Privileges. *The Colonial Advocate*, September 12, 1833.
9. Mackenzie as Mayor. *The Advocate*, April 10, 1834.
10. Mackenzie the Oppressor. *The Advocate*, June 5, 1834.
11. Enterprises Unlimited. *The Constitution*, July 19, August 10, November 12, 1836.
12. A Target for Assassination. *Mackenzie's Gazette*, [Rochester], October 19, 1839.
13. The Death of His Mother. *Mackenzie's Gazette*, [Rochester], December 29, 1839.
14. The *Gazette* Closes. *Mackenzie's Gazette*, [Rochester], December 23, 1840.
15. Fugitive Editor and People's Lawyer. *The Volunteer*, [Rochester], January 24, 1842.
16. An Appeal for Votes and Funds. *Mackenzie's Weekly Message*, July 7, 1853.
17. On the Hustings. *Mackenzie's Weekly Message*, July 17, 1854.
18. Mackenzie's Last Almanac. *Toronto Weekly Message*, January 7, 1859.
19. Disillusionment. *Toronto Weekly Message*, October 1, 1859.
20. A Personal Homestead from the People of Upper Canada. *Toronto Weekly Message*, January 28, 1860.

SECTION II Political Ideas

A. *British and American Whig, 1824-30*

1. British and American Liberty. *The Colonial Advocate*, May 18, 1824.
2. Agrarian Democracy and America. *The Colonial Advocate*, May 18, 1824.
3. Verse Satire on the Family Compact. *The Colonial Advocate*, May 27, 1824.
4. Anti-Americanism. *The Colonial Advocate*, October 7, 1824.
5. Libel or Satire? *The Colonial Advocate*, May 18, 1826.
6. British North American Union. *The Colonial Advocate*, December 14, 1826.
7. A Colonial Peerage. *The Colonial Advocate*, April 26, 1827.

8. "The Slayer of Ambrister" – Andrew Jackson. *The Colonial Advocate*, April 26, 1827.
9. The Social Sources of British Legislative Superiority. *The Colonial Advocate*, May 7, 1827.
10. "We the People...". *The Colonial Advocate*, January 3, 1828.
11. The Homely Virtues of John Quincy Adams. *The Colonial Advocate*, January 31, 1828.
12. The Lessons of 1688 and 1776 Compared. *The Colonial Advocate*, July 26, 1829.
13. On English-speaking Revolutions. *The Colonial Advocate*, March 11, 1830.
14. A Treatise on Aristocracy. *The Colonial Advocate*, September 16, 1830.

B. *Transatlantic and Colonial Reformer, 1830-1836*

15. France and the Transatlantic Revolution. *The Colonial Advocate*, March 26, 1831.
16. North America Applauds the Great Reform Bill. *The Colonial Advocate*, August 18, 1831.
17. A National Guard for Britain. *The Colonial Advocate*, December 29, 1831.
18. Political Unions for Upper Canada. *The Colonial Advocate*, December 13, 1832.
19. Scottish Politics. *The Colonial Advocate*, January 17, 1833.
20. Responsible Government. *The Colonial Advocate*, May 16, 1833.
21. The Colonial Office Defended. *The Colonial Advocate*, August 1, 1833.
22. The Family Compact Named. *The Colonial Advocate*, September 26, 1833.
23. Egerton Ryerson's Defection. *The Colonial Advocate*, October 26, 1833.
24. Honest Farmer-Government. *The Advocate*, March 13, 1834.
25. Joseph Hume and Revolution. *The Advocate*, June 12, 1834.
26. A Political History of *The Colonial Advocate*. *The Advocate*, November 4, 1834.
27. Reform Principles, 1834. *Correspondent and Advocate*, December 18, 1834.
28. The Grievance Committee Report. *Correspondent and Advocate*, May 7, 22, 1835.
29. Search for a Responsible Constitution. *Correspondent and Advocate*, March 28, 1836.

C. *Republican and Revolutionary, 1836-1837*

30. Ohio and Upper Canada Compared. *The Constitution*, August 24, 1836.
31. Colonial Precedents for Revolt. *The Constitution*, October 12, 1836.
32. Rousseau and Republicanism. *The Constitution*, February 15, 1837.
33. Response to Lord John Russell's Ten Resolutions. *The Constitution*, April 19, 1837.
34. Thomas Paine's *Common Sense* Printed. *The Constitution*, July 12, 19, 1837.
35. "Babylon Is Falling" – A Jacksonian Manifesto. *The Constitution*, July 26, 1837.
36. A New Constitution for Canada. *The Constitution*, November 15, 1837.
37. Sympathy for Lower Canadian Rebels. *The Constitution*, November 22, 1837.
38. A New Social Order. *The Constitution*, November 22, 29, 1837.
39. Mackenzie's Rebellion Broadside. *Mackenzie's Gazette*, [New York], August 18, 1838.

D. *American Exile, 1838-1843*

40. Fresh Breezes off the Hudson. *Mackenzie's Gazette*, [New York], July 7, 1838.

41. Lord Durham and the French Canadians. *Mackenzie's Gazette*, [New York], July 14, 1838.

42. Divine Right. *Mackenzie's Gazette*, [New York], August 4, 1838.

43. Lords and Ladies Undressed. *Mackenzie's Gazette*, [New York], August 11, 1838.

44. Louisiana and French Canada Contrasted. *Mackenzie's Gazette*, [New York], November 24, 1838.

45. Disillusionment with Republicanism. *Mackenzie's Gazette*, [Rochester], January 11, 1840.

46. Declaration for the Democrats in 1840. *Mackenzie's Gazette*, [Rochester], September 26, 1840.

47. The End of Republicanism in North America. *Mackenzie's Gazette*, [Rochester], December 23, 1840.

48. Conventions and the Repeal of the United Canadas. *The Volunteer*, [Rochester], April 17, 1841.

49. Responsible Government: a sham. *The Volunteer*, [Rochester], May 15, 1841.

50. A Democratic Manifesto. *The Volunteer*, [Rochester], June 19, 1841.

51. Mackenzie vs. Van Buren. *The New York Examiner*, October 7, November 11, 1843.

E. *The Old Reformer, 1852-1860*

52. Man's Progress. *Mackenzie's Weekly Message*, December 25, 1852.

53. Upper Canadian Sectionalism. *Mackenzie's Weekly Message*, June 9, 1853.

54. Independence or Colonial Representation? *Mackenzie's Weekly Message*, October 27, 1853.

55. An Open Letter to Lord Elgin. *Mackenzie's Weekly Message*, March 3, 1854.

56. America's Promise and Isolationism. *Mackenzie's Weekly Message*, March 24, 1854.

57. The Virtues of American Simplicity. *Mackenzie's Weekly Message*, January 12, 1855.

58. Dissolution of the Union and Elective Institutions. *Mackenzie's Weekly Message*, December 7, 1855.

59. On Governor Head and French Canadians. *Mackenzie's Weekly Message*, December 14, 1855, February 8, 1856.

60. An Old Reformer's Manifesto. *Mackenzie's Weekly Message*, January 11, 1856.

61. A General Convention in Upper Canada. *Toronto Weekly Message*, May 22, 1857.

62. The Indian Mutiny. *Toronto Weekly Message*, July 17, August 14, 1857.

63. The British Monarchy Praised. *Toronto Weekly Message*, February 19, 1858.

64. Old Wine and New. *Toronto Weekly Message*, August 30, 1859.

65. The Reform Convention of 1859. *Toronto Weekly Message*, November 19, 1859.

66. The Reformers on Union and Annexation. *Toronto Weekly Message*, December 31, 1859.

SECTION III Economic Ideas

A. *Agriculture, Improvements and Industry*

1. The Canada Company. *The Colonial Advocate*, December 16, 1824.

2. American and Canadian Canals. *The Colonial Advocate*, September 27, 1824.
3. The Welland Canal and John Beverley Robinson. *The Colonial Advocate*, February 21, 28, 1825.
4. Growing Disenchantment with the Welland. *The Colonial Advocate*, June 26, 1828.
5. Agricultural Protection against the United States. *The Colonial Advocate*, November 24, 1831.
6. Farmers vs. Merchants. *The Colonial Advocate*, March 1, 1832.
7. St. Lawrence Navigation: another Compact job. *The Advocate*, January 11, 1834.
8. Reciprocity with the United States. *The Constitution*, February 1, March 22, 1837.
9. Free Enterprise vs. Government Subsidies. *Mackenzie's Weekly Message*, November 17, 1853.
10. Railway Progress: two views. *Mackenzie's Weekly Message*, November 24, December 1, 1853.
11. A Native Steel Industry. *Toronto Weekly Message*, October 24, 1856.
12. Native Manufactures. *Toronto Weekly Message*, July 2, 1858.
13. Immigration and Land Values. *Toronto Weekly Message*, March 6, 1857.
14. Homesteads: Canada and the United States. *Toronto Weekly Message*, February 18, May 5, 1860.

B. Money and Banking

15. Banking, Speculation and Gambling. *The Colonial Advocate*, August 8, 1827.
16. Against Paper Money. *The Advocate*, February 20, 1834.
17. William Gouge on Banks as Corporate Monopolies. *The Advocate*, April 10, 1834.
18. The Banks Rated. *Correspondent and Advocate*, July 16, 1835.
19. The Farmers' Bank Bubble. *Correspondent and Advocate*, July 30, 1835.
20. The Bible and Banking. *Correspondent and Advocate*, August 6, 1835.
21. The Ill-Gotten Rothschild Fortunes. *The Constitution*, October 13, November 16, 1836.
22. Labour Theory of Value. *The Constitution*, May 24, 1837.
23. Go for Gold and Silver! *The Constitution*, May 17, 1837.
24. Mackenzie's Canadian Banking Policies Reviewed. *Mackenzie's Gazette*, [Rochester], September 7, 1839.
25. New Forms of Extortion. *Mackenzie's Weekly Message*, March 10, 1853.
26. Free Banking Laws in the United States. *Mackenzie's Weekly Message*, November 24, 1853.
27. Mackenzie and the Public Accounts. *Toronto Weekly Message*, January 25, 1858.

SECTION IV Social Attitudes

A. Labourers, Slaves and the Poor

1. Anti-Slavery. *The Colonial Advocate*, November 25, 1830.
2. Poverty in Great Britain. *The Colonial Advocate*, July 27, 1833.

3. Mackenzie and His Printers. *The Constitution*, October 26, 1836.
4. Negroes, Reformers and Bond Head. *The Constitution*, September 26, 1837.
5. Rich vs. Poor. *The Constitution*, November 1, 1837.
6. White Slaves and Black. *Mackenzie's Gazette*, [Rochester], May 11, 1839.
7. Abolition with Compensation. *Mackenzie's Gazette*, [Rochester], September 7, 1839.
8. Relief for Debtors in New York. *The Volunteer*, [Rochester], May 1, 1841.
9. Wage Slavery on the Railways. *Mackenzie's Weekly Message,* February 10, 1853.
10. Labour and the High Cost of Living. *Mackenzie's Weekly Message*, September 22, 1853.
11. Workers vs. Capitalists. *Mackenzie's Weekly Message*, August 25, 1854.
12. The Poor and the Depression of 1858. *Toronto Weekly Message*, March 5, 1858.
13. Free Trade in Occupations. *Toronto Weekly Message*, April 30, 1858.

B. *Religious Toleration and Minorities*

14. A Plea for Religious Tolerance. *The Colonial Advocate*, April 7, 1825.
15. Quaker Society. *The Colonial Advocate*, February 22, 1827.
16. Moses Swartz, the Wandering Jew. *The Colonial Advocate*, October 9, 1828.
17. In Defence of York's Catholics. *The Colonial Advocate*, January 1, 1829.
18. Brutalization of Indians. *The Constitution*, October 19, 1836.
19. The New Testament vs. Church Establishment. *The Colonial Advocate*, November 8, 1832.
20. Clergymen Denounced. *Mackenzie's Gazette*, [New York], December 8, 1838.
21. Religion in American Politics. *Mackenzie's Gazette*, [Rochester], September 26, 1840.
22. The Gavazzi Riots in Quebec. *Mackenzie's Weekly Message*, June 16, 1853.
23. Civil Marriages. *Toronto Weekly Message*, February 13, 1857.
24. Popes, Priests and Canadian Politics. *Toronto Weekly Message*, February 12, 1858.

C. *Moral and Social Reform*

25. Suicide and Social Disintegration in Upper Canada. *The Colonial Advocate*, July 29, 1829.
26. The Social Sources of Insanity. *The Colonial Advocate*, September 10, 1829.
27. On Raising Industrious Daughters. *The Colonial Advocate*, April 21, 1831.
28. Freedom to Breathe. *The Colonial Advocate*, June 14, 1832.
29. Sobriety and Honest Government. *The Advocate*, June 26, 1834.
30. Temperance for the Working Class. *The Constitution*, September 21, 1836.
31. Prohibition vs. Licensing. *The Volunteer*, [Rochester], April 25, 1842.
32. Feminism: a satirical affirmative. *Mackenzie's Weekly Message*, July 28, 1853.
33. Sabbatarianism. *Mackenzie's Weekly Message*, October 6, 1854.
34. The Maine Law and Prohibition. *Mackenzie's Weekly Message*, November 3, 1854.
35. The Lunatics: who will pay? *Mackenzie's Weekly Message*, February 10, 1854; April 16, 1858.

36. The Evils of Gambling. *Toronto Weekly Message*, January 4, 1858.
37. Prostitution and Its Remedy. *Toronto Weekly Message*, February 18, 1858.
38. Liquor Distilling for Export. *Toronto Weekly Message*, May 5, 1860.

D. *Education and Science*

39. A University for Upper Canada. *The Colonial Advocate,* May 18, 1824.
40. On American Colleges for Canadian Youth. *The Colonial Advocate,* May 27, 1824.
41. The Natural History Society of Montreal. *The Colonial Advocate,* July 23, 1829.
42. Mind, Morals and Education. *The Colonial Advocate,* November 19, 1829.
43. Anti-Scientific Toryism. *The Colonial Advocate,* July 9, 1831.
44. Industrial Revolution in Upper Canada. *The Colonial Advocate,* July 4, 1833.
45. Colonial Ignorance. *The Constitution*, December 19, 1836.
46. A Geological Survey of Upper Canada. *The Constitution*, July 19, 1837.
47. Free Thinking Defended. *Mackenzie's Gazette*, September 22, 1838.
48. American Education Appraised. *The Volunteer*, May 10, 1842.
49. The Nature of Disease. *Mackenzie's Weekly Message*, February 10, 1853.
50. Education and Civilization. *Mackenzie's Weekly Message*, September 29, 1853.
51. The Technology of Print. *Mackenzie's Weekly Message*, October 20, 1853.
52. An Interview with William Logan. *Mackenzie's Weekly Message*, June 23, 1854.
53. Electrical Cures for Cholera. *Mackenzie's Weekly Message*, August 18, 1854.
54. American Educational Reforms for Canada. *Mackenzie's Weekly Message*, February 1, 1856.
55. Agricultural Education. *Mackenzie's Weekly Message*, February 22, 1856.
56. Disenchantment with Logan. *Toronto Weekly Message*, June 4, 1858.
57. Higher Education. *Toronto Weekly Message*, December 24, 1858.

A Note on the Documents

Unless otherwise noted, the documents reproduced below conform, in spelling, grammatical usage and punctuation, to the originals. Since CANADIAN HISTORY THROUGH THE PRESS is, in a limited sense, a history of Canadian journalism, it has seemed advisable to preserve contemporary usage, however questionable it might appear to be, in order to illustrate the changing quality of Canadian journalistic writing.

TO BE SOLD BY PRIVATE BARGAIN,
The Presses, Types, and Printing
MATERIALS
Of the Office of the
COLONIAL ADVOCATE,

Consisting of

[1st.] The following articles purchased of Geo. Bruce & Co. N. York, in Oct. last, new and of excellent quality:

327lbs. Long Primer,
314lbs. Bourgeois,
25lbs. Pearl,
14lbs. Double Pica Antique,
9lbs. Double Pica Open Black,
About 25lbs. Minion Black, Long Primer Italian, two line, and title, 2 line Bourgeois, Pica Black, & Space Rules.
12lbs. Meridian Border,
22lbs. Leads, 6, 8, & 10 to Pica,
1 Sett of Braces,
10 Pairs New York made Cases,
A great variety of Ornaments,
120 Advertisement Rules 22 long primer ems wide intended for an enlarged edition of this newspaper.
48 Single Dashes, ditto,
36 Double, Double Single, and Single Rules,
36 Swell Dashes, and 4 Head Rules,

[2nd.] One Keg, 40lbs., finest Book Ink, from Morrison, N. Y. also about 40lbs. good news ink.

[3rd.] The establishment of the Advocate as I found it on my return from England, consisting of

1 Smith's Imperial Patent Press, (with 2 friskets,) in excellent order,
1 Second Hand Demi Ramage Press,
1 Handsome Foolscap Press, lately made by Ramage of Philadelphia,
3 Wrenches—1 Sheaves Foot—a Composition outside and 2 inside Kettles and Mould—2 cores for Rollers, and a Handle—an Ink Block—2 Ink Brayers and 2 Shovels—1 Imposing Stone and 2 drawers—a Bank and 2 horses.
1 Large and powerful Standing Press, with 20 walnut Boards, sorted sizes, from imperial down to post, and the necessary apparatus for screwing and unscrewing.
2 Demi Chases—2 Foolscap Chases—2 Half Chases Imperial—1 Card Chase—1 Chase for small Press.
5 Single and 4 Double Frames.
18 Cases of Long Primer, upper & lower case, in excellent order, partly worn—the Advocate will serve as a specimen of the quality—with a full upper & lower case of Italic, the whole estimated to weigh about 8 cwt.
12 Cases of Minion, upper & lower case, and 1 Case, upper & lower of Italic do., estimated to contain about 4 cwt. Specimen—the Advocate advertisements.
6 Cases of Pica and 1 of Italic—about 250lbs, and very little used.
1 Pair full Cases, Great Primer Script,
1 Fount Double Pica, Roman and Italics,
1 do. do. Small Pica do. do.

[From *The Colonial Advocate*, November 28, 1833]

Section I

Newspapers and Biography

1 A FAMILY HISTORY

The Constitution,
February 8, 1837

An elaboration upon an earlier article appearing in *The Colonial Advocate*, June 10, 1824.

"WHO IS THIS MACKENZIE?"

"A hardworking newsmonger of the Town of Toronto, who, like 'P. P. parish clerk,' might be of importance enough to himself to induce him to indite his own memoirs, but could scarcely expect that any body else would take the trouble to read them."

Such a question might reasonably expect such an answer. But it would be altogether too self-denying. W. L. Mackenzie is a far more significant character than Swift's "P. P." for he has become important to other people. His life and adventures adorn the columns of the truth telling *Patriot* of Toronto; his birth and parentage are retailed as commercial intelligence in the Montreal *Morning Courier*; while the St. Thomas *Liberal*, in the kindness of its heart wonders if so very little a fellow could have risen to so *high* a station;!! and, admitting the probability of the thing, reminds "the London world" that Daniel Defoe was a hosier, Columbus a weaver, Rear Admiral Shovel a shoemaker's 'prentice, Homer a beggar, [he should have said a ballad singer,] and the author of Don Quixotte neither more nor less than a private in a marching regiment!

". . . If all my subscribers, and they are many, had read the old Advocate, they would need no sketch from me of the origin of 'the little agitator' who made even a Major General shake in his shoes, although his name was Colborne, but as news readers, like the passengers in a stage coach, are made up of comers and goers, we shall suppose the vehicle going slow & easy, French fashion, while I gratify their curiosity as briefly as possible. My Mother, whom Mr. Dalton* wantonly and very ungenerously insults, is the oldest female inhabitant of this City, being now in her 86th year. Mr. Dalton is surely the first person who ever mentioned her name without kindness and friendly feelings. She has been a member of the Scottish Presbyterian Church for nearly three quarters of a century, and a woman of more unaffected piety and blameless deportment is seldom to be met with. Her father, Donald Mackenzie, who was of a highly respected Highland family near the Castletown of Braemar, in Scotland, took up arms for Charles Stuart, held a Captain's commission at the battle of Culloden, proved a trusty friend to his lawful Prince, accompanied him to the low countries, partook of his fortunes on the continent of Europe, returned to the highlands of Perthshire when it was safe to do so, and married Miss Elizabeth Spalding daughter of Mr. Spalding of Ashintully Castle, in Strathardale, a branch of the Glenkilrie family. – Her cousin, Mr. Spalding of Glenkilrie, married Miss Nairn the niece of Sir Wm. Nairn, Lord Dunsinane, and inherited his estates, another of her cousins, a Spalding, was the mother of the late Patrick Chalmers of Auldbar, and grandmother to Colonel Chalmers who, if I recollect right, is at present member for Montrose in the place of Mr. Hume. My mother is the eldest but one of ten children.

"My paternal grandfather, Colin Mackenzie, was a Farmer in comfortable circumstances, residing near the Spittal of Glenshee, also in the highlands of Perthshire – he obeyed the commands of Lord Seaforth, accompanied my maternal grandfather, and fought for the true King at Culloden, for which he afterwards suffered severely, in his worldly circumstances. His youngest son was foolishly advised to join the enemies of human freedom in the American war, and fell in battle warring by the side of a band of German mercenaries against Washington and liberty. My father's eldest brother Robert, married the oldest daughter and heiress of the Laird of Bermony, on the Isle of Strathmore, near Cupar; and, with his wife, died within a year and a half of their marriage. . . . within a few days of his brother's death, [my father] also died, leaving [my mother] in poverty, with myself, an infant of three weeks old. I was named after a relation of the Glammis family, and although my mother had to contend with many difficulties, she knew the value of a good education, and did not neglect mine. If her circumstances were straitened, the recollection has taught her son to take part with the humble – if I received early lessons in the school of adversity, those who have been witnesses of my public and private conduct will admit that they were not thrown away.

"Is the Chief Justice deserving of censure because his family, respectable and honorable as I learn it was, came to poverty by taking part with the King in what they considered a good cause? Is Mr. Hagerman, whose amusing family history at the time of my expulsion, enlivened the dulness of that weary trial; is he disgraced because his father was, by the fortune of war, left with a very small share of this world's means?

"I got an excellent education – several of my school-fellows are inhabitants of this city. Two of my uncles, with my mother's consent, articled me as a clerk to George Gray, the wealthiest as he was one of the oldest merchants of Dundee. I was at 15 admitted a member of the Commercial Reading-room. Before I arrived at that age I was an active member, and for some time Secretary of a Scientific Society, of which the late Mr. Edward Lesslie was the Vice-President. We were members together for several years.

"Although early instructed in the principles of religion and good morals, and kept constantly at school under excellent masters from the time I was five years old, I acknowledge that at seventeen I was reckless, wild, a confirmed gambler, and somewhat dissipated, (more so perhaps than I would like to own). But, even at that age my thirst for useful knowledge was unquenchable. At twenty-one I paused, threw down cards and dice for ever, and became temperate. Over twenty-one years have now nearly elapsed since I began to exercise that salutary self-control, leaving me a constitution so hale and sound that I hope to be able to weather the storms of *twice twenty one years more.*

"I was several years in Canada before I got so angry with the conduct of the executive as to resolve to step out of my way to oppose it. My Toronto neighbors first knew me when I had a share in the profits of the business now carried on here by the Messrs. Lesslie – next, as a person in business at Dundas, under the firm of 'Mackenzie & Lesslie,' and afterwards on my own account.

A thousand copies of No. 1, of the old '*Advocate,*' brought me at once before the Canadian people as a supporter of their rights, and in that capacity I have since enjoyed their confidence, and received the highest honors in their gift.

"My wife and I are natives of the same Scotch town – we were school-fellows – the Rev. Mr. Easton, of Montreal, married us in that city – and she has brought me a family of nine children. . . ."

* The vitriolic and ultra-tory editor of the Toronto *Patriot*. [ed.]

2 A BLACK DAY IN THE LIFE OF A NEWSPAPER EDITOR

The Colonial Advocate,
April 27, 1826

The life of a Farmer compared with that of a Printer.

The death of Thomas Smith,* with the circumstances that attended it, have in no small degree increased the dislike I have long entertained to the manner in which a country newspaper is and must be conducted in a small community. To publish a small political paper draws the attention of no one, and is care and labour uselessly bestowed. – To publish a large one, as I have done for some time, induces a great number of respectable persons to subscribe; and so far all is well. But the proprietor and editor is and must be a slave. – He toils from day to day to get forward; he perceives that his ideal profits are accumulating; that the list of his debtors is *rapidly* augmenting; that his prospects are *slowly* brightening; but he still must remain a *slave*. What with writing for the paper, dunning careless subscribers in all directions, receiving and answering letters, reading foreign journals (as a task,) correcting the press, attending to the directions, or weekly addressing an immense number of papers to hundreds of post-offices, collecting ways and means for carrying on his business and maintaining those whose dependence is placed upon him, sitting up on one or two nights of the week to superintend his publication, giving an every day's constant attention on the spot, entering accounts and posting his banks in a business carried on entirely by the leger, and where very few indeed think of paying him in advance, continually displeasing some of those he wishes most to please, and pestered with their ungenerous and angry expostulations, independent only that he may be the more acutely made to feel his daily dependence on all classes. Such is his life for six days in the week *all the year round*; and how think you is the seventh disposed of? If I would speak for myself I might truly say, that I am often so wearied and fatigued with the toils of the working days as to be perfectly unable to enjoy the rest provided by a kind providence on the Christian Sabbath. That instead of being fit to attend church, read the scriptures, or in any way engage in the duties of divine appointment, I am glad to lay me down on my bed or on a sofa, as a temporary relief from the effects of incessant toil. All this is bad enough, but there is one circumstance connected with a country newspaper which is still worse: Namely, the slavish dependence of masters upon their journeymen. A large newspaper requires many hands; if one or two desert you, you are most awkwardly situated. Of journeymen printers there are, perhaps, more than in a great many other trades, of what may be fairly termed *tipplers*; men who will be sober one day, tippling the next, and useless for one or two days in the week, all the year round.

In Upper Canada there is no choice except Hobson's, "this or none." A master printer is not like a carpenter or a shoemaker, who can at all times find abundance of working people in his calling. There are but few operatives; and consequently you must oftentimes introduce among your apprentices men who will make the printing house a scene of drunkenness and disorder; and, if you quarrel with them, your paper stops, and yourself must go off to the United States to hire at any price Yankee "helps" in their place, real water drinkers, but as stiff, as self-important, and as calmly insolent in their behaviour, as if they had, each in his own proper person, achieved their national independence, and brought about the peace of '83. These are facts in newspaper printing which I have long tried to disguise even from myself....

* A young journeyman printer formerly with the *Advocate*. [ed.]

3 THE NECESSITY OF ADVERTISING

The Colonial Advocate,
June 21, 1827

ADVERTISE FREQUENTLY

There is nothing in the line of our business which fills us with so much surprize as the indisposition to advertise in the newspapers which seems to be universal within this colony. This hostility to the press is by no means confined to those government journals, which, as a matter of course, have a very limited circulation, but extends itself to every establishment within the colony without exception. And here we mean to speak particularly of the advertising of storekeepers. If you take up an English country paper, or a Yankee paper, or a Quebec or Montreal paper, whether of administration or anti administration politics, you will find it studded with these printers' gems, "storekeepers advertisements." In the Lower province advertising is not confined to houses of yesterday, nor to individuals not yet fully established. – No. The oldest, the most respectable dry goods, or grocery, or hardware stores, inform the public through the news, when they receive new supplies, some briefly, some at great length, some for a week, some for a year. And they study their interest by doing so. A dozen lines continued in a newspaper for a month costs only a dollar and some odd pence to the advertiser, and he is by this means, and without the least trouble to himself, enabled to tell nearly the whole of his neighbourhood that he has received by the last steam-boat, such and such goods, which he will sell low for cash. If you do not read to day's paper, you may that of this day week. If you miss that also, the notice stands ready for a third and a fourth week, – and who will say that a brief account of your store thus displayed before town and country will not gain for you far more in sales than the paltry sum you pay the printer? ...

The advertiser has nothing to do with the politics of the papers he publishes in. If he chooses the Advocate and U.E. he is not thereby converted either into a whig or a tory, – he is merely aware that by means of his advertisements the articles he vends will become still more extensively known to the public, and that as a matter of course his gains will be increased, which is the chief end of a mercantile life. We would not wish a monopoly of mercantile advertising, but we would like to see it increase, and in that increase, of course we would hope for a share. The Colonial Advocate is to be found in every corner of the province – in town and in country – on the tables of the rich, and in the cottages of the poor – as well in the lieutenant governor's study, as in that of his greatest political opponent. It is read by all classes, and taken by all sides and parties. ...

4 GOOD AND BAD NEWSPAPERS

*The Colonial Advocate,
September 16, 1830*

... One important means of Education is the periodical press. Seven years ago, perhaps not more than 2000 newspapers a week were distributed in all Upper Canada – now, there are at least 8000, and the number is rapidly increasing. Sometimes their editors libel me, and sometimes they libel you – still, it would not do to muzzle the press: – "The free opportunity of censuring public measures is to the government a salutary admonition; to the people it is peace and freedom. As hostile to a government founded on a right basis it is nothing. Breathe against a rock and it will fall before you, when the pen of the most artful and daring libeller can shake a government worthy of public confidence."

I greatly regret that the periodical press has been degraded in this province, by being made the dernier resort of the venal, the profligate, and the unprincipled in society – of men ready to sell their mercenary labours to any party or faction likely to pay for them; it is a great evil. The public journalist, if he has "abandoned principle, if honesty of purpose, and a quiet conscience are not his, poisons the fountain and it sends forth bitter waters; fills the atmosphere around him with contagion, pestilence, and sorrow, and hurls amid the people 'firebrands, arrows, and death.' He becomes a gangrene to society, and rapidly consumes all that is fair, and all that is lovely. His corrupt and corrupting influence reaches even the children and youth, for they will read his columns, and he trains them up to depravity, wretchedness, and disgrace. Such a pest is the unprincipled editor to the community; such a pestilential atmosphere does he cast around him." It is among the young, the unexperienced and uninformed, that proflicacy [sic] commits the greatest ravages. It is unto the minds of the unguarded, the unsuspecting, that the unprincipled editor infuses the poison of his own, thus blighting the hopes of our country and spreading desolation around. Let parents then take care that no journal conducted by such a man, falls into the hands of their children. Let them take care that no such pestilence comes near their dwelling. It may mar the fair prospects of their children, may embitter the close of their own lives, and, its effects may be seen in the ruin of their families long after their heads shall have slumbered in the grave.

"The station which the editor of a public Journal holds is one of great responsibility. If he be a man of genius, of independence, of industry, and above all of principle, his Journal becomes to the community around him, an unfailing fountain of amusement and instruction. He gives to his fellow citizens more enlarged, more liberal views of moral, political, and intellectual subjects. He spreads before them from week to week a map of no common value, gives a healthy tone to public sentiment, corrects the misapprehensions of the people, and leads them onward to higher degrees of happiness and prosperity." ...

5 MACKENZIE EMBATTLED

The Colonial Advocate,
July 8, 1830

A Report of the meeting to organize the Home District Agricultural Society on May 15, 1830, in the Grand Jury Room, York.

There was a public meeting, open to all, free to all. The resolves of the previous assemblage were only provisional, and until the country could be brought to act in concert with the two dozen movers. No constitution or original established government had been adopted; the public or such of them as chose to attend were then met there to establish a society and frame laws and ordinances for its government. It was competent for the persons then present to say what should be the qualifications of a member, whether a 5s. subscription, or a freehold qualification, a seat in the Legislative Council, or House of Assembly, or any other modes of distinction they chose; and to whatever established system the majority might have voted or determined upon, the minority and of course the country would have submitted. – Had even the four farmers and the *aristoi* who were with them, agreed to a constitution or established the principles of a society on the 15th of May, we should have smiled at their assurance in applying for the public funds, but they waited for a little more of the public countenance – they advertised for it and they got it.

Before the question was put on the 2nd clause, *Mr. Mackenzie* rose and observed, that probably it would be difficult to get 60 directors advised to come together every time a board was called: – 60 persons scattered over perhaps fifty townships would require to have circulars sent them, and perhaps a smaller number would be more convenient for the transaction of business.

On this the Hon. John Elmsley, Sqr. Wood, Capt. or Lieut. O'Brien, D'Arcy Boulton and others of the official *gentlemen* round the table set up a loud shout in opposition to the speaker being allowed to make any observations. They hissed and clapped, and some beat with their feet. *Mr. Mackenzie*, however, refused to give way. If there was a question of order he would willingly see it discussed and abide by the opinion of the meeting as to the event. Mr. *Elmsley* replied that he should not allow him (Mr. Mackenzie) to speak to a question of order or any thing else. He (Mr. M.) was very obnoxious to the majority of the meeting – and he (Mr. Elmsley) was determined he should not speak. *Mr. Mackenzie* insisted (amidst a shower of hisses and groans from the official *gentlemen*) that he was as much a member as any individual there present, that the present meeting was called for the express purpose of declaring who should and who should not be members, and that if the public money had been given to it, as be that evening understood, that he (Mr. M.) had a good equitable right to come there and assist in making the constitution as liberal, useful and comprehensive as possible; that altho' his conduct in the legislature and out of it made him obnoxious to placemen, it did not hinder him from attempting to prevent them from having the sole management of the £100 per annum. But if what he proposed should be negatived, he would be content with having done his duty, for he certainly wished the society to be so constituted as to be useful.

These remarks met with great opposition.
...

During these attacks, the High Sheriff, and the other Honourable gentlemen, magistrates, &c. looked on and evidently enjoyed the riot. The hissing and yelling gave the scene a colouring as it were, quite in character with the actors. Mr. Mackenzie was only once struck at – by he believes, Mr. Gapper, – and as the cry of violence had been raised against him of old, by those whose conduct he had from time to time commented on, he had to bear even this assault, while held fast by the cabinet and the bench. . . .

6 TORY INVECTIVE AND MACKENZIE'S FIRST EXPULSION

The Colonial Advocate,
December 29, 1831

A report on the events in the Provincial Parliament.

Substance of the Defence Made by Mr. Mackenzie to Messrs. Willson and Samson's Charge of Breach of Privilege.

". . . it cannot even be alleged by my judges, the public agents for the Gore Mercury, (Messrs. Mount, Burwell, Shade, Ingersol and Robinson) owned by the learned member opposite (Mr. McNab) that that newspaper has changed and become more violent at the onset. Mr. McNab told us in his first that, 'Believing decency and good manners to compose some part of virtue, we shall endeavour to exclude from our columns all selections and communications having a contrary tendency. All personal reflections, private scandal, and vituperative attacks upon individual character, we openly declare we wish never to have even sent to us.' And in the very same number he gave several *delectable* verses at his own definition of this 'virtue' 'decency' and 'good manners.' I may as well give the House a specimen from his opening number, where he speaks of the [Reform] majority of the last House of Assembly:

> 'Each post of profit in the house
> To greedy sharks assigned,
> And public records of the state,
> Clandestinely purloined.
>
> The Attorney from the Senate House
> Endeavour'd to expel,
> Whose Hall they made look like a room
> Where raving drunkards dwell.
>
> For months this ribald conclave
> Retail'd their vulgar prate,
> And charged for two dollars each per day
> For sporting billingsgate.
>
> Two years their saintships governed us
> With lawless despot rule,
> At length a sudden change broke up
> The League of knave and fool.'

"After apportioning to your predecessor in that chair a due share of this decent poetry, the learned gentleman opposite, informed the people of Wentworth that their late representatives, of whom I was one, were so many 'juggling illiterate boobies – a tippling band – a mountebank riff-raff – a saintly clan – a saddlebag divan – hackneyed knaves'. . ."

---

7 TORY OPPRESSION AND RE-EXPULSION

The Colonial Advocate,
January 12, 1832

The annexed address, together with the paragraphs about the House of Assembly, in the "impeachment" of Thursday last, constitute the *libels* for which Mr. Mackenzie was re-expelled!!!

TO THE PEOPLE OF CANADA.

FRIENDS, COUNTRYMEN
AND BROTHERS!

Let it never be forgotten by you, that it is to the possession of a Free and Independent Press that Great Britain owes her greatness: that but for the absence of the censorship France would have ere now relapsed into her ancient despotism under the iron sway of Charles the 10th and that a shackled Press in Upper Canada would speedily convert your fifty representatives into fifty tyrants, in close and unholy alliance with trained bands of public robbers *elsewhere*. Remember, that wherever the Press is not free the people are poor abject degraded slaves; that the Press is the life, the safeguard, the very heart's *blood* of a free country; the test of its worth, its happiness, its civilization; and that thirty individuals "dressed up in a little brief authority," aimed a deadly thrust at this great palladium of your rights. The members of your legislature who contributed their aid to put down the free expression of public opinion, by violent means, in the case of the expulsion of Mr. Mackenzie, are ☞ J. H. Samson (with whom the dark proceeding originated), ☞ his seconder Asa Werden, ☞ Absalom Shade, ☞ Hugh Christopher Thomson!

☞ William Morris, ☞ Christopher A. Hagerman, ☞ W. B. Robinson, ☞ John Willson, ☞ William Willson, ☞ Henry J. Boulton, ☞ William B. Jarvis, ☞ Allan N. McNab, ☞ Richard D. Frazer, ☞ Alexander Fraser, ☞ William Berczy, ☞ George Boulton, ☞ William Chisholm, ☞ William Crooks, ☞ William Elliott, ☞ Henry Jones, ☞ Alexander McMartin, ☞ Charles Ingersol, ☞ Charles Duncombe, ☞ Roswell Mount, ☞ John Warren, ☞ Philip VanKoughnet, ☞ John Lewis, ☞ John B. Macon, ☞ John Brown, & ☞ Mahlon Burwell.

NOBLE CANADIANS! – See that ye inscribe their names and deeds in your most sacred family records; publish them in your schools and colleges; and teach your children and your children's children, that as they would desire to avoid bringing misery and destruction upon their beloved country, to take warning and avoid the pernicious example of these misguided men.

8 TORY NEWSPAPERS AND POSTAL PRIVILEGES

The Colonial Advocate,
September 12, 1833

It is well known that from its establishment, in 1829, until the present hour, THE PATRIOT, first published at Kingston and now at York, by *Mr. Thomas Dalton*, a director of the first Kingston Bank and late member for Frontenac, has had a considerable circulation by mail; but it is not so well known that during that period His Majesty's Government have ordered the Deputy Postmaster General to pass it through all the post offices of British North America free of all mail charges, an exemption not granted even to the official gazettes of the two provinces. – We find by reference to the returns of last July, signed "T. A. Stayner, D. P. M. G.," that, in 1829, *the Patriot* paid £5, or for 12 months' postage of only 20 newspapers; that in 1830, the paper passed free altogether, and that in 1831 it paid £6, or at the rate of 24 subscribers by mail!! Will Mr. Dalton be pleased to inform the public what were the secret services, other than his votes and his writings, which induced the government to frank his members through the country, while even the Courier had to pay postage! Mr. Dalton could see nothing amiss in the post office department last winter. There he stood alone. Was he hired to publish the offensive articles which appeared in his journal? It is well known that the late tory government tampered with the catholic priesthood of Canada, but it is not so well known that the violent newspaper printed by Mr. Dalton for the Catholics, was franked through all the colonial post offices by royal authority, and that for 1830 and 1831 "THE CATHOLIC," like the Patriot was an engine of the government under its especial care, passing through America post-free. Those who doubt these facts may see more by referring to the official documents on our table, and which we intend speedily to publish as our voucher for these assertions. If the Patriot shall explain we will publish the explanation; but if the answer consist of vulgar abuse, let the people look to it. . . .

9 MACKENZIE AS MAYOR

The Advocate,
April 10, 1834

THE CITY ELECTION

Last Thursday the election for a Mayor of this city, was held in the city hall, when 9 Aldermen and 10 Common Councilmen attended, and William Lyon Mackenzie, Esq. was elected Mayor by a vote of 10 to 8, (Mr. Mackenzie did not vote.) The minority did not intend to propose any other than a liberal candidate – they would have preferred Dr. Rolph to Mr. M., but that gentleman had withdrawn himself altogether from the corporation.

A special meeting or session of the City Council has been called by the Mayor and sits daily. It has already disposed of a great deal of important preliminary business, and we have no doubt that every exertion will be made by its members to promote to the utmost the welfare of the city and the prosperity and comfort of its inhabitants.

10 MACKENZIE THE OPPRESSOR

The Advocate,
June 5, 1834

A DECLARATION OF WAR, BY GEO. MONRO!!!

To William Lyon Mackenzie, Esquire,
  Mayor of the City of Toronto
    in the Province of Upper Canada.
SIR:

I do hereby, as the attorney of and for George Monro of the City of Toronto, Esquire, duly authorised in that behalf according to the form of the Statute in such case made and provided, give you notice that the said George Monro, will, at or soon after the expiration of one calendar month, from the time of your being served with this notice, cause a writ of capeas ad respondendum to be sued out of His Majesty's Court of King's Bench, for the Province of Upper Canada, against you, at the suit of him the said George Monro, and proceed thereupon according to law.

For that you, the said William Lyon Mackenzie, on or about the first day of April last, with force and arms, caused an assault to be made upon him the said George Monro, to wit at the City of Toronto aforesaid, and then and there caused him to be apprehended and seized and laid hold of, and to be forced and compelled to go from and out of a certain public room commonly called "The Town Hall," situate and being in the said City of Toronto, into the public street, there and also, to be then and there forced, compelled to go in, through and along divers public streets and places, to a certain police office, situate and being in the said City of Toronto, and to be unlawfully imprisoned and kept, and detained in prison without any reasonable or probable cause whatsoever, for a long space of time then next following contrary to the laws and customs of this province, and against the will of him the said George Monro, whereby he the said George Monro, was then and there not only greatly hurt, bruised and wounded, but was also thereby greatly exposed and injured in his credit and circumstances, to wit at the City of Toronto aforesaid.

And also for that you, the said William Lyon Mackenzie, on or about the day and year aforesaid, with force and arms, &c., caused an assault to be made upon him the said George Monro, to wit at the City of Toronto aforesaid, and caused him to be then and there beat, illtreated, apprehended and imprisoned, kept and detained in prison without any reasonable or probable cause for a long time then next following contrary to the laws and customs of this province, and against the will of him the said George Monro, and other. wrongs to him the said George Monro did to his great damage and against the peace of our Lord the now King.

Dated this twenty-third day of May in the year of our Lord one thousand eight hundred and thirty four.

  Yours, &c.
  Wm. H. DRAPER
Of the City of Toronto, Attorney
for the above named George Monro.
  Filed, 31st May, 1834.

11 ENTERPRISES UNLIMITED

The Constitution,
July 19, August 10, November 12, 1836

"The Constitution."

THE price of this Journal is *Four Dollars* per annum, whether called for at the Bookstore, delivered in town, or sent by mail, payable, yearly or half yearly, always in advance. No extra charge will be made for newspaper postage.

Companies of 6, 12, or more, desirous to subscribe for *the Constitution* by the quantity, and disposed to pay in advance will receive such a discount as may be agreed on at the time of subscribing.

Advertisements without specific directions, (which ought to be in writing) will be inserted until forbid, or until the day of sale in Auction notices, and charged accordingly. Orders for discontinuing advertisements are to be given to the Editor, or left in writing at the Book-store.

All letters, and communications, are to be

addressed to the Editor, at Toronto, and to be post-paid if sent by mail. . . .

*****

S. FISHER of London's Editions of the Following Works, for sale by W. L. MAC-KENZIE, *King Street*, viz:

BY ANN RADCLIFFE:
1–Mysteries of Udolpho, 2 vols. 9s.
2–Romance of the Forest, 4s. 6d.
3–Sicilian Romance, 2s. 6d.
4–Castles of Athlin and Dunbayne, 2s. . . .

*****

FOR SALE, by W. L. MACKENZIE, *King Street*, price One Dollar and a Quarter, THE CITY OF TORONTO AND HOME DISTRICT COMMERCIAL DIRECTORY, with Almanac and Calendar for 1837. . . .

*****

"CANADIAN EDITION OF THE SCRIPTURES."

W. L. MACKENZIE has imported from New York a copy of the OLD AND NEW TESTAMENTS on stereotype metal plates, in beautiful order, warranted under the hand of the agents of the Protestant Episcopal Church in New York, to be perfectly correct and of the approved version in use in the Protestant churches, and as printed in Scotland and England under royal authority. This Bible consists of about 900 pages 12mo. (or small 8vo.) and will be found very suitable for schools or private families. The types are in excellent order, and will print off any number of copies, from one to one hundred thousand, either of the Bible and New Testament or of the New Testament by itself.

Mr. M. would agree with a binder or with any person having on hand a large quantity of paper of a suitable size, to print such a number of copies as might be agreed on, and he trusts that those associations and individuals who exert themselves in circulating bibles, will extend their patronage to the first edition, he believes, ever printed within Upper Canada.

A specimen of the print and type will probably accompany the next number of this Journal.

King Street, July 18. . . .

*****

"PATENT MEDICINES, &c."
SOLD by W. L. MACKENZIE, at his store in *King Street*:
Soda and Seidlitz Powders.
Cheltenham Salts.
Whitehead's Essence of Mustard.
Hill's Pectoral Balsam of Honey.
British Oil – Godfrey's Cordial. . . .

12 A TARGET FOR ASSASSINATION

*Mackenzie's Gazette, [Rochester]
October 19, 1839*

From the Rochester Democrat, Oct. 15,

Narrow Escape. – On Saturday last about noon, Mr. Mackenzie of Toronto, now confined in the Jail of this city, went up to the window of his apartment and laid three letters on the cill, which he intended should be conveyed to the Post Office by his friend Mr. Kennedy, whom he expected at the front of the prison a little before noon. He had not been looking out more than half a minute, and was turning about, when a bullet came whistling through one of the panes of glass. Mr. Mackenzie instantly opened the window and called to the Jailer's youngest boy, who stood in the area, to tell him who had fired at the window. The lad, who had heard the report, said he did not know, and no one else was in view except a person near the stair of the brick blacksmith's shop opposite. On examination, the mark where a bullet had passed through the plaster was visible in the wall opposite the window, leaving the inference that the shot was fired from the other side of the mill-race. The Jailer, on inquiry, learnt that a tall stout man with a large fowling piece and a dog, was seen, in the direction whence the shot must have proceeded about that time; and he also found that a hole had been made with buckshot (which he has) in one of the panes in an adjoining window. To suppose that any one would mistake the grated bars of Mr. Mackenzie's windows, in the 3rd story of a large jail, for wild game is absurd. He is however truly grateful for his preservation.

REMARKS. – The *Democrat*, in another

number, thinks that because *day* and not night was chosen, the shot might have been the careless aim of some sportsman. That is impossible. The boy says, the shot came against the jail like a handful of gravel stones, and that one buckshot passed through a pane of glass and window blind in the room below Mr. Mackenzie's. Let any one look at the prison, and judge for himself, whether for the first time since it was built a sportsman could have selected noon on a gloomy Saturday; the moment when the stone-breakers and their overseers were out of the way; the very minute Mr. Mackenzie approached and looked out thro' the window; and when none was near but a little boy, to send a bullet past his ear, through one of the panes close to which he stood; across his room; and through the plaster opposite; scattering buckshot, breaking three other panes in his window and one in the window below? Who so credulous as believe this? Then, as to the choice of the day – Is there not a succession of reports from blasting rocks all the day round, so that people are used to such noises? – And did not Slippery Jack and the other rogues find broad daylight the safest time for escape? – And might not this tall *sportsman* with the fowling piece have pleaded *accident* had Mr. M. been beyond the prison bars and able to trace him at the moment? – Another curious fact is, that this very suspicious *accident* should happen within an hour or two after the publication and sale of last Saturday's Gazette. It co'd not have been done with a pistol; and judging by the course the ball took, the shot must have been fired from beyond the mill-race, whence any one could go where they pleased. We thought once, that if Mr. M. did not entirely lose his health from confinement he was safe from assassination in the strong box of old Monroe, but there may be doubts even as to that. The *Democrat* assumes that it was not a rifle shot. Who can say that it was not?

13 THE DEATH OF HIS MOTHER

Mackenzie's Gazette, [Rochester]
December 29, 1839

DIED

At Rochester Sunday last, at half past four in the afternoon, after a short illness, ELIZABETH MACKENZIE, widow of Daniel Mackenzie of Glenshee, in the highlands of Perthshire, Scotland, and mother of the editor of this Gazette, in the 90th year of her age.

REMARKS – My mother accompanied my wife from Scotland many years ago, and has ever since resided with me. As soon as the troubles in Canada permitted my family to leave it, she safely accomplished the journey from Toronto to New York, and when we removed to Rochester last January by land, she did not appear to suffer by fatigue. After my unjust punishment here she came four times on foot from our dwelling, a mile distant, to see me, and the impression seemed strong on her mind that as a family we were reserved for still more severe trials. For four months, I never once wrote to Mr. Van Buren, but as she said she was willing to undertake another journey to the south provided she could see me at liberty, I sent a memorial offering security to leave the country. The President paid no attention to it, three young children took ill, and at last my mother, whose strength I had supposed equal to many years of life, for her health was uninterruptedly good, took to her bed also. The moment she was taken ill I wrote to the President to permit me to see her, but had no hope that he would interest himself in doing so. Many persons who thought it cruel that an aged woman who had expressed the utmost anxiety to see an only son only for a few moments and be within a few minutes walk of her bedside, applied to Mr. Sheriff Perrin; but as Garrow the Marshal and Judge Conklin were in favor of the most severe construction of the sentence against me, the sheriff declined. At length the expedient was suggested that as I was a material witness in a certain case, it might be tried at my dwelling and I removed thither by writ of habeas corpus, which was done. The sheriff and jailer carried me home, the court was opened, and while the judge was hearing the pleadings, I was allowed to converse with my afflicted parent. The interview gratified her beyond expression; and fortunately she was as clear in the intellect as at any former period of life, and able to speak though slowly. After I returned to the prison she became speechless, and so continued till her death. It is right I should here state that the Sheriff's conduct throughout was kind, courteous, gentlemanly, and humane. He and the jailer behaved in this matter so as to deserve my grateful commendations and those of my family.

My mother was one of the oldest members of the Scottish Presbyterian Secession Church, – perhaps for about three quarters of a century. My father died while I was yet very young, but I cannot remember that any mother ever [?] in the many years she was my protector and instructress, or after I came to man's estate, to worship, God by singing, prayer, and reading the scriptures every morning and evening. She was unaffectedly pious, and a firm believer in the doctrines she professed. I asked her on her deathbed if she had that comfort for the future which she expected in former years, and found that she was as happy in the prospect of a blessed eternity as the most steadfast martyr of ancient days.

Her remains will be carried to Mount Hope for interment tomorrow, Wednesday, by strangers in a land of strangers. I only see the hearse pass but dare not accompany it. This is unjust and cruel in the government, which acts by partial not by general laws; but it is strong, and I fear too regardless of high principle, and I am weak and feeble, having for the last fortnight been afflicted by a wasting fever, a natural consequence of the painful confinement I am enduring, so foreign to my previous active habits of life, and so unsuitable to my advanced years.

Tuesday Dec. 24.

14 THE *GAZETTE* CLOSES

Mackenzie's Gazette, [Rochester]
December 23, 1840

THREE YEARS IN THE UNITED STATES

This Gazette is brought to a close, because I am unable to continue it, without such a weekly loss as would soon turn myself and my family out of doors, and because I am really somewhat doubtful whether mankind are enlightened enough to fulfil the duties that would be required of them under a system of political and social equality, which ours here is not. He makes a bad courtier who cannot flatter where praise seems undeserved, and a worse one who always blames justly. Perhaps the privations of the last three years, exceeding all I ever knew before, have blinded my vision in some of the beauties of American Democracy, and made the comparison with limited and absolute Monarchy and the Colonial yoke, less favorable to the former than heretofore. However this is, I am really and truly disappointed. To have kept clear of American politics would have shewn worldly wisdom, but I leant towards the party whose views appeared really favorable to the principle of self-government nor did I regret discussing general questions of state policy any where until I saw our prostrate millions fall down and worship their base enslavers. . . .

I have been compelled to dispose of my small establishment at one-third of its cost, and to abandon the Almanack and other publications. The support this paper gave to Van Buren and Johnson enraged the frontier people, and ruined it while a strong party felt indignant at my private and public remonstrances against the foolish project of an invasion at Detroit. In that city I had over 100 subscribers; they are reduced to six! In Watertown, Oswego, St. Alban's, Utica, Lewiston, Ogdensburgh, Lockport, Massillon, Port Ontario, and Cape Vincent, I had 200 subscribers, and have not now 30 in them all! . . .

15 FUGITIVE EDITOR AND PEOPLE'S LAWYER

The Volunteer, [Rochester]
January 24, 1842

TO SUBSCRIBERS FOR THE VOLUNTEER, & PERSONS INDEBTED TO ME. –

Those who have overpaid the Volunteer will receive another newspaper for the difference. Those in my debt will please to pay, when convenient. No letters for me should ever be mailed in a Canada Post Office.

. . . Little did I dream in those days of hope and fond expectation for freedom to all America, that I should live to beg in vain for a breath of the fresh air, after many months close confinement in a Rochester Jail, or that the legal monopoly I had abhorred in youth for its intolerance to worthy Americans, would be found enthroned at Albany and Rochester, in Supreme and County Courts, as exclusive, as partial, as aristocratic in principle and practice as in Canada.

"Why did you try to revolt, if this is so?" will be asked by the Canadian Loyalist.

Because the people CAN afford a remedy here, while in Canada they dare not even attempt it.

LAW OFFICE, ROCHESTER, N.Y.

Having opened a central office – No. 20½ State street, next door to Messrs. Gay & Stevens – for the practice of the Law, (so far as the honorable profession of an Advocate of the rights of the innocent and injured, in the Courts of this State, is not converted into a gainful monopoly for a few individuals,* by depriving the great body of the citizens of an equality of rights, in strict imitation of the worst usages of the British monarchy,) I respectfully invite some attention to the following statement: . . .

W. L. MACKENZIE.

---

* Mackenzie had been refused admission to the bar of the State of New York in December of 1840 on the grounds that he was not a counsellor at law before he arrived in the state. He continued to study law and perform minor legal services in the hope that he would be admitted when he became a citizen. [ed.] See L. Gates, "W. L. Mackenzie's *Volunteer*," *Ontario History*, LIX, 3, (September 1967), 164, 182.

---

16 AN APPEAL FOR VOTES AND FUNDS

Mackenzie's Weekly Message,
July 7, 1853

AN APPEAL TO UPPER CANADA REFORMERS SECOND HALF-YEAR OF THE MESSAGE

There are those who believe that the people are fickle, capricious and changeable: – that no length of service, no faithfulness to their cause, no amount of risk or loss, privation, insult, or suffering, borne or incurred on their behalf, can ever secure that public man who has never betrayed their interest, but always placed his trust in their gratitude or good will from sinking under their apathy and neglect.

My experience in Upper Canada during a public career of more than thirty years, leaves me as truthful and confident as any former period of my political journey. Often have I asked the people's suffrage for offices in their gift – never has it been refused – as a schoolmaster (for what else is an editor?), I have always had plenty of pupils. When sad adversity was my lot, those who might have gained wealth and honor as betrayers, preferred loss and injury as my friends. When the wages of years gone by were asked from York, Ontario, and Peel they were cheerfully paid with interest. Six months since, I asked, as a proof of their good feelings the signatures of a prosperous community to a public journal not then in existence and two thousand dollars were instantly placed at my disposal, by way of commencement, and nobly has the country thus far sustained The Message, though neither in the Senate House, nor as a public journalist, has its public conduct truckled to faction, whether in office, or as its expectant.

During the last two years you have witnessed my conduct in the Assembly – my opinion upon men and things have been spread before you, through an independent Press, frank, free, and fearless.

We may differ in a few things – some of us perhaps in many things – but in the winter of life I can occupy no more suitable position in life while at all able to work, than in maintaining and defending with tongue and pen those cherished rights and liberties of Canada, which I lived in youth, and have assisted in teaching tens of thousands of Canadians to value and uphold, as the source of enduring national wealth and greatness. Nor will many of you regret in the distant future – fair and lovely may it dawn upon a virtuous distinguished and prosperous race – that with all its faults and failings (and I wish he had fewer of them) you generously contributed to sustain the closing efforts of your oldest servant in the fourth estate of the Press, at a time when heated partizans would have consigned him to political oblivion.

I have worked hard since I had the pleasure of asking you to take hold of the subscription lists of the last six winter months, – and I think that cheered on as I am by thousands whose worth I have long known, I can work still harder during the summer months. Other papers have their travelling agents, a systematic scheme for increasing their subscription roll, large capital, gainful official patronage, I trust alone and solely to the active good will of old forgiving and constant friends. . . .

17 ON THE HUSTINGS

Mackenzie's Weekly Message,
July 17, 1854

A WEEK'S ELECTIONEERING

I attended Mr. Hinck's meetings at Ingersoll, Mount Elgin, Otterville, and Norwich – held other meetings in the forenoons at Tillsonburgh, &c – did my best to give South Oxford into Hincks' true character, and was most attentively listened to by very large audiences, many of the hearers in which were old and sincere friends. Hincks *may* be elected – I do not say he will not – but my impression is that no majority of electors can be found to endorse such conduct as his has been. Rolph & Co. should have checked his career, or quit office, but they sacrificed principles, and at the proper time will try to say why. I'll help them somewhat.

Early last Friday morning I rode twenty miles across from Norwich to Woodstock – took the cars there – hired a cab at the Falls of Niagara, and addressed a large assemblage of the farmers of Welland, Fo.–hill [?], in opposition to Street. Thence rode twelve miles to Port Colborne same night. Spoke next day at Dunnville, Haldimand – travelled a little through the country – visited Brant, &c. – returned to Toronto – and started for Cayuga to attend the nomination on Thursday, July 20th.

18 MACKENZIE'S LAST ALMANAC

Toronto Weekly Message,
January 7, 1859

"ALMANAC OF FREEDOM AND INDEPENDENCE, FOR 1860."

It will be for sale next Monday.

My true friend for the last 40 years, Charles Hill of Malahide, wrote me on 17 Nov. last, as an apology for not ordering more Almanacs, that so many came free, with patent medicines, the demand had lessened.

But mine is a political Almanac, with no puffs of unknown drugs in it. It enters upon the great questions of the future of Canada and the United States; the way to escape war and dissension; the Union proposed by Mr. Brown to the Convention; the Galt-Brown federation; Pure and Simple Dissolution; Terrill, Galt, Rose and Holton's Annexation; the integrity of the American Republic; and the impossibility of going on as we are.

If those who may read and approve of its principles and objects would but buy and spread among the people, according to their means, the whole of this edition, they would furnish thousands with facts whereon to argue from, and help to bring about that Union of purpose which is so essential to our future welfare. Free discussion is as yet allowed – let us benefit Canada thereby.

"Let us be united!" is the cry of the leaders of two factions, struggling for the control of places and pelf, and for nothing else – "let us rally round our principles." The poor fellows who follow these cunning rogues find that when one set of sharpers get the patronage, they unblushingly betray their trust, while the knaves they have ousted, promptly take up the cries of their predecessors or invent additional plausible stories. As Sir A. MacNab said "there is no principle involved."

The Almanac is cheap, to suit all classes: Five Cents per copy; 36 cents per dozen; $3 per 100; $25 per thousand. Send in your orders.

I printed Almanacs here some thirty years since; my latest Almanac, and it will be my last, is now offered.

W. L. M.

19 DISILLUSIONMENT

*Toronto Weekly Message,
October 1, 1859*

In the progress of society we have, in a measure, dropped the physical part of the business; and instead of punching, scratching, kicking, biting, and knocking, down one another, true to the original principles of our nature, we are all endeavoring to circumvent one another. Every body is trying to take every body in; the moment that one of us has got together a thing or two, he is pounced upon by his neighbor, who in his turn falls a prey to another, and so in endless succession. We cannot help ourselves, though we are splitting our heads to discover devices, by way of law, to restrain this propensity of our nature: it will not do! we are all overreaching, cheating, swindling, robbing one another, and, if necessary, are ready to maim and murder one another in the preservation of our designs.

20 A PERSONAL HOMESTEAD FROM THE PEOPLE OF UPPER CANADA

*Toronto Weekly Message,
January 28, 1860*

THE MACKENZIE HOMESTEAD

Altho' we expressed a desire by advertisement in the Toronto Daily papers that the Homestead subscription should cease,* and the account be closed, all the lists had not been given in; we have now therefore to acknowledge lists and money, additional, as follows:

3259.	John Wallace,	Esquesing	$ 5.00
3260.	William Barber, Esq.	......do....	5.00
3261.	James Ferrie	..............do....	2.00
3262.	R. L. Johnson	................do....	4.00
3263.	Duncan Kennedy	..........do....	2.00
3264.	Duncan Kennedy, Jr.	...do....	3.00
3265.	Robert Kennedy	............do....	1.00
3266.	Lauchlan Macdonald	......do....	4.00
3267.	Charles Hill	................do....	4.00
3268.	.... Grant	.............do....	4.00
3269.	Archibald Campbell	......do....	4.00
3270.	Malcolm Macpherson	....do....	2.00
3248.	Late R. A. Parker, Yorkville	..............do....	50.00
3272.	X. Y. Z., Toronto	..........do....	50.00
3274 and 3273. Andw. Thompson & T. Grover, Wardsville			3.00
3275.	Port Rowan		4.00
3276.	James Hume Sen. Esq., Scotch Block		10.00
3277.	James Hume, Junr.	........do....	4.00
3278.	James Kinnear, Esq., Decewsville		10.00
3279.	Late Donald Campbell, Esq., balance of $419 collected by him for Homestead, to close the account		11.00

Thus far, the money paid to Mr. Lesslie, before he closed his trust, to the Committee who bought the Homestead, and to myself personally, amounts to $7,000. The unpaid subscriptions were, say, $2500 more.

* Mackenzie quarrelled with the Committee raising the fund, wishing to travel to Scotland on a portion of the Homestead money and it was denied him. See W. Kilbourn, *The Firebrand* (Toronto: Clarke Irwin, 1964), p. 226.

Section II
Political Ideas

A. British and American Whig, 1824-1830

1 BRITISH AND AMERICAN LIBERTY

The Colonial Advocate,
May 18, 1824

THE EDITOR'S ADDRESS TO THE PUBLIC

... Sincerely attached to freedom, we yet think it not incompatible with a limited monarchy. We would never wish to see British America an appendage of the American Presidency; yet would we wish to see British America thrive and prosper full as well as does that Presidency. We trust to see this accomplished, if Britain does not fall into the error of considering her colonists as much her slaves as Virginia does her negroes.

We dislike much to hear Mr. Daniel Webster, of Massachusetts, gibe us "as the distant dependency of a distant monarchy," &c. &c. and hope the time will come when Canada will be pointed out as a model for other countries – not pointed at with scorn, as the King's printer has it.

We like American liberty well, but greatly prefer British liberty. British subjects, born in Britain, we have sworn allegiance to a constitutional monarchy, and we will die before we will violate that oath.

It has often occurred to us to enquire, while we perused the works of a political writer, or national historian, what religion did he profess? of what church was he a member? In some instances we could divine this ourselves from the bias he gave to his writings. But we have read authors, Protestants, aye, and Catholics too, who did in no instance suffer their religious creed to interfere with their political writings, and we are ambitious of being found amongst the latter class. It may not be amiss for us here to state, that we are Calvinists, and profess to believe the Westminster confession of faith as now adopted by the church in the northern part of our native island of Great Britain. ...

2 AGRARIAN DEMOCRACY AND AMERICA

The Colonial Advocate,
May 18, 1824

On you alone, farmers, does Canada rely. You are the sole depositories of civil and religious liberty. If you look to the provincial executives, they are foreigners, having an interest differing widely from yours, and are hardly able, even if we grant that they have the will, to reconcile jarring interests arising from a crooked colonial policy; but possessing patronage and power, having in their gifts, offices and emoluments, honours and dignities, lands and heritages; influence immense, if we consider the size of the country.

To yourselves, therefore, Farmers, in the hour of trial, must you look for aid. The eyes of the whole Colonies, and of America, are fixed on you. You are the only true nobility that this country can boast of. Through you only, by your Representatives, can the real state of things become known in the British senate. If ye choose the wisest, the honestest, the most esteemed of your body; men who have been long known as tried patriots, in whose souls the voice of freedom is not yet extinct; who hold no offices under, or receive any gifts from the Crown; and who, as fathers, as husbands as members of society, are kind and brotherly minded; men of cultivated minds and discreet demeanour, *fearing God and hating covetousness.* If to such as these ye trust your liberties, there is yet hope for your country, that such representatives will assert your rights, recover your due influence, and be a means to consolidate your freedom. But if ye will, as heretofore, choose collectors and king's advocates, ambassadors, parasites and sycophants, to manage your affairs, you will dearly rue it; you and the generations that shall be hereafter. Look at Spain – Look at Greece – Look at Revolutionary France – behold the sad effects of misgovernment, and beware! – The errors were in the princes in the end, but sprang from an effeminacy in the people in the beginning.

Compare Napoleon Buonaparte as emperor and king, or as exile and prisoner, with the untitled Washington, the free citizen of a free government; or with Franklin, the asserter of civil and religious rights. Read Lord Byron's beautiful lines, and say whether you would not rather that your sons should imbibe a portion of the disinterested energy of soul and noble principle which characterized the American chief, "the tyrant-tamer," and the *amor patriæ*, and untaught philosophy, that has immortalized the Bostonian printer than that they should become such selfish, gilded, unhappy things, as are emperors and kings: . . .

Assuredly, Farmers, Mr. Washington going to town in his market cart was a more "noble creature" than Napoleon Buonaparte in his chariot and surrounded by the pomp and splendour of almost Oriental magnificence. For, as the Grecian sage so truly remarks, it is not the office which dignifies the possessor, but the MAN which renders honourable the office. . . .

---

3 VERSE SATIRE ON THE FAMILY COMPACT

The Colonial Advocate,
May 27, 1824

THE COUNTIES OF YORK AND SIMCOE.

An Address written and published by H. J. B--lt--n, h-s M-j-sty's s-l-c-t-r g-n-r-l of Upp-r C-n-da, to the Free and INDEPENDENT Freeholders of YORK AND SIMCOE.

He had written much blank verse, and
   blanker prose,
And more of both than any body knows.
He had written Wesley's life: – here turning
   round
To Satan, "Sir, I'm ready to write yours,
"In two octavo volumes, nicely bound
"With notes and preface, all that most
   allures
"The pious purchaser; and there's no
   ground
"For fear, for I can choose my own reviewers:
"So let me have the proper documents
"That I may add you to my other saints."

Satan bowed and was silent "Well, if you,
"With amiable modesty decline
"My offer what says Michael? There are few
"Whose memoirs could be rendered more
   divine.
"Mine is a pen of all work; not so new
"As it was once, but I could make you shine
"Like your own trumpet; by the way, my
   own
"Has more of brass in it and is as well blown.
. . .
"But talking about trumpets, here's my" --*

ADDRESS

Dear Tom, and Dick, and Harry,
What makes you all so merry,
At the expense of Solicitor Dandy O?
Who wishes and who hopes
You'll all prove such nincompoops
As to swallow all his blarney and his
   Brandy O!

Prior to making my profession,
I have waited a whole session,
Ere I bolted out that I am so handy O!
But see what a clever fellow
Without "leather or prunella"
Is your mixture of *water and brandy O!*

Dull Charlie Fothergill
May bawl about
And taunt brother Georgey so handy O,
About Ridout's U. C. m--p
There the head it fits the cap:
"And shall we not then wasnt a little
   Brandy" O! . . .

To see townships full of people,
Without parson, church or steeple,
Or a shilling for to buy a gill of brandy O!
To see clients we oppress,
Shews the freedom we possess,
The merry life that's led by your Dandy O.

No man can me control,
I'm a happy little soul,
Quite as independent as "a hungry lawyer"
   well can be O;
I'm quite competent to join
The representatives divine:
The Hagermans and Robinsons are the
   dandies O!

If collector Sherwood should,
For reasons good conclude

To disuse his three-cock'd *chapeau* so grand,
  heigh ho!
For to shew you that I'm ready
To preside like my old daddy,
I'll be speaker of the house of – cherry
  Brandy O!

Playter, Denniston and Small,
May give in one and all,
Justice Thompson must bow to the
  Dandy O;
For I two masters can
Serve, as well as any man;
First *myself* – then – the Governor of
  Candy O!

Like Goessman, I'll not sell
Nor buy your votes pell mell;
It would not look well, nor be handy O!
Of my blarney I am *vogue*,
For I've got none of the brogue,
So when I've got your votes you'll have the
  Brandy O!

The original copy of the address of this modest gentleman is in our possession, and will be shewn to the incredulous. – When it is considered that he is the 15th candidate, and that it is as difficult for a 15th candidate to write a good address as for the last of 15 barristers employed on one side in the same case to make a good speech, we cannot but allow that he has made the most of his brandy and water text, and we wish him all the success he deserves. . . .

* Byron's vision of Judgement [Mackenzie's note – ed.]

4 ANTI-AMERICANISM

The Colonial Advocate,
October 7, 1824

AMERICAN GRATITUDE – *La Fayette.*
AMERICAN INGRATITUDE – *Barton.*

I am afraid, that, like many other native subjects of the king of England, I have hitherto been disposed to think too well of the American government, and to overlook some of those peculiar characteristicks which render it more beautiful in theory than virtuous in practice. Its encouragement of slavery in Missouri; its federal constitution allowing new states to introduce the cursed slave system; its connexion with two millions of our fellow creatures by only one tie, that of the tyrant over the oppressed, the strong over the weak, the slave owner over the slave, grieves and distresses me. I have, of late, perused very carefully some of the leading journals of the Union, and in many instances where I anticipated pleasure from learning the wise enactments of a virtuous community, I have been shocked with accounts of political fraud, bribery, and corruption; I have seen the Albany and New-York journals accuse the members of the legislature of that state of political quackery and chicanery; I have read of *"management and intrigue, for which Albany has become notorious throughout the Union;"* I have heard of republicans in high places being accused of successfully *bribing with money* members of their assemblies, to induce them to vote for incorporating novel banks and air-bubble associations; I have seen their highest officers calling the people "a rabble;" I have been told of the wise men, the virtuous representatives of the great state – the enlightened state of New-York, wresting from their constituents the elective franchise, saying, "we and not you shall elect the first officer in the Union" – in short, the result of my observation is, that the love of power and place is nowhere more predominant than in the citizens of the twenty three American free republicks. Were the English constitution introduced into the colonies, in all its purity, and with such alterations as suits our local situation and scattered population, I, for one, truly believe that we should see little to envy in the boasted codes of law and justice, liberty and equality, which exist on the other side of the Niagara river; . . .

5 LIBEL OR SATIRE?

The Colonial Advocate,
May 18, 1826

A meeting of the *Advocate*'s "subscribers," Peter Russell, Esq.; Caleb Hopkins, Capt. Humphrey Clod, Dr. Andrew Tod, Adam Brown, Tom Moore, reported by Andrew Wylie. This article in conjunction with further abuse of John

Beverley Robinson and J. B. Macaulay on June 8, 1826, caused a violent retaliation by the young members of the Compact who wrecked Mackenzie's presses.

A faithful account of the proceedings at a general meeting of the contributors to the Advocate, held in Macdonell's Parlour on the evening of Monday, May 1st, 1826.

"O Beverly! O Virginia! thou dost shame
That bloody spoil: Thou slave, thou wretch, thou coward:
Thou little valiant, great in villainy! . . ."
                                King John

The sudden and unexpected announciation [sic] in the Colonial Advocate of the 27th ultimo, that the editor intended to reduce the size and price of his journal, close the door upon political discussions, and for ever shut out even religious articles, fell upon the ears of the people of Upper Canada like a clap of thunder or an earthquake. . . .

In the meanwhile the contributors to the Advocate, seriously alarmed, took horse each man of them, and as if impelled by a simultaneous impulse reached the city of York within a very short time of one another, they met by common consent, first in Mrs. Jordan's large room, and from thence adjourned their sitting to Macdonell's blue parlour, a quiet and retired situation immediately in the rear of the Advocate Office, with its windows embracing a delightful view of Lake Ontario, the Bay of York, the Lighthouse &c. – In this right pleasant place, with a dozen of French Claret on the table, for the double purpose of drowning care and quenching thirst, they proceeded to business, on the evening of Monday 1st of May.

. . . Caleb Hopkins . . . The Times will tell you that Mr. Canning was the son of mother Hunn the actress, but the delicacy of our York Belles would be shocked if reminded that the present Attorney General of this Province is the hopeful offspring of mother Beeman who kept the cake and beer shop in King-street, York, that the Honourable Peter Robinson whose pranks and Peterboroughs, we hear so much of, with his learned brother the Declaimer General against the Americans, were paupers of the lowest class for whom people now in York taking pity on their forlorn condition, went about and begged handfuls of meal and York sixpences to keep them from actual starvation. The reputed father of these worthies was likewise an original in his way, and when he took his hopeful family into the boat with him for a very remarkable purpose, it would have been no loss to society if the heart of flint in the bosom of his son had then found a bed in the bottom of the deep, where the hardest pebble, has a softer texture. This Virginian descended of Virginians has not forgotten the unshaken pride of his country, has he forgotten that it was long the botany bay of the British Kingdoms, the unhallowed receptacle of thieves, rogues, prostitutes & incorrigible vagabonds, have the Robinsons any thing to boast of in their Virginian descent? Is their boasted loyalty of a purer and more exalted rank than that of those who pursue in this colony a less odious line of conduct? – What was their origin and ancestry? – Where is the table of their line of descent? – Is it a secret in these parts that many, very many such Virginian nobles as the Robinsons assume themselves, were descended from mothers who came there to try their luck and were purchased by their sires with tobacco at prices according to the quality and soundness of the article? And is it from such a source that we are to expect the germ of liberty? Say rather is it not from such a source that we may look for the tyranny engendered, nursed and practised by those whose blood has been vitiated and syphilized by the accursed slavery of centuries. . . .

Mr. Caleb Hopkins – . . . The ugliest faces I ever saw were those of the infidels Paine and Voltaire, – both had shocking countenances, and the turned up nose, wolf like jaws, and gruesome eyes of this *stink trap* of government not a little resemble theirs. It is only by his appearance that you can know a wolf from a lamb, and if he is a bleater, I marvel much, seeing that "upon his eyeballs vengeful tyranny sits in grim majesty to fright the world."

BROWN. – It is a wonder how so ordinary a fellow as this Macaulay got into the Council, or into any situation above that of a bum bailiff.

DOCTOR TOD. – I can give you a reason

for his nose being crooked upwards, and a very good one it is. His father intended him at first for his own trade of an apothecary and kept him pounding stinking gum for hysteric pills to old women, until the horrid smell of the drug actually turned his nose into a peg, whereon his grandfather might have safely hung up his fiddle. ...

6 BRITISH NORTH AMERICAN UNION

The Colonial Advocate,
December 14, 1826

A Confederation of the British North American Colonies

The Albion lately favoured its readers with an account of certain contemplated *changes in the Governors* of these colonies, which from all that we can learn has not the slightest foundation in fact – that journal however proceeds in its series (paper of Nov. 25th) to give a chapter of *changes among the governed*; and really we are afraid the news are too good to be true. – Right glad should we be indeed if the confidential information received by the Albion should prove correct – We have written much and often, advocating an effective united government for the colonies, in the bonds of amity and relationship with England, – we have sent hundreds of copies of our journal to Europe to distinguished persons, with that project specially marked and noted – But were always afraid that the idea would be treated as "an idle chimera," even by the wisest and ablest of British Statesmen. – It would however be the best and safest policy; for England can continue to hold Cabotia only by the ties of friendship, amity and mutual advantage, – ties which, with the divine blessing would be greatly strengthened, were *the talent*, the resources, the enterprize of all the colonies fully brought into action in a liberal, enlightened and *united* general Government. ...

7 A COLONIAL PEERAGE

The Colonial Advocate,
April 26, 1827

The Union of Great Britain and British American recommended; here is a series of letters addressed to His Excellency the Governor in Chief.

LETTER FIRST

To the Right Honourable,
    The Earl of Dalhousie.
MY LORD,
    ... I have long been satisfied that if the North American colonies were rid of these inferior and subordinate legislatures, which are and must be for ever inefficient for the purposes for which they were intended; and allowed instead thereof a due weight in both branches of the British parliament, it would prove the foundation of their permanent and true happiness. A colonial peerage has been ridiculed, but my lord, Mr. Pitt saw its usefulness, and if merit either on the bench or in the army and navy has deserved a Scottish or Irish coronet, it surely would not be less prized by a Canadian or Nova Scotian. The people would submit to taxes imposed by themselves through their representatives, the aristocracy would add to the national dignity, and be a blessed exchange for legislative councellors [sic] whose honours are consigned to the tomb with them who wear them. ...

When the Canadas received their present constitution, the theory of which has not proved good in practice, that great statesman Mr. Fox, whom no man charged with ultra-royalism,

"laid it down as a principle never to
"be departed from, that every part of
"the British dominions ought to pos-
"sess a government, in the constitution
"of which, monarchy, aristocracy, and
"democracy, were mutually blended
"and united, nor could any govern-
"ment be a fit one for British subjects
"to live under, which did not contain
"its due weight of aristocracy, be-
"cause THAT he considered to be
"the proper poise of the constitution,

"the balance that equalized the pow-
"ers of the two other branches, and
"gave stability and firmness to the
"whole." To this doctrine Mr. Pitt most willingly subscribed, and joined with his great
political rival in the manly and delicate
compliment he had paid to the British constitution. . . .

8 "THE SLAYER OF AMBRISTER" – ANDREW JACKSON*

The Colonial Advocate,
April 26, 1827

A further extract from the first letter to Lord Dalhousie on a closer Union of the Colonies and Great Britain.

. . . What your lordship may think of this short paragraph [from the Washington *National Intelligencer*] I cannot tell, but to my Scottish feelings it was rather annoying to see our Canadian *miseries* becoming so conspicuous, and I took the pains to look out a few evidences of the *blessings* of their republican system in order to place them before your lordship and the country by way of contrast. I shall say nothing about governor Troup and the "troubles in Georgia," nor of governor Giles, and the "troubles in Virginia" for your lordship and all the world have heard enough of these troubles already, nor will I attempt to describe those "signs of the times," in their Intelligencer which go to shew that "a corrupt faction" are exerting every nerve and invoking every shade of slumbering grievance to fright their present ruler from his stool of office, and to make room thereon for the slayer of Ambrister. . . .

* Richard Ambrister and Alexander Arbuthnot were two British subjects who had the misfortune to be in the military post at St. Marks, East Florida in 1818 when Andrew Jackson burst into Spanish territory allegedly in the pursuit of Seminole Indians. They were charged with inciting Indians against whites by a court martial and summarily executed.

9 THE SOCIAL SOURCES OF BRITISH LEGISLATIVE SUPERIORITY

The Colonial Advocate,
May 7, 1827

Letter Second to the Right Honourable Lord Dalhousie.

. . . The United States have a union but it is badly cemented – their ruler is elective, and unlike the monarch of Britain, is blamed for every misfortune which happens to his country; the English language is ransacked for terms of abuse to heap on the head of the American president for the time being, and to strangers it would appear, that as the king can do no wrong, so the president can do nothing that is right. With an aristocracy of more imperishable materials than at present exists, with a ruler less responsible, less liable to be changed at the caprice of the opposition for the time being, and with a house of representatives less tramelled by countervailing state laws, the U.S. might prosper. But it is with me one of the strongest arguments which can be adduced against the abolition of the British primogeniture laws, that in those republics where they have been abolished, and where more equalizing laws of inheritance obtain, a less independent and less valuable class of persons usurp the places of the country gentleman of education, manly principle and honourable family. For instance the majority of Congress of the United States is composed of practising attorneys and popular men of law, while in the British house of commons the far greater number of members are country gentlemen, merchants of the first respectability, naval and military men of long experience and high character, manufacturers of wealth and opulence, with a few bankers, and some lawyers of eminence in their profession and who in nine cases out of ten are the younger sons of ancient families, or themselves possessed of a large estate. I have observed in those places in Great Britain where the elective franchise is most widely extended, that country gentlemen are oftenest preferred to be sent to parliament. . . .

10 "WE THE PEOPLE..."

The Colonial Advocate,
January 3, 1828

STATE OF THE COLONY

... The English parliament, some thirty or forty years ago, passed an act, without the consent of the people of Canada, by which these provinces are to be governed until it shall please the same wise body to pass another act, (will we nill we) to alter, take away, or add to the rights of this conquered territory. This is not a constitution, it is not freedom, it is a government which will be submitted to, much upon the same principle on which Ireland is managed, but it is not a constitution.

The constitution of a country is not the act of its government, nor of any distant authority, but of the people constituting a government suited to their necessities — A constitution contains the principles on which the government shall be established, the manner in which it shall be organized, the powers it shall have, the mode of elections, the duration of parliaments, assemblies, or congresses; the authority to be given the executive, and the principles on which it shall be bound. "A constitution, therefore, is to a government, what the laws made afterwards by that government are to a court of judicature." The court acts according to the laws made, and the government is governed by the constitution.

Were the people of the Canadas asked whether the mode of government set over them in 1791 was agreeable to their wishes, or did the more efficient argument of a military force settle the question without a popular appeal?

We have the example of the late colonies to convince the doubtful, that the ancient mode of reasoning about constitutions is not considered binding by the people; and the old whigs of England, with Lord Chatham at their head, held it as a principle, that resistance to such a system was lawful and right. Mr. Galt to the contrary, notwithstanding ... if the people shall ask for leave to mould their internal government it will be conceded to them, we purpose in our next to consider further the state of the colony, and of the necessity which exists for a constitutional form of government.

11 THE HOMELY VIRTUES OF JOHN QUINCY ADAMS

The Colonial Advocate,
January 31, 1828

At the head of the Administration, is John Quincy Adams, President of the United States – a man who is alike distinguished for his eminent talents and long public services, at home & abroad. His name is connected with most of the great events of our country for the last thirty years; who, as a statesman, has no rival; as a patriot, no superior; a man who loves his country, and glories in its free institutions, and devotes his time and attention to promoting and securing its best, its dearest, and its greatest interests; a man approaching to the age of sixty, and grown grey in the service of his country. He divides and employs his time with all the economy of Franklin; his morality has all the austerity of the patriot, Samuel Adams; he possesses the purity and self-denial of Madison; and I do verily believe he is the plainest man that ever was President of the United States. He is seldom seen out of his house except on foot, mingling with his fellow-citizens, and is then only to be distinguished by the humility of his deportment.

12 THE LESSONS OF 1688 AND 1776 COMPARED

The Colonial Advocate,
July 16, 1829

... The historic page is open to all mankind: the pulpit orator quotes and illustrates such passages as best suit his purpose; so does the lawyer; *so do we.* From that day on which the glorious revolution of 1688 dawned upon benighted Britain, Englishmen regarded themselves as the arbiters of their destiny. "From that day they considered the institutions of their country as made for them and not them for the institutions.

From that day, the right of thinking, and of delivering their thoughts, both respecting government, and respecting religion, they assumed as their own; and spurned the advocates of slavery, who would rob them of that invaluable possession." The government of William III., and still more strongly the government of the House of Hanover, nourished this spirit among the people, and advocated the propriety of revolting against established power, "whensoever an evil or the producer of evil." Hence the writings of Locke on government, "laying the will and approbation of the people as its only legitimate foundation." Hence Burnett's elegant, instructive and manly pages. Hence too the adherence of the English Colonies to the glorious principles of representative government and civil and religious freedom; hence the ability, high-toned independence and manly feeling displayed in the address of Congress in February 1776, to their friends and countrymen and fellow subjects. They were firmly attached to the first and best principles of the British constitution: – so are we; so are the inhabitants of British America. Let the Canadians of our times read the important document we this day present to their notice, and feel justly proud of the noble minded men America has produced. Let persons in power read it also and retrace their steps ere it be too late: – let them shun injustice and eschew oppression, so shall they escape the gulph which yawned for their predecessors three score years ago.

13 ON ENGLISH-SPEAKING REVOLUTIONS

*The Colonial Advocate,
March 11, 1830*

..."Freedom" observes the biographer of Wesley, "is of slow, and silent, and gradual growth. It must pass through the successive stages of infancy and youth ere it reaches the maturity of manhood, and long before the people have, so to speak, committed the first overt act of freedom in the establishment of free institutions, there has been a silent and perhaps unnoticed progress which, though unseen, has been felt, and the last step is only the termination of a journey which commenced at a period now long forgotten." – Although this description of the progress of liberty, will not altogether apply to the formation of Upper Canada into a separate government, yet the general principle must be admitted even in a country the first settlers of which were peculiarly distinguished for their veneration of regal government, and their fierce opposition to the American Revolution, and the measures of the great majority of their countrymen. The United Empire Loyalists, as they were called, carried with them into the wilds and forests of Canada, an unqualified hatred to American independence; – they had boldly opposed the public will in the old colonies – they had stood, side by side with the warlike native of the Scottish mountains, and the phlegmatic hireling of Hanover, to maintain what they had been taught to consider as paternal government, and to overwhelm the noblest band of patriots that ever unsheathed the sword in defence of that fair and glorious inheritance of human kind, "civil and religious liberty."

The American revolution was a noble era in the annals of British freedom. It was a memorable struggle of christian freemen – of men who trusted in the God of Heaven, who revered his Sabbaths, and, by their representatives in Congress, set apart days of fasting and humbled themselves before Him, in that period of doubt and darkness. The British Colonists of '76 fought, with their Bibles in their knapsacks – they had learned to prize the sweets of liberty, and panted, not after worldly wealth and distinction but after the freedom of interpreting the Bible for themselves and following its precepts. History affords a few similar glorious examples of disinterested devotion to the true principles of liberty – not in Greece nor in Rome but on the plains of the United Provinces; at Bannockburn; and on the mountains of Switzerland, at the battle of Morgarten. . . .

14 A TREATISE ON ARISTOCRACY

The Colonial Advocate,
September 16, 1830

An Appeal to the People of Upper Canada, "From the Judgements" of British and Colonial Governments Respecting That Province.

ARISTOCRACY

... By education and habit, I have been an admirer of an aristocracy, in which talent, virtue, wealth and ancient lineage, were (as I had been taught) combined – I have supposed such an independent body essential to good government. But nearly eleven years' experience of your manners and customs, and habits and opinions, has fully satisfied me that the English landed aristocratic system will not soon take root in Upper Canada. Power and property will gravitate to each other by an unerring law of nature, but it is evident you will make them change hands oftner than in Great Britain.

Darwin has enumerated pride of family among the diseases of volition in his Zoonomia;* he describes it as a species of insanity: ...

"Aristocracy is, nevertheless, most perversely inherent in human nature; and all the raillery, in pen, ink, and paper, will not eradicate it." The passion for artificial distinctions, and the ready submission of many to its claims, are independent of institutions. They are as discoverable in an American trading town as in London or Vienna. The worthy citizens of the United States are quite as liable to split into castes and circles, as their brothers of the mother country; and as long as distinctions exist in society, (and distinctions of wealth and education must subsist even in the most republican communities,) the desire to participate in them will prevail. ...

... There is a natural aristocracy among men, founded on virtue and talents; and there is an artificial aristocracy, founded on wealth and birth, without either virtue or talents. Perhaps in place of such of the latter class as fill the offices of your government, and obtain the chief seats in your senate house, it would be wise to select the natural aristocracy of the country, for the instruction, the trusts, and the government of society! Mr. Fox, in his remarks on the Quebec bill, recommends a middle course for the Canadian Senates, an aristocracy to be elected from among men of property only. At all events, the working of the present system has, during a period of thirty or forty years, clearly demonstrated, to your entire satisfaction, that of the three sorts of aristocracy, Upper Canada in her Councils has by far the worst. ...

PRIMOGENITURE LAWS

The present laws of primogeniture are manifestly opposed to the divine command, to do to others as we would have them to do to us. On this continent, the father by the constant habits of industry, guided by information, acquires wealth, rears up the children in luxury, and dies, leaving his property divided among his heirs who waste and spend it, returning to that numerous class from which their parent rose by his industry. In England those results are prevented by artificial restraints. The continuation of property in families, and its consequent accumulation in individuals, by entails, is a provision of aristocracy in order to secure its power. The very provision itself argues a consciousness of natural weakness. It is evident, that it is as unjust, as it is opposed to our common affections, to make one child affluent at the expense of half a dozen others. No man, left to the operation of natural feeling would do so cruel an act. "In the United States, a man may devise his property to his eldest son to the injury of the rest of his family – still no man does it. And even if one father could be found who would do so great injustices to his descendants, still he has no pledge that his son will be as absurd as himself." Your representatives have often passed bills for the repeal of the laws of entail, but in vain – they were lost in the Council. And unless the next House shall display great firmness and perseverance in all their proceedings, with perfect union among themselves, they will be unable to do the good they otherwise might. To obtain this desirable union, you will have to recommend mutual concessions of individual opinion, and that the repeal of the entail and half blood laws and every other leading measure should be well considered before it is introduced. The policy of your Government cannot be mistaken; it would keep the disposal of all places and honours and emoluments as much as possible in its own hands – it would increase the men of talent and ambition, and share with them its political power – keep the state united with the church for the sake of political influence, and throw every possible obstacle in your way whenever you attempt to obstruct its proceedings.

* *Zoonomia* (1794-96) was written by Erasmus Darwin, the English poet and physician, and father of the naturalist, Charles Darwin.

B. Transatlantic and Colonial Reformer, 1830-1836

15 FRANCE AND THE TRANSATLANTIC REVOLUTION

The Colonial Advocate,
March 26, 1831

FRANCE AND FREEDOM

Altho' I dislike war and bloodshed, I must owe that the late intelligence from Europe does not all displease me. – General LaFayette (like Samson with the Philistines of old) seems determined to make one other effort to crush the Hydra heads of arbitrary power in Europe before he dies; and the hearts and hands of his gallant countrymen are with him. Louis's ministry would rather wait patiently until the tyrant of the north had subdued the brave Poles, and Austria crushed in the dust the friends of freedom in the land of Cicero and Cincinnatus; they would then expect the aid of the allied despots to prevent the French from consummating their revolution and reuniting with Belgium; and would invite to their aid a prostituted priesthood, who like ours would, as heretofore, answer for spies and informers to the mock liberal government, and under the hypocritical mask of christian forbearance and pious submission, teach their flocks the exploded creed by which European tyrants long have thriven. But it will not do. France is arming. Already she can count 500,000 well disciplined troops, able officered, and united as one man in the cause of freedom. Italy is with her. The oppressed Poles look upon her as on the morning star of their coming day. The brave and generous Belgians are eager to fight their old oppressors under her banners. Ireland, whose ill-treated millions have for ages sighed in vain for civil and religious equality, will rejoice in every victory obtained by the genius of France; and Scotland my native land whose choicest patriots and truest friends were murdered and banished and fined and imprisoned and tortured by the tyrants and blood hounds of 179..., in solemn mockery of the first principles of eternal justice, will offer up before the throne of the omnipotent, the daily prayers of her pious and long suffering children for success to "the cause of truth upon the earth." England, whose glorious and oft repeated efforts in favour of rational freedom, first illumined the benighted soil of France; England, the free spirit of whose institutions (tho' now perverted by the few) first taught America to rejoice in the enjoyment of self-government; England, once happy and prosperous, but now depressed by the efforts of a despicable aristocracy of wealth without merit, a faction hostile to every principle of virtue, justice and christianity; England too will be with France, and the Birmingham artist while he fashions the weapon of war with which the fortress of continental darkness are destined to be attacked, and, we would fain hope, for ever overthrown, will rejoice that he too had been made instrumental in bringing the glorious cause of human right to a happy consummation. Of the warm and generous feelings of the Canadians I surely need not speak; and the United States have testified their gladness at the progress already made in the good work of regeneration. It is honourable to our nation that we have now a ministry at the helm who sympathize with Frenchmen in this their day of renovation; and I trust that the machinations of the titled traducer of the gallant Moore, and the depraved and dissolute oligarchy by whom he is surrounded, will in vain seek their downfall. I have ever had the fullest confidence in the truly noble ministry now guiding the reins of state in Great Britain.

But who are they who will dare to oppose the progress of freedom in France? Who are they who would seek to crush her gallant sons while fighting on the plains of Europe the battles of the human race! – I can tell, for I have marked them well. They are they who seek to hold power solely for their own aggrandizement; that few who long have triumphed in the misery of, and trampled to the dust, the millions; that few who have in all ages striven to keep mankind ignorant, divided and debased.

Established priesthoods; titled misers and titled spendthrifts and debauchers; arbitrary monarchs, and the venal throng who bask in the guilty sunshine of their power; government brokers, bankers, and Jewish state creditors; Ambitious and unprincipled politicians; the proud, the haughty and the overbearing of all countries – these, with few exceptions, will make common cause against the people, and in secret conclave enter into a unholy alliance to perpetuate European bondage. Grave senators and princes, titled priests and hireling legislators, from Charles and his Cardinal in Holyrood, from Arthur Wellesley and his partizans at Strathfield, say down even as low as Father Strachan at York and his hopeful pupil John Robinson in the palace of *justice*, (with the very meanest of their tribe of provincial sycophants,) will view with horror and dismay the glorious attempts that are now making and about to be made in Europe to establish on a broad foundation the rights of man equal to laws and all their emissaries will be at work underground in the dark and midnight hour sowing discord in the people's camp....

16 NORTH AMERICA APPLAUDS THE GREAT REFORM BILL

*The Colonial Advocate,
August 18, 1831*

GLORIOUS NEWS FOR CANADA.

By the favour of our attentive correspondents on the Niagara Frontier, we have received per the Steam Packet *Canada* the New York Commercial of the evening of the 10th current, containing London advices of the 7th and Liverpool of the 8th July, by the Sheffield, with the gratifying intelligence that the whigs have triumphed over the old tories by a most overwhelming majority.

The Reform Bill was ordered for a second reading on the 4th of July, on which day the Wellington & Peel, or old Tory High Church party, put forth their whole united strength, and to the joy of the People of England, Ireland, and Scotland, received a signal defeat. In the House of Commons the vote was as follows:

FOR THE REFORM BILL
(*second reading,*)
367;
AGAINST REFORM
231;
MAJORITY FOR THE
PEOPLE'S RIGHTS
136;

The Bill was to be considered in detail in committee of the whole *on the 12th of July.*

17 A NATIONAL GUARD FOR BRITAIN

*The Colonial Advocate,
December 29, 1831*

In reading over the English journals we are struck by the extraordinary fact, that the Ministerial papers recommend the embodying throughout England of a National Guard on the model of that of France and the formation of "political unions" or societies in all the principal towns. Should these two measures take effect, we should say, that a great political change must follow. They will throw all the power in the hands of the people and make the people sensible of it. "Political unions" or societies on similar principles, have frequently been attempted in England, but never acquired strength and were always confined to the lower classes because the Government not only discountenanced them, but put them down, when they could find an excuse for so doing. Now, the papers in the interest of the Government, speaking, it may be supposed, the wishes of the King's ministers, recommend these institutions as necessary to the welfare of the country.

18 POLITICAL UNIONS FOR UPPER CANADA

The Colonial Advocate,
December 13, 1832

Political Union – We this day lay before our readers the Constitution of the Upper Canada Central Political Union as adopted on the 26th of November and signed by 66 persons on the spot.

We formerly stated them at about 50, but it was merely from guess work.

When it is considered that England and Scotland is indebted to the Political Unions for passing the Reform Bill, which has emphatically been termed "a bloodless revolution," and which certainly is a renovation, or at least a foundation for a renovation of the Constitution of Great Britain, of course when all this considered every friend to true British principles must rejoice to see such a beneficial institution established in the country. We shall expect to see the list of membership swelling by the addition of the names of every true friend to British rule in Canada. We should be glad, as we are sure every friend to Upper Canada would be, to see a union of this sort established in every county in the province....

19 SCOTTISH POLITICS

The Colonial Advocate,
January 17, 1833

Letter 24 to Randal Wixson of the *Advocate* by W. L. Mackenzie, dated London, October 25, 1832.

... There never was, nor never will be a more gallant race of people than the Scotch, but their government, like that of the Canadas, has up to this date been altogether in the hands of the aristocracy, the landed proprietors of great estates, and their connexions and dependants, who like to see a set of serfs about them in order to set off their *greatness* to better advantage. – These Scotch aristocrats, bankers, entailed lairds and else, are, as a body, the meanest and most worthless of God's creatures – they have oppressed their countrymen for centuries, and condescended to acts of sycophancy, servility, aye and tyranny to retain their power, the very recollection of some of which makes me shudder. It is to them, and their spawn in Montreal and Quebec, that Scotland owes the character, often unjustly given her, of being sycophantic and servile, a nation of such men as *Andrew Fairservice*. And the generality of the Scotch sent to the Assembly in Upper Canada have not done much to wipe out the stain. Yet, few countries have produced braver men or more devoted patriots than Scotland; and now that the people, and not the dregs of a feudal aristocracy among them, as heretofore, will be represented in the Imperial Parliament, Scotland will shew her spirit and temper, and prove that if many of her sons are poor, there are comparatively few of them that would stoop to meanness to increase their stores of this world's wealth.

"Let posts and pensions sink or swim, with
   them who grant them;
If honestly they canna come – far better
   want them."

20 RESPONSIBLE GOVERNMENT

The Colonial Advocate,
May 16, 1833

THE EXECUTIVE COUNCIL

This body so far as we can learn still continue to sit, we are informed, and there can be no doubt, that every artifice will be resorted to for keeping as many of the old materials together as possible. The Strachanic organ says there is only to be a change of men and not a change of measures. But this will never do; nothing less than a change of men and measures can ever satisfy an insulted and injured colony. Nothing less will ever answer the purpose; we must have men who will so alter and amend measures, as that every public officer will be compelled to exhibit all the accounts of his office in detail, for the information of the public. We must have men to advise His Majesty's representative in whom the colonists can confide; and continue them in office no longer than they can obtain a majority in the House of Parliament. Then will we begin to enjoy something like a "Constitution the very image and transcript of that of Great Britain." Make all public officers accountable to the people through their representatives, and then if the people do not elect good representatives it will be their own fault; and if they elect good ones they and their children after them will reap the benefit by having good laws, a cheap and economical government; good roads will follow as a matter of course and every thing soon be placed in a happy and prosperous condition. All these things are fast coming if the people do but bestir themselves at the next election and not allow themselves to be deceived with any professions of zeal for the public welfare, where there has been no former proof of such services on any former occasion.

21 THE COLONIAL OFFICE DEFENDED

The Colonial Advocate,
August 1, 1833

Letter to Mr. John McIntosh, dated London, May 31, 1833.

Dear Sir: – I am informed that His Majesty's Government have carefully considered the Charters or Acts for the Incorporation of Banks at Kingston and York; they have also allowed me ample opportunity to state my objections, both personally and in writing, and it has been at length decided and determined to disallow and annul both these Acts. This you will find to be the deliberate opinion of the Lords of the Treasury, the Board of Trade, and the Secretary of State for the Colonies. It is not by any means intended to prevent these joint stock companies from continuing in operation if possessed of capital; but well advised measures will be taken to protect the landowners and inhabitants from the effects of future mismanagement on the part of the Directors. Of course, the question will come once more before the House of Assembly, and doubtless such instructions, will be transmitted to Canada by the Government as will prevent all attempts at monopolizing for political and personal ends the currency of the country. That His Majesty in Council has disallowed these Acts is a fact on which you may place the most implict [sic] dependance; and the people of Upper Canada ought to be for ever grateful to the Crown for this especial mark of its wisdom and goodness. I may be told that it is an act of interference with our domestic legislation. So it is: and such acts of interference must and will and ought to continue so long as our Legislature is liable to be unduly influenced, and led to do those things which might bring ruin on thousands of the population. In short, while we are a colony, the interference of the Crown for the protection of the subject against ruinous and dangerous monopolies, will not cease to be implored on every occasion which may seem to demand it. In the present case there was no other alternative. With respect to the Colonial Post Office and the charges for newspaper-postages, I had the honour sometime since to submit a plan to the Secretary of State, containing the view I take of the question; and Mr. Stanley, by whom I was favoured with an audience of an hour and a half, a few days since, informs me that His Grace the Post Master General has sent to Quebec to request Mr. Stayner the Colonial Deputy Post Master General's attendance here, with the view of making such arrangements as would be most advantageous and satisfactory to the people of British America. ...

22 THE FAMILY COMPACT NAMED

The Colonial Advocate,
September 26, 1833

SUPPLEMENT TO THE COLONIAL ADVOCATE, Thursday, Sept. 26, 1833. [From Mackenzie's *Sketches of Canada and the United States.*]

UPPER CANADA – KING, LORDS, AND COMMONS.

"It may easily be seen to what fate a colonial governor is exposed. He may become the instrument of the ambition or of the interest of those whose advice he is obliged to take. These latter escape as well censure as punishment, whilst he is answerable for errors and injustice which are the means of their acquiring honours and emoluments which should be the recompense of services, the reward of merit." – Letter – The Hon. D. B. Viger to Viscount Goderich in the matter of Attorney General Stewart.

A Political Union

The following curious but accurate statement will convey to the minds of liberal Englishmen a tolerably fair picture of colonial rule. When I left Upper Canada last year, some of the offices, sinecures, and pensions of the government were divided as follows: –

No. 1. *D'Arcy Boulton,* senior, a retired pensioner, £500 sterling.

2. *Henry,* son to No. 1, Attorney-General and Bank Solicitor, £2400.

3. *D'Arcy,* son to No. 1, Auditor-General, Master in Chancery, Police Justice, etc. Income unknown.

4. *William,* son to No. 1, Church Missionary, King's College Professor, etc., £650.

5. *George,* son to No. 1, Registrar of Northumberland, Member of Assembly for Durham, etc. Income unknown.

6. *John Beverley Robinson,* brother-in-law to No. 3, Chief Justice of Upper Canada, Member for life of the Legislative Council, Speaker, £2,000.

7. *Peter,* brother to No. 6, Member of the Executive Council, Member for life of the Legislative Council, Crown Land Commissioner, Surveyor-General of Woods, Clergy Reserve Commissioner, etc. Income £1300.

8. *William,* brother to Nos. 6 and 7, Postmaster of Newmarket, Member of Assembly for Simcoe, Government Contractor, Colonel of Militia, Justice of the Peace, etc. Income unknown.

9. *Jonas Jones,* brother-in-law to No. 2, Judge of the District Court in three districts containing eight counties, and filling a number of other offices. Income about £1000.

10. *Charles,* brother-in-law to No. 9, Member for life of Legislative Council, Justice of the Peace in twenty-seven counties, etc.

11. *Alpheus,* brother to Nos. 9 and 10, Collector of Customs, Prescott, Postmaster at ditto, Agent for Government Bank at ditto, etc. Income £900.

12. *Levius P. Sherwood,* brother-in-law to Nos. 9, 10, 11, one of the Justices of the Court of King's Bench. Income £1000.

13. *Henry,* son to No. 12, Clerk of Assize, etc.

14. *John Elmsley,* son-in-law to No. 12, Member of the Legislative Council for life, Bank Director, Justice of the Peace, etc.

15. *Charles Heward,* nephew to No. 6, Clerk of the District Court, etc. Income £100.

16. *James B. Macaulay,* brother-in-law to Nos. 17 and 19, one of the Justices of the Court of King's Bench. Income £1000.

17. *Christopher Alexander Hagerman,* brother-in-law to No. 16, Solicitor-General. £800.

18. *John M'Gill,* a relation of Nos. 16 and 17, Legislative Councillor for life. Pensioner, £500.

19. and 20. *W. Allan* and *George Crookshanks*, connexions by marriage of 16 and 17, Legislative Councillors for life, the latter President of the Bank. £500.

21. *Henry Jones*, cousin to Nos. 9, 10, etc., Postmaster at Brockville, Justice of the Peace, Member of the Assembly for Brockville. Income unknown.

22. *William Dummer Powell*, father of No. 24, Legislative Councillor for life, Justice of the Peace, Pensioner. Pension £1000.

23. *Samuel Peters Jarvis*, son-in-law to No. 22, Clerk of the Crown in Chancery, Deputy-Secretary of the Province, Bank Director, etc. Income unknown.

24. *Grant*, son to No. 22, Clerk of the Legislative Council, Police Justice, Judge Home District Court, Official Principal of Probate Court, Commissioner of Customs, etc. Income £675.

25. *William M.*, brother to No. 23, High Sheriff Gore District, Income from £500 to £800.

26. *William B.*, cousin to Nos. 23 and 25, High Sheriff, Home District, Member of Assembly. Income £900.

27. *Adiel Sherwood*, cousin to No. 12, High Sheriff of Johnstown, and Treasurer of that district. Income from £500 to £800.

28. *George Sherwood*, son to No. 12, Clerk of Assize.

29. *John Strachan*, their family tutor and political schoolmaster, archdeacon and rector of York, Member of the Executive and Legislative Councils, President of the University, President of the Board of Education, and twenty other situations. Income, on an average of years, upwards of £1800.

30. *Thomas Mercer Jones*, son-in-law to No. 29, associated with No. 19 as the Canada Company's Agents and Managers in Canada.

This family connexion rules Upper Canada according to its own good pleasure, and has no efficient check from this country to guard the people against its acts of tyranny and oppression. It includes the whole of the judges of the supreme, civil and criminal tribunal (Nos. 6, 12, and 16) – active Tory politicians. Judge Macaulay was a clerk in the office of No. 2, not long since. It includes the President and Solicitor of the Bank, and about half the Bank Directors; together with shareholders holding, to the best of my recollection, about 1800 shares. And it included the crown lawyers until last March, when they carried their opposition to Viscount Goderich's measures of reform to such a height as personally to insult the government, and to declare their belief that he had not the royal authority for his despatches. They were then removed; but with this exception the chain remains unbroken. This family compact surround the Lieutenant-Governor, and mould him like wax to their will; they fill every office with their relatives, dependants, and partisans; by them justices of the peace and officers of the militia are made and unmade; they have increased the number of the Legislative Council by recommending, through the Governor, half a dozen of nobodies and a few placemen, pensioners, and individuals of well-known narrow and bigoted principles; the whole of the revenues of Upper Canada are in reality at their mercy; – they are Paymasters, Receivers, Auditors, King, Lords, and Commons! ...

23 EGERTON RYERSON'S DEFECTION

The Colonial Advocate,
October 26, 1833

ANOTHER DESERTER!

The Christian Guardian, under the management of our rev. neighbour Egerton Ryerson, has gone over to the enemy, press, types, & all, & hoisted the colours of a cruel, vindictive tory priesthood. His brother George when sent to London became an easy convert to the same cause, and it appears that the parent stock were of those who fought to uphold unjust taxation, stamp acts, and toryism in the United States. The contents of the Guardian of tonight tells us in language too plain, too intelligible to be misunderstood that a deadly blow has been struck in England at the liberties of the people of Upper Canada, by as subtile and as ungrateful an adversary, in the guise of an old and familiar friend, as ever crossed the Atlantic. The Americans had their Arnold and the Canadians have their Ryerson;

and oppression and injustice, and priestly hypocrisy may triumph for a time and wax fat and kick, but we yet anticipate the joyful day as not far distant in which the cause of civil and religious freedom shall win a great and lasting victory in this favoured land.

The thorough defection of THE GUARDIAN and the RYERSONS will leave York without a Newspaper having the least pretence to independence of principle, during the ensuing Winter, and my remarks of tonight may lessen my chance of success in the Toronto riding next General Election, and *perhaps* render it expedient for me to decline being a candidate for the County in the case of an expulsion next month. But I hesitate not a moment, in expressing my sentiments – deceit and hypocrisy under the broad mantle of religion have not vanquished me. No, I was the dupe of a jesuit in the garb of a methodist preacher, and believed Egerton that I had been in error in opposing the Union, the fruits of which are so very soon ripened, but he and his new allies the church and state gentry shall now have me on their rear. Of course my plan of operations must be changed, for I feel that I am unable in my present position to contend against such powerful odds. I held out in the good old radical cause as an editor as long and well as I could.

24 HONEST FARMER-GOVERNMENT

The Advocate,
March 13, 1834

THE CONVENTION*

We this day publish as many of the resolutions and proceedings of this body as it is at present deemed prudent to place before our readers. The farmers present will long remember the day. How peaceful their proceedings! How unanimous all their votes! So also would it be in the House of Assembly if the yeomanry could but be made to believe the important truth that nothing more is required to qualify a representative of their rights than common honesty, the most ordinary business acquirements, and a knowledge by each member of the wants and wishes of the neighbourhood by which he is returned. There will always be leaders and talkers enough, but the difficulty is to get a steady band of plain men to go with them for the general good. It is roads and bridges, and schools, and salaries, and militia laws, and justice court laws, and such like that are to be considered, and is not a plain man fit to judge of such matters better than a person paid to mystify truth? We are well pleased with the choice made by the Convention, of Messrs. Morrison, Gibson and Mackintosh as candidates, and consider their election as perfectly sure. They will make as firm independent members as any who will set foot in the next legislature.

* The General Convention of Delegates of the Metropolitan District of Upper Canada held in York, February 27, 1834.

25 JOSEPH HUME AND REVOLUTION

The Advocate,
June 12, 1834

A reference to Joseph Hume's "Baneful Domination" letter denouncing British colonial rule.

(*For the Advocate.*)
I have been so constantly employed of late in attending to the duties imposed on me by my fellow citizens, that I had not so much leisure as formerly either to read or reply to newspaper paragraphs. I find, however, that the British Whig, the Hamilton Free Press, the Courier, Guardian, Patriot, Western Mercury, and the Quebec Gazette and Mercury are displeased with the contents of a letter addressed to me by Mr. Hume, and dated at London the 29th of March last. I beg to state that my reason for giving publicity to that letter was a belief that it would be attended with the most beneficial results. I am satisfied of the truth of the statements made by Mr. Hume and heartily accord with the sentiments and opinions he expresses concerning the present condition and future prospects of the Canadas....

... As to Mr. Hume's reference to the

example of America in 1776, it does indeed furnish an excellent and salutary lesson to the statesman – and with regard to his prediction that freedom from life legislators, military domination, land jobbing, established priesthoods and irresponsible government must be the result of the continued misconduct of the authorities here and their abettors in the Colonial Office, I do sincerely believe it is the truth. I am sure I have been acting the part of a sincere friend of the empire to which I belong while seeking the independence of Canada from the baneful domination of the Colonial Office. If revolution, violent revolution is to be avoided – if an honorable and beneficial connexion with Great Britain is to be maintained it must be in the way proposed by Mr. Hume, namely, by conciliating the people and allowing the colonists the management of their internal concerns. – Those who hold a different language are manifestly working to drive Canada into the arms of the United States.

W. L. MACKENZIE.
June 9th.

26 A POLITICAL HISTORY OF THE COLONIAL ADVOCATE

The Advocate,
November 4, 1834

A FEW WORDS AT PARTING.

It is now nearly eleven years since I wrote the first number of *the Colonial Advocate*, and ventured on its publication after reading it word for word to my worthy friend Mr. Beardsley of Niagara, who, as a whole, was pleased to approve of it. In my opening address I avowed my whig principles, eschewed radical reform, favored the principle a [sic] of hereditary peerage, as the most suitable for England, leant a *very little* towards the specious scheme of supporting the several religious denominations by Clergy Reserves, plainly expressed the unqualified contempt I felt for Sir Peregrine Maitland's administration of the provincial government, and while giving utterance to sincere and anxious wishes that Canada might thrive and rival the U. S. avowed the predilection I felt for the continuance of a political connexion with the country of my birth.

. . . After wearing the dress of a Whig for some years, I conscientiously adopted that of a radical reformer, ceased to put confidence in the inherent wisdom of hereditary peers, or to express admiration of the constitutional balance, and began my legislative labours in the House of Assembly by a notice for the abolition of the law of primogeniture. I continue a steady advocate of the representative system of government, a disunion of church and state, the abolition of monopolies, entails and perpetuities; and in proportion as England advances in the career of useful reform and improvement, in like proportion does my anxiety increase for a permanent settlement of the political connexion upon mutually advantageous terms. . . .

27 REFORM PRINCIPLES, 1834

Correspondent and Advocate,
December 18, 1834

OBJECTS AND RULES OF THE
CANADIAN ALLIANCE SOCIETY,
AGREED TO AT A
GENERAL MEETING
Held in the Society's Rooms,
Market Sqr. Toronto,
On TUESDAY, 9th DECEMBER, 1834

"WHEN BAD MEN CONSPIRE,
GOOD MEN MUST UNITE"

THE CANADIAN ALLIANCE

Resolved,– That a Society be now formed, with branches in the Canadas and elsewhere, to be known by the title of "the CANADIAN ALLIANCE."

The objects for the attainment of which the Society is established are these:

1. A responsible representative system of Government, and the abolition of a Legislative Council the members of which are nominated for life by the Colonial Governors.

2. The prevention of a Legislative Union of Upper and Lower Canada.

3. A Written Constitution for Upper Canada, embodying and declaring the original principles of the government.

4. The abolition or gradual extinction of all licensed monopolies.

5. A more equal taxation of property.

6. A less complicated and expensive Law System.

7. The amendment of the Jury Laws.

8. The abolition of the Law of Primogeniture.

9. A total disunion of Church and State; the ministers of religion to depend on their congregations.

10. The sale of, and disposal of the proceeds arising from, the Clergy and Crown Reserves, under the control of the representatives of the people, for extending the blessings of education, improving the roads and diminishing the public debt.

11. The control of the whole Public Revenue to be in the representatives of the people.

12. The gradual liquidation of the Public Debt.

13. To lessen the taxation on labour; increase the security of property; and enable the colonists to turn their skill, industry and capital to the best advantage.

14. To oppose all undue interference by the Colonial Office, Treasury, or Horse Guards, in the domestic affairs of the Colonists.

15. The diffusion of sound political information by tracts and pamphlets.

16. The extinction of all monopolizing Land Companies.

17. A speedy, efficient and cheap communication between the Provinces by a responsible Post Office.

18. To watch the proceedings of the Legislature and enforce economy and retrenchment in the expenditure of the Revenue.

19. To support honest, faithful and capable Candidates for all public situations of honor and emolument, power and trust, especially for the office of representative of the people.

20. A Free Press and an amendment of the Libel Law.

21. The Vote by Ballot in the election of representatives, Aldermen, Justices of the Peace, &c.

22. To preserve the public peace and order, and cimeously [sic] to remonstrate whenever the rights, liberties, and interests of the people of the North American Colonies are invaded.

23. To enter into close alliance with any similar Association that may be formed in Lower Canada or the other Colonies, having for its object "the greatest happiness of the greatest number."

W. L. Mackenzie,
Corresponding Secretary

28 THE GRIEVANCE COMMITTEE REPORT

Correspondent and Advocate,
May 7 and 22, 1835

IN ASSEMBLY, 10th APRIL, 1835
SEVENTH REPORT FROM THE
COMMITTEE ON GRIEVANCES

To the Honorable
the Commons House of Assembly

The Select Committee on Grievances, to whom were referred the Despatch of Lord Viscount Goderich, His Majesty's Principal Secretary of State for the Colonies, of date the 8th of November, 1832, with the Message of His Excellency the Lieutenant Governor, and several letters, petitions, and other Documents which had been addressed by William Lyon Mackenzie, Esquire, to the Secretary of State, accompanying the same – the Message of His Excellency the Lieutenant Governor in reply to the address of the House of Assembly for information concerning the dismissal and re-appointment to office of Mr. Solicitor General Hagerman the appointment of Mr. Jameson as Att'y General in the room of Mr. Boulton, and relative to the expulsion of the said William Lyon Mackenzie from the House of Assembly in a former Parliament – and certain other messages, petitions and documents on various subjects of grievance and public and private wrong – have, in obedience to the orders of the House, made some enquiry on the several subjects referred to them, and agreed to the following Report: ...

... The class of persons who are in favor

of elective institutions contend, that they were found to work well in the old North American colonies while in a colonial state – that the people of Upper Canada are entitled to the enjoyment of institutions equally free with those enjoyed by the old colonists during the time they were colonial, and under British protection – that few politicians are now found contending that these continental colonies, capable of containing a large population, will for a long series of years be required to submit to the inconveniences resulting from perpetual interference by the Home Government in their internal concerns – that in the House of Assembly many useful bills are proposed and carried for many successive sessions which are continually thrown out in the Legislative Council, of which the return moved for in the House of Commons by Mr. Hume and appended hereto gives particulars up to the year 1832 – that it is the wisdom of the aristocracy to try to make the people fearful of themselves, by raising idle cries about loyalty, republicanism, jacobinism, and revolution – that birth, office, or peculiar privileges ought not to give to a few superiority over the many – that the legislative council neglect and despise the wishes of the country on many important matters which a council elected by the freeholders would not – that the people, if united in claiming their privileges to constitute the second branch of the legislature, would obtain it, and that it is weakness and wavering among their representatives which alone can make them timid as to claiming the enlargement of their liberties. . . .

This country is now principally inhabited by loyalists and their descendants, and by an accession of population from the mother country, where is now enjoyed the principles of a free and responsible government; and we feel the practical enjoyment of the same system in this part of the empire to be equally our right; without which it is vain to assume that we do or can possess in reality or in effect "the very image and transcript of the British Constitution."

The House of Assembly has, at all times made satisfactory provision for the civil government, out of the revenues raised from the people by taxation, and while there is cherished an unimpaired and continued disposition to do so, it is a reasonable request that His Majesty's adviser in the province and those about him should possess and be entitled to the confidence of the people and their representatives, and that all their reasonable wishes respecting their domestic institution and affairs should be attended to and complied with.

Your Committee would respectfully recommend that, besides the usual number for the Journals, a large edition of this report, with the evidence and other appended documents, should be printed in a portable form, as early as possible and distributed among the members of the House, for general circulation throughout the colony. – And, as the affairs of the Canadas will probably occupy a large share of the attention of the Imperial Parliament during its present session, it might perhaps be advisable to transmit to London a certain number of copies for distribution among those members of the Legislature who take an active interest in Canadian affairs.

W. L. MACKENZIE, CHAIRMAN,
T. D. MORRISON,
DAVID GIBSON,
CHARLES WATERS.

Committee Room, House of Assembly, 10th April, 1835.

29 SEARCH FOR A RESPONSIBLE CONSTITUTION

Correspondent and Advocate, March 28, 1836

County of York Meeting over the role of the Governor in the Constitution.

. . . One party says it was intended by it to provide a responsible government in Canada, the other, that the Governor is a branch of the Legislature, and the only responsible minister of that branch, or of the government, and that his responsibility is not to the country but to a person living in a certain street in London, to whom all appeals are to be made. If we have not a constitution to protect our persons and property, it is time we had one; and I hope to meet as many of you as the state of the roads will permit at the County Meeting on Saturday next, there to receive your instructions, which I am sure I shall have very great satisfaction in obeying.

Yours faithfully,
W. L. MACKENZIE.

C. Republican and Revolutionary, 1836-1837

30 OHIO AND UPPER CANADA COMPARED

The Constitution,
August 24, 1836

... In old times and older nations the common people were continually deceived with names. Uneducated and ill-informed on government, they seldom referred to first principles, but were obliged to labour hard and fare poorly by whichever faction ruled in the state. In America more correct notions have prevailed; the labourer and mechanic, no longer deceived by high sounding titles, ask themselves why it is that Ohio and Michigan prosper while Upper Canada is depressed. They hear a great deal about reform, revolution, republicanism, democracy, and so forth, and are told that self-government is a dreadful thing, almost too awful to name. Still, they ask, why does property rise in value, in Ohio, and emigration pour into Michigan while the Canadas are torn with faction and their progress to a prosperous condition marred? It is admitted that we are the same people, having the same native energy, the same origin, and speaking the same language. – Where then the difference? Let their civil institutions be compared with ours, and the great secret of our poverty and their grandeur, of our dependence and their wealth, is at once told and

for ever. To this object then we intend to devote an occasional column of *The Constitution*, by which means that busy class who think, *or say they think*, our institutions perfection itself, will be enabled to offer proofs if they have any such, while those of a different stamp will be furnished with such convincing arguments as the case affords. . . .

31 COLONIAL PRECEDENTS FOR REVOLT

The Constitution,
October 12, 1836

Our Own Notions.

Having promised to re-state, with plainness and candour, our political sentiments, as soon as the course taken by the people of Lower Canada should become known, we hasten to redeem our pledge.

We are personally of opinion, that the conduct of the executive towards the people of Upper and Lower Canada has been such as in effect to absolve them from an allegiance, the principle of which is reciprocal obligations not deadly injuries. But this extreme view is perhaps not taken by the majority of the people, nor do we, for the present, see the utility of further considering it.

Allowing, for the sake of argument, that the tie of allegiance remains unbroken, the reasoning of some of our correspondents over real or fictitious signatures, that the prices of grain, flour or other of our staple commodities are higher in the United States market than here, and that the regulations of trade are vexatious, are not proper grounds for urging a dissolution of the Union of the *Crown* of England with these Colonies. Nor would we recommend to Reformers that course of proceeding, although we will not hesitate to publish what can be said in favor of it.

In 1774, the 13 Colonies, now the United States, asserted the great principle that representation must accompany the power of imposing taxes upon them – that they neither were nor could be represented in the Parliament of England – and that to taxation by that Parliament they would not submit. Taxes laid on by their representative Assemblies, agreed to by the King, who as the head of the empire might be expected to guard against the imposition of duties which would prejudice the interests of other portions of his dominions, they were ready to pay. In the assertion of this principle, Lord Chatham and the Whigs fully concurred with them, but the British Legislature expended one hundred and forty millions, sterling, with the view of forcing them to submit to taxation without representation and then declared them an independent nation. . . .

We are of opinion, that the Acts of the Imperial Parliament, imposing excise and customs duties, external and internal taxation, and, in some cases, placing prohibitions on the trade of the Canadas, whether at Quebec, Toronto, or elsewhere, are illegal, unconstitutional, and ought to be resisted in our courts of law, and the questions they involve discussed, brought before juries, and the arguments laid before the people, to whose welfare they are of such vital importance. . . .

32 ROUSSEAU AND REPUBLICANISM

The Constitution,
February 15, 1837

REPUBLICS VERSUS MONARCHIES – "If the good government of a state be a matter of difficulty under any mode of administration, it is more particularly so in the hands of a single person; and *every body knows the consequences when a king reigns by substitutes.* Again, there is one essential and unavoidable defect which will ever render a monarchical government inferior to a republic; and this is, that in the latter the public voice hardly ever raises unworthy persons to high posts in the administration; making choice only of men of knowledge and abilities, who discharge their respective functions with honour; whereas those who generally make their way to such posts under a monarchical government, are men of little minds and mean talents who owe their preferment to the meretricious arts of flattery and intrigue. The public are less apt to be deceived in their choice than the prince; and a man of real merit is as rarely to be found in the ministry of a king, as a blockhead at the head of a republic. Thus when, by any fortunate accident, a genius born for government takes the lead in a monarchy, brought to the verge of ruin by such petty rulers, the world is amazed at the resources he discovers, and his administration stands as a singular epoch in the history of his country."
– *Rousseau.*

33 RESPONSE TO LORD JOHN RUSSELL'S TEN RESOLUTIONS

The Constitution,
April 19, 1837

SLAVERY FOR CANADA

The secret is told at last. – The screens and councils and constitutions, the pledges and kingly declarations, the proclamations and acts of parliament & ministerial statements, to which the judge on the bench, the representative in the legislature, and the loyalist in his family circle referred as proofs that colonists were freemen are swept away in one instant by an almost unanimous resolution of the House of Commons of England, agreeing to rob, plunder, steal and defraud the people of Lower Canada of their money, the produce of taxation, to apply that money to purposes the people by their representatives would not consent to apply it, and to refuse them all substantial redress of the grievances under which they have so long and so patiently laboured. First, the parliament of England imposes taxes on the Canadians without their consent and in opposition to their solemn remonstrances; next, Lord Glenelg, keeps in authority a Council in Canada which taunts the people with their ignorance at the very time it tramples on their bills to provide for public education, and refuses their bills of supply because these bills provide that while the Chief Justice gets £1500 of their money as Chief, he should not get another £1000 as Speaker of the Council, and checks other monstrous pluralities; and thirdly, the parliament of England resolves that the Chief of the Colonial Office may empower the governor of Canada to put his hand in the Treasury of Canada, rob it of its contents, and without consulting the colonial legislature, pay it in thousands and tens of thousands to the host of placemen, pluralists and sinecurists who have been impeached by the country as unworthy of trust, and are protected and upheld only by the Bayonets of the Garrison of Quebec and the terrors of civil war with a cruel and unsympathising European power.

The resolves of the House of Commons may be opposed by the people of England before they become a law, but they shew nevertheless the true character of the plausible villains who were enabled to ride into power by offering England a reform bill, who were kicked out of it again for offering to gag and coerce Ireland, and who screamed against negro slavery in the West India Colonies while they were forging the fetter for the bondsman with a white skin in "conquered Canada." We thank God that he has given us the sense and feeling to despise and abhor the mercenary immoral wretches who, whether their names were Lord John Russell, Thomas Spring Rice, or Henry Labouchere, could degrade the legislature of our native land, and expose its rottenness and corruption, by proposing for its adoption, resolutions more suitable for the Meridian of Russia in its dealings with Poland, resolutions to barter the honour and good name of the United Kingdom for the purpose of giving temporary repose to the Whig government at the expense of British justice....

34 THOMAS PAINE'S *COMMON SENSE* PRINTED

The Constitution,
July 12 and 19, 1837

We have commenced the publication of an edition of twelve hundred copies of the far famed political publication, "Common Sense," a pamphlet which has received more praise and more abuse than almost any other similar work in our language. – It has passed through upwards of two hundred editions in Europe alone; it has been condemned by kings, courts, parliaments, judges and juries; it has been praised by peers and peasants – Fox, Sheridan, Erskine, Mackintosh, Lord Grey in his youth, Pitt before he took office, Horne Tooke, Major Cartwright, the Duke of Richmond, the celebrated Muir, Lord Jeffrey, La Fayette, and many other distinguished men in Europe, greatly admired it – its effect in America is recorded in the annals of the world.

Unlike other political works of its day, it studiously avoids personalities, adhering closely to principle throughout. The author, although afterwards led away by the example of French Philosophy, expresses himself throughout with the most reverential deference for the scriptures of truth, and the revelations of Christianity, and the Editor of this Journal respectfully recommends to those of his readers who have the means to spare, to purchase "Common Sense" by the score or dozen and circulate copies in their several localities, as an antidote to the high church doctrines of the pensioned clergy of the Church of England, and as a groundwork for the contemplations of the people on the question of government, and a written constitution.

We have departed from our original design so far as to use a large type, which increases the expense. The price will be one dollar per dozen, or 7½d. for a single copy. Copious extracts will be given in this newspaper; and it is hoped that in this day of unexampled difficulty, calm appeals to the "Common Sense" of the farmers, merchants, and labourers of Upper Canada will not be without beneficial effects.

** Six hundred copies are already purchased and paid for.

35 "BABYLON IS FALLING" – A JACKSONIAN MANIFESTO

The Constitution,
July 26, 1837

This extract is partially taken from Orestes Brownson's *Babylon Is Falling, A Discourse Preached in the Masonic Temple to the Society for Christian Ethics and Progress* (Boston, May, 1837). See Lillian Gates, "The Decided Policy of William Lyon Mackenzie," *Canadian Historical Review*, XL (September, 1959), p. 197.

Canadians! It has been said that we are on the verge of a revolution. We are in the midst of one; a bloodless one, I hope, but a revolution to which all those which have been will be counted mere child's play. Calm as society may seem to a superficial spectator, I know that it is moved to its very foundations, and is in universal agitation. The question which is now debated, and to which entire humanity listens, is one which reaches infinitely further than the most celebrated of the questions heretofore debated. The question to day is not between one reigning family and another, between one people and another, between one form of government and another, but a question between privilege and equal rights, between law sanctioned, law fenced in privilege, age consecrated privilege, and a hitherto unheard of power, a new power just started from the darkness in which it has slumbered since creation day. THE POWER OF HONEST INDUSTRY. The strange name borne by this new-born power, may deceive some as to its strength and merits, but though they may deem it an infant, they may be assured they will find it a Herculean one. The contest is now between the privileged and the unprivileged, and a terrible one it is. The slave snaps his fetters, the peasant feels an unwonted strength nerve in his arm, the *people* rise in stern and awful majesty, and demand in strange tones their ever despised and hitherto denied rights. They rise and swear in a deep and startling oath that JUSTICE SHALL REIGN. Let Hagerman, Head, Strachan, Ryerson, and all those who feed on the labours of others hear, and know, that not with a look or a word will they frighten or charm them down.

Not to this country and continent alone, nor chiefly, is this revolution confined. It reaches the old world. The millions downtrodden for ages by kings, hierarchies, and nobilities, awake. Kings put their hands to their heads to feel if their crowns be there; hierarchies lash themselves and cry mightily unto Baal; nobilities tremble for their privileges; time-cemented and moss covered state fabrics reel and totter; all who live on abuses seem to themselves to see the handwriting on the walls of their palaces, and to feel EVERY THING GIVING WAY BENEATH THEM. . . .

BROWN'S REFORMING. RECEIVER GENERAL LEMIEUX FOUND ASLEEP IN HIS CABINET

"The obstinate wrong-headedness and downright *vis inertiæ* of Mr. LEMIEUX. * * * The difficulty is how to get rid of him! * * * If we had an institution for the encouragement of SLEEP, Mr. LEMIEUX might do very well for Chief Superintendent."—*Globe*, Oct. 31, 1887.

"Mr. Drummond's sharp words had something of the effect on his colleague [LEMIEUX] that the apparition of the Angel had of BALAAM'S ASS. It made him speak!"—*Globe*, April 15, 1856.

[From *Toronto Weekly Message*, June 25, 1859]

The Remedy, A Convention of the People of Upper Canada.

The Wrong and

LEGISLATIVE ASSEMBLY'S CHAMBER,
TORONTO, Monday, May 18, 1857.

To the Inhabitants of Upper Canada:—

DEAR FRIENDS.—This day thirty-three years, (after reading my manuscript at Niagara to Mr. B C Beardsley, and obtaining his hearty approbation of the scheme,) I issued the first number of a public newspaper, devoted to progress in religion and morals, and to such an educational training as would enable the rising generation to prize useful knowledge and free institutions.

You are my witnesses, this day, that I have neither sought honours nor offices; that I have bartered no principle for gain—that I have not gambled in your lands, your banks, your railways, or your municipal trusts—that I have not forgotten the pledges with which I have set out in public life—but toiled as hard for my living as the poorest laborer, suffering exile, imprisonment, impoverishment, and the loss of this world's goods, for the sake of a cause I believed to be just.

While I gratefully acknowledge the magnificent gift of more than eight thousand dollars, recently bestowed upon me as a token of regard by more than 2,700 of my fellow citizens, and justly appreciate the generous feelings which dictated so unusual a present, I trust that I shall be forgiven, if, at your oldest journalist, as a true and faithful friend, and as a representative who entered the Legislative Assembly the earliest but one of any now there for either Canada, I anxiously and most earnestly entreat you to bestow an unusual degree of attention on the present condition of the public affairs.

That the rulers of the State and leaders of this people are shamelessly profligate and corrupt no sane man can help seeing. No new election or legislature under the present system will, in my opinion, afford a real remedy; neither is it right to allow the country to fall a prey to moon-day knavery in the hope that matters will mend of themselves—that would be doing evil that good may come.

We are now in the midst of peace, our towns, counties and estates adjoin each other, our fates are linked together, by honesty and industry, with intelligence, Canada may greatly prosper, but if we neglect our common obligations I fear the results. In the following paper, which I will endeavour to place on the Assembly's Journal, as a substantive proposition, I have tried clearly to explain my views, and the remedy I have suggested in a Convention of Representatives of your townships, towns, and cities at some central place, in order that the mind of the people may be made known with reference to those great and weighty affairs which urgently require a peaceful, prudent, speedy adjustment.

In no other way known to me can the public rapid be concentrated, or its decision given. In Union there is surely great strength.

There is no novelty in Congresses, Conferences, Conventions: they are the most effectual remedy known in such emergencies as that in which Canada is now placed. Monarchs, republicans, nations, confederacies, religious societies, have recourse to them, and if you conclude to call a convention, and if you choose faithful, earnest, true men, to attend its sittings, I may yet see the whole country going hand in hand to promote the common welfare, after concurring as to measures. I remain, your faithful servant,

W. L. MACKENZIE.

[From *Toronto Weekly Message,* May 22, 1857.]

36 A NEW CONSTITUTION FOR CANADA

*The Constitution,
November 15, 1837*

This constitution, as noted in J. E. Rea, "William Lyon Mackenzie – Jacksonian," pp. 233-34, was an amalgam of the American Constitution, the constitution of the State of New York, Jacksonian economic ideas, and Mackenzie's own strictures against corporate privilege. [ed.]

To the Convention of Farmers, Mechanics, Labourers, and other Inhabitants of Toronto, met at the Royal Oak Hotel, to consider of and take measures for effectually maintaining in this colony, a free constitution and democratic form of government.

The Committee appointed to report a popular Constitution, with guards suitable for this Province, in case the British system of government shall be positively denied us, respectfully submit the following draft:

WHEREAS the solemn covenant made with the people of Upper and Lower Canada, and recorded in the statute book of the United Kingdom of Great Britain and Ireland, as the thirty-first chapter of the Acts passed in the thirty-first year of the reign of King George III., hath been continually violated by the British Government, and our rights usurped; *And Whereas* our humble petitions, addresses, protests, and remonstrances against this injurious interference have been made in vain – We, the people of the State of Upper Canada, acknowledging with gratitude the grace and beneficence of God, in permitting us to make choice of our form of Government, and in order to establish justice, ensure domestic tranquillity, provide for the common defence, promote the general welfare, and secure the blessings of civil and religious liberty to ourselves and our posterity, do establish this Constitution.

1. Matters of religion and the ways of God's worship are not at all intrusted by the people of this State to any human power, because therein they cannot remit or exceed a tittle of what their consciences dictate to be the mind of God, without wilful sin. Therefore the Legislature shall make no law respecting the establishment of religion, or for the encouragement or the prohibition of any religious denomination.

2. It is ordained and declared that the free exercise and enjoyment of religious profession and worship, without discrimination or preference, shall forever hereafter be allowed within this State to all mankind.

3. The whole of the public lands within the limits of this State, including the lands attempted, by a pretended sale, to be vested in certain adventurers called the Canada Company (except so much of them as may have been disposed of to actual settlers now resident in the State), and all the land called Crown Reserves, Clergy Reserves, and rectories and also the school lands, and the lands pretended to be appropriated to the uses of the University of King's College, are declared to be the property of the State, and at the disposal of the Legislature, for the public service thereof. The proceeds of one million of acres of the most valuable public lands shall be specially appropriated to the support of Common or Township schools.

4. No Minister of the Gospel, clergyman, ecclesiastic, bishop or priest of any religious denomination whatsoever, shall, at any time hereafter, under any pretence or description whatever, be eligible to, or capable of holding a seat in the senate or house of Assembly, or any civil or military office within this state.

5. In all laws made, or to be made, every person shall be bound alike – neither shall any tenue, estate, charter, degree, birth, or place, confer any exemption from the ordinary course of legal proceedings and responsibilities whereunto others are subjected.

6. No hereditary emoluments, privileges, or honors, shall ever be granted by the people of this State.

7. There shall neither be slavery nor involuntary servitude in this State, otherwise than for the punishment of crimes whereof the party shall have been duly convicted. People of Colour, who have come into this State, with the design of becoming permanent inhabitants thereof, *and are now resident therein,* shall be entitled to all the rights of native Canadians, upon taking an oath or affirmation to support the constitution.

8. The people have a right to bear arms

for the defence of themselves and the State.

9. No man shall be impressed or forcibly constrained to serve in time of war; because money, the sinews of war, being always at the disposal of the Legislature, they can never want numbers of men apt enough to engage in any just cause.

10. The military shall be kept under strict subordination to the civil power. No soldier shall, in time of peace, be quartered in any house without the consent of the owner, nor in time of war but in a manner to be prescribed by law.

11. The Governor, with the advice and consent of the Senate, shall choose all militia officers above the rank of Captain. The people shall elect their own officers of the rank of Captain, and under it.

12. The people have a right to assemble together in a peaceful manner, to consult for their common good, to instruct their representatives in the Legislature, and to apply to the Legislature for redress of grievances.

13. The printing presses shall be open and free to those who may wish to examine the proceedings of any branch of the government, or the conduct of any public officer; and no law shall ever restrain the right thereof.

14. The trial by jury shall remain for ever inviolate.

15. Treason against this State shall consist only in levying war against it, or adhering to its enemies, giving them aid and comfort. No person shall be convicted of Treason unless on the testimony of two witnesses to the same overt act, or on confession in open court.

15A. No ex post facto law, nor any law impairing the validity of legal compacts, grants, or contracts, shall ever be made; and no conviction shall work corruption of blood or forfeiture of estate.

16. The real estate of persons dying without making a will shall not descend to the eldest son to the exclusion of his brethren, but be equally divided among the children, male and female.

17. The laws of Entail shall be forever abrogated.

17A. There shall be no lotteries in this State. Lottery tickets shall not be sold therein, whether foreign or domestic.

18. No power of suspending the operation of the laws shall be exercised except by the authority of the Legislature.

19. The people shall be secure in their persons, papers, and possessions, from all unwarrantable searches and seizures; general warrants, whereby an officer may be commanded to search suspected places, without probable evidence of the fact committed, or to seize any person or persons not named, whose offences are not particularly described, and without oath or affirmation, are dangerous to liberty, and shall not be granted.

20. Private property ought, and will ever be held inviolate, but always subservient to the public welfare, provided a compensation in money be first made to the owner. Such compensation shall never be less in amount than the actual value of the property.

21. *And Whereas* frauds have been often practised towards the Indians within the limits of this State, it is hereby ordained, that no purchases or contracts for the sale of lands made since the .... day of .... in the year ...., or which may hereafter be made with the Indians, within the limits of this State, shall be binding on the Indians and valid, unless made under the authority of the Legislature.

22. The Legislative authority of this State shall be vested in a General Assembly, which shall consist of a Senate and House of Assembly, both to be elected by the People. ....

51. The Legislature shall have power to pass laws for the peace, welfare, and good government of this State, not inconsistent with the spirit of this Constitution – To coin money, regulate the value thereof, and provide for the punishment of those who may counterfeit the securities and coin of this State.

I. To fix the standard of Weights and Measures.

II. To establish a uniform rule of Naturalization.

III. To establish uniform laws on the subject of Bankruptcies.

IV. To regulate Commerce.

V. To lay and collect Taxes.

VI. To borrow money on the credit of the State, not, however, without providing at the same time the means, by additional taxation or otherwise, of paying the interest, and of liquidating the principal within twenty years.

VII. To establish Post Offices and Post Roads.

52. Gold and Silver shall be the only lawful tender in payment of debts. . . .

54. There shall be no sinecure offices. Pensions shall be granted only by authority of the Legislature.

55. The whole public revenue of this State, that is, all money received from the public, shall be paid into the treasury, without any deduction whatever, and be accounted for without deduction to the Legislature, whose authority shall be necessary for the appropriation of the whole. A regular statement and account of the receipt and expenditures of all public money shall be published once a year or oftener. No fees of office shall be received in any department which are not sanctioned by Legislative authority.

56. There shall never be created within this State any incorporated trading companies, or incorporated companies with banking powers. Labor is the only means of creating wealth.

57. Bank Notes of a lesser nominal value than .... shall not be allowed to circulate as money, or in lieu thereof.

58. The Executive power shall be vested in a Governor. He shall hold his office for three years. No person shall be eligible to that office who shall not have attained the age of thirty years.

59. The Governor shall be elected by the people at the times and places of choosing Members of the Legislature. The person having the highest number of votes shall be elected; but in case two or more persons shall have an equal, and the highest number of votes, the two Houses of the Legislature shall, by joint vote, (not by ballot,) choose one of the said persons for Governor. . . .

65. The Judicial power of the State, both as to matters of law and equity, shall be vested in a Supreme Court, the members of which shall hold office during good behavior, in District or County Courts, in Justices of the Peace, in Courts of Request, and in such other Courts as the Legislature may from time to time establish.

66. A competent number of Justices of the Peace and Commissioners of the Courts of Request shall be elected by the people, for a period of three years, within their respective cities and townships.

67. All courts shall be open, and every person for any injury done him in his lands, goods, person, or reputation, shall have remedy by the due course of law; and right and justice shall be administered without delay or denial.

68. Excessive bail shall not be required; excessive fines shall not be imposed, nor cruel and unusual punishments inflicted. . . .

76. After this Constitution shall have gone into effect, no person shall be questioned for any thing said or done in reference to the public differences which have prevailed for some time past, it being for the public welfare and the happiness and peace of families and individuals that no door should be left open for a continued visitation of the effects of past years of misgovernment after the causes shall have passed away.

76A. For the encouragement of emigration, the Legislature may enable aliens to hold and convey real estate, under such regulations as may be found advantageous to the people of this State.

77. The River St. Lawrence of right ought to be a free and common highway to and from the ocean; to be so used, on equal terms, by all the nations of the earth, and not monopolized to serve the interests of any one nation, to the injury of others.

78. All powers not delegated by this constitution remain with the people.

79. Such parts of the common law, and of the acts of the Legislature of the Colony of Upper Canada, as together did form the law of the said colony on the ...... day of .... shall be and continue the law of this State, subject to such alterations as the Legislature shall make concerning the same. But all laws, or part of laws, repugnant to this Constitution are hereby abrogated.

80. The Senators and Members of the House of Assembly, before mentioned, and all Executive and Judicial Officers within this State, shall, before entering upon the duties of their respective offices or functions be found, by an oath or solemn affirmation, to support the Constitution; but no religious

test shall ever be required as a qualification to any office or public trust under this State.

81. This Constitution, and the laws of this State, which shall be made in pursuance thereof, and all treaties, made, or which shall be made under the authority of this State, shall be the supreme law of the land, and the judges shall be bound thereby.

Several clauses for the carrying a Constitution like the above into practice are omitted, the whole being only given in illustration of, and for the benefit of a comparison in detail, with other systems.

We have not entered upon the questions whether any, and if so, what restrictions ought to be laid upon the right of voting, or as to residence in the State, taxation, performance of militia duty, &c. These matters, however, might be advantageously discussed by the public press.

HENRY GRATTAN,
JOHN LOCKE,
ALGERNON SYDNEY, [sic]
BENJN. FRANKLIN.*

Committee Room, Royal Oak Hotel,
13th Nov., 1837.

* A diverse appeal to republican and revolutionary thought: Sidney was a seventeenth century English revolutionary and participant in the Puritan Commonwealth; Locke a political theorist used in justification of the Glorious Revolution of 1688 and the American Revolution of 1776; Franklin a signator to the American Declaration of Independence; and Grattan an advocate of British Parliamentary reform for Ireland in the 1780's and 1790's. [ed.]

37 SYMPATHY FOR LOWER CANADIAN REBELS

The Constitution,
November 22, 1837

Look Deeply and Consider!!!
PEOPLE OF UPPER CANADA

... You are told, the Lower Canadians are French, by your enemies. Suppose their ancestors were French, does that make them the worse? No, certainly not. The truth is they are born Canadians like ourselves; their fathers were born in Canada – they are free-minded Americans, therefore, they will not be slaves!! Many of them are Englishmen, and Irishmen and the descendants of them. Whatever country they are fighting for the rights of freemen, therefore, they deserve *our sympathy*! You are told they are Catholics, and speak French. Suppose they do; they are none the worse for that. Their opposition to injustice – their acts – their meetings – all shew they desire to improve – to tolerate and support civil and religious liberty; – by their fruits you must judge them. Has not France produced some of the greatest men that ever lived – Patriots, Philosophers, and friends of man? Did not the French Lafayette cross the Atlantic with Frenchmen to support the struggling American people in the revolutionary war? The struggle of the Americans, then *Upper Canadians*, was like that of the Lower Canadians now. They would not suffer England to tax them – they opposed it – England imported troops, soldiers, to put them down – they opposed and gained their liberties!!! ...

I was astonished when I saw the British government act as they did to Lower Canada. They have subverted a free government – they have trampled, upon every right dear to freemen and Englishmen. Why should Lower Canada, if it is a small province, be trampled upon and deprived of the rights of a free people? – I have always (until now) been taught to believe it was the beauty of the British government to respect the weak as well as the strong; but, is this the case with Lower Canda? [sic] No, because they are a weak and brave people England oppresses them. ...

In conclusion, let me advise every friend of the people to provide himself with a rifle, or a musket or gun; let meetings be called, either exclusively among reformers or otherwise; societies every where formed; and let *union* exist among you; *keep your eyes on Lower Canada*; be prepared for martial law from Governor Head. It is not at all unlikely but he will take your fire-arms from you, or will cause you to march down to Lower Canada, to put down a people contending for their rights. ...

38 A NEW SOCIAL ORDER

The Constitution,
November 22 and 29, 1837

THE NEW AGE

Considering now that all public power was suspended, and that the habitual restraint of the people had suddenly ceased, I shuddered with the apprehension that they would fall into the dissolution of anarchy; but immediately a voice was heard to say:

"It is not enough that we have freed ourselves from tyrants and parasites, we must prevent their return. We are men, and experience has abundantly taught us that every one is fond of power, and wishes to enjoy at the expense of others. It is necessary then to guard against a propensity which is the source of discord; we must establish certain rules of duty and of right: but the knowledge of our rights and the estimation of our duties are so abstract and difficult as to require all the time and all the faculties of a man. Occupied in our own affairs, we have not leisure for these studies; nor can we exercise these functions in our own persons. Let us choose then among ourselves such persons as are capable of this employment. To them we will delegate our powers to institute our government and laws; they shall be the representatives of our wills and of our interests. And in order to attain the fairest representation possible of our wills and our interests, let it be numerous, and composed of men resembling ourselves."

Having made the election of a numerous body of delegates, the people thus addressed them: "We have hitherto lived in a society formed by chance, without fixed agreements, without free conventions, without a stipulation of rights, without reciprocal engagements; and a multitude of disorders and evils have arisen from this precarious state. We are now determined on forming a regular compact; and we have chosen you to adjust the articles; examine them with care what ought to be its basis and its conditions; consider what is the end and the principle of every association; recognise the rights which every member brings, the powers which he gives up, and those which he reserves to himself; point to us the rules of conduct, and equitable laws; prepare us a new system of government; for we feel that the one which has hitherto guided us is corrupt. Our fathers have wandered in the paths of ignorance; and habit has taught us to stray after them: every thing has been done by fraud, violence and delusion, and the true laws of mortality and reason are still obscure; clear up then their chaos; trace out their connexion; publish their code, and we will adopt it."

Scarcely had he finished these words when a great noise arose in the west; and turning to that quarter, I perceived in one of the nations of Europe, a prodigious movement; such as when a violent sedition arises in a vast city, a numberless people rushing in all directions, pour through the streets and fluctuate like waves in the public places. My ear, struck with the cries which resounded to the heavens, distinguished these words:

"What is this new prodigy? what cruel and mysterious scourge is this? We are a numerous people, and we want hands! we have an excellent soil, and we are in want of subsistence! we are active, and laborious, and we live in indigence! we pay enormous tributes, and we are told they are not sufficient! we are at peace without, and our persons and property are not safe within! Who then is the secret enemy that devours us?"

Some voices from the midst of the multitude, replied: "Raise a discriminating standard, and let all those who maintain and nourish mankind by useful labors gather round it, and you will discover the enemy that preys upon you."

The standard being raised, this nation divided itself at once into two unequal bodies, of a contrasted appearance: one, innumerable, and almost total, exhibited in the general poverty of its clothing, in its emaciated appearance and sun burnt faces, the marks of misery and labor; the other, a little group, an imperceptible fraction, presented in its rich attire bedaubed with gold and silver, and in its sleek and ruddy faces, the signs of leisure and abundance....

And then the people immediately raised a great standard, inscribed with these three words, in three different colours. They displayed it over the pyramid of the legislator, and for the first time the flag of universal justice floated on the face of the earth; and the people raised before the pyramid a new altar, on which they placed golden scales, a sword, and a book with this inscription:

To equal Law, which judges and protects.

And having surrounded the pyramid and the altar with a vast ampitheatre, [sic] all the nation took their seats to hear the publication of the law. And millions of men, raising at once their hands to heaven, took the solemn oath to live free and just; to respect their reciprocal properties and rights; to obey the law and its ministers regularly constituted.

A spectacle, so forceful and sublime, so replete with generous emotions, moved me to tears, and addressing myself to the Genius: "Let me now live," said I, "for in future I have everything to hope."

39 MACKENZIE'S REBELLION BROADSIDE

Mackenzie's Gazette, [*New York*]
August 18, 1838

INDEPENDENCE FOR CANADA!

I find in page 160 of a folio volume on Canadian affairs printed last July by order of the House of Commons of England, a copy of the handbill which was circulated in the country back of Toronto, on the Monday of the revolt. A few days before that I sent one of Mr. Maxwell of the Bowery's portable printing presses, with type, balls, cases, a chase, and paper, up from the city. On Friday morning, while breakfasting in Markham, I hastily wrote and sent back the following handbill, Mrs. Mackenzie's brother set it in type, the press was hastily corrected, 1,000 copies circulated, generally on beautiful paper, and all was going well, for never was a secret better kept, when the news that, by a verbal message, Mr. Lount and his friends had been called out, caused great uneasiness among us, and we countermanded the order when too late. For us no shrewd messenger, no letter was sent; the people of the north supposed that the day had been altered by agreement, and came towards the city openly, and in such a way that before the half of them had reached Montgomery's the bells of Toronto were ringing an alarm. But it is better as it is – as the end will show. My handbill is offered to the reader as a record of a revolt, which will be most gloriously successful, and that before long.

[From the Journals of the
English Parliament, 1838]

INDEPENDENCE!

There have been nineteen strikes for independence from European tyranny on the Continent of America; they were all successful! . . . Brave Canadians! God has put it into the bold and honest hearts of our brethren in Lower Canada to revolt, not against "lawful" but against "unlawful authority." The law says we shall not be taxed without our consent by the voices of the men of our choice; but a wicked and tyrannical government has trampled upon that law, robbed the exchequer, divided the plunder, and declared that, regardless of justice, they will continue to roll their splendid carriages and riot in their places at our expense; that we are poor, spiritless, ignorant peasants, who were born to toil for our betters. But the peasants are beginning to open their eyes and to feel their strength; too long have they been hoodwinked by Baal's priests, by hired and tampered-with preachers, wolves in sheep's clothing, who take the wages of sin and do the work of iniquity, "each one looking to his gain in his quarter."

Canadians! Do you love freedom? I know you do. Do you hate oppression? Who dare deny it? Do you wish perpetual peace and a government founded upon the eternal heaven-born principle of the Lord Jesus Christ, a government bound to enforce the law to do to each other as you would be done by? Then buckle on your armour, and put down the villains who oppress and enslave our country; put them down in the name of that God who goes forth with the armies of his people, and whose Bible shows us that it is by the same human means whereby you put to death thieves and murderers, and imprison and banish wicked individuals, that you must put down, in the strength of the Almighty, those governments which, like these bad individuals, trample on the law and destroy its usefulness. You give a bounty for wolves' scalps; why? because wolves harrass you. The bounty you must pay for freedom (blessed word) is to give the strength of your arms to put down tyranny at Toronto. One short hour will deliver our country from the oppressor, and freedom in religion, peace and tranquillity, equal laws and an improved country, will be the prize. We contend that in all laws made, or to be made, every person shall be bound alike; neither should any tenure, estate, charter, degree, birth or place, confer any exemption from the ordinary course of legal proceedings and responsibilities whereunto others are subjected. . . .

D. American Exile, 1838-1843

40 FRESH BREEZES OFF THE HUDSON

Mackenzie's Gazette, [New York]
July 7, 1838

THE KNICKERBOCKER-RADICALISM-
HOBOKEN-FOURTH OF JULY

Among the pleasures of New York, there are few who can forget in June, the Elysian Fields over at Hoboken. When tired of hard stone walks, and red brick houses – wearied of the ceaseless din of hacks and omnibusses, carts, cars, and charcoal bawlers – the poor and rich can find rest and a ride in Neptune's chariots, periodically despatched from Canal, Kitt, and Barclay streets, to the shady groves of dear, delightful Hoboken. London has its Parks and the Seine is, at best, but another Goose Creek. – True, there are no stray cents of ferriage to be paid, but neither do we inhale the fine, cool, fresh, river breeze which invigorates and enlivens the ferryboat passenger, while wafted across the mighty Hudson. As to the groves of trees, the hill and dale scenery, and the sweep of a vast expanse of water to the south, there is nothing like these in the Capitals of England and France. Quebec and Edinburgh are indeed more splendid, but a walk up the higher road, and down the lower – an ice-cream, a dish of strawberries, &c, *"The Knickerbocker,"* for June, and the shade of an acacia – are these insufficient to fortify the mind against the inroads of dull care for the time? If so, the mental disease will perchance baffle the most radical of the three faculties, we mean the medical. . . .

Most earnestly do we wish that this Union, and the radical utilitarian principles on which a constellation of stars such as seldom appear together in the ascendant in the political firmament of any country, were enabled to found it, may be preserved and extended until pure democracy shall form the bond of good government as well on the mountains of Astoria, as on the shores of the Pacific – but if those who influence society in America shall successfully deceive its people by holding up gilded slavery in any of the anti-radical, bewitching forms it can so craftily assume, the benevolent intentions of the Franklins, the Jeffersons, and the Washingtons of other days will be frustrated forever, and the yoke of a hundred different warring and contending states and sovereignties, principalities and powers, will exhibit to posterity on this continent about as much of republicanism or radicalism, as the mitre, income, powers, privileges and pretensions of an Archbishop of Canterbury in England, does of the mild, generous, gentle and most acceptable religion of the meek and lowly Jesus of Nazareth, on which English anti-radical established clerical power professes to be founded.

41 LORD DURHAM AND THE FRENCH CANADIANS

Mackenzie's Gazette, [New York]
July 14, 1838

BREACH OF FAITH ON THE PART OF LORD DURHAM

The plan resorted to by Lord Durham to gratify the cravings of the Ultra Tories in Canada for revenge, shews that he is not very scrupulous of means so the end be gained which he wishes to accomplish. The manner in which he has entrapped Dr. Wolfred Nelson and his seven associates is a proof of this. By means of agents and spies, his Lordship learned that there was no chance in Lower Canada of obtaining a jury to find these worthy men guilty of treason. The plan, therefore, says the Montreal *Herald* of the 7th inst., was *"to get them to plead guilty."* With this base purpose Lord Durham sent an official agent to the prisoners with a draft of a petition for them to sign, in which they were made to plead guilty as his Lordship desired. Full of honied professions, this agent represented to them that the petition was a mere matter of form. The prisoners, however, had their suspicions, and refused to sign the paper which was brought to them, but Dr. W. Nelson and 7 others, now on their way to Bermuda, drew up a paper in which they avowed that they had offered resistance in defence of their personal liberty and character, but disclaimed all guilt as *rebels*. In order to make surety doubly sure, they obliged the Government agent to give them a certificate to the effect that they had not pleaded guilty, as required by a law passed by Colborne, which would give Durham the power of transporting them.

With this paper Durham's agent returned to his employer, and the latter forthwith called his automatons around him, passed an ordonnance declaring that Dr. W. Nelson, &c., had pleaded guilty to the charge of high treason, although they had the agent's certificate in their possession to prove the contrary, and ordering them to be "transported during her Majesty's pleasure!"

This trait in the character of the Autocrat of the Canadas is sufficient to assure us that he will fail in settling the difficulties which exist in those provinces. In public as in private life, "honesty is the best policy." Trick is a sign of a low and feeble mind – His Lordship has succeeded in expatriating Nelson and others, but the means by which he has attained his object have been such as to destroy all confidence in his honesty, justice, or promises. The Canadians will doubt hereafter every one of his professions. – Those who are in jail will be glad to get rid of their dungeons. Those in exile may not be sorry to return to their homes, but as long as Wolfred Nelson's name shall be remembered by the people of Canada, it will be a monument, *ære perennius*, of the bad faith of Governor Durham. He and his administration will never possess the confidence of the Canadian people, who have now an additional reason to induce them to wish to be rid of a connexion from which nothing is obtained but slavery for themselves, and banishment and exile for the best lovers of their country.

42 DIVINE RIGHT

Mackenzie's Gazette, [New York]
August 4, 1838

WHAT IS A QUEEN?

"If a king deserves to be opposed by force of arms, he deserves death; if he reduces his subjects to that extremity, the blood spilt in the quarrel lies on him." – Horace Walpole.

And what's a queen? – Come tell us now –
   And what is "right divine?"
What sits upon Victoria's brow,
   More royally than thine?
A diadem, and gay attire,
That witlings crave and fools admire.

Her *"sacred person!"* save the mark!
   Must rot with Time's decay;
She can't see further in the dark
   Than other people may.
Her Majesty must eat and drink,
Do all the needs of life save – THINK!

Her "right divine" for doing wrong
   We're bold enough to doubt;

And thus we raise our simple song
   To find the matter out;
If queens may slaughter subjects, why
Our "*Monarch*" has a mind to try.

But we are made of sterner stuff,
   We'll just see how we fare –
Of wrongs we've surely had enough,
   And cry aloud beware;
When thus a nation's held in thrall,
We'll think how Charley* left Whitehall.

* Charles I, the royal despot who attempted to coerce the people. [Mackenzie's note – ed.]

43 LORDS AND LADIES UNDRESSED

Mackenzie's Gazette, [New York]
August 11, 1838

Morality of the English Aristocracy – Judge Turton, Lord Durham's favorite at Quebec, is pretty well hauled over the coals for being a whoremonger and an adulterer. It seems his wife and her sister lived with him, and he debauched the sister, on which the wife got divorced from him, and he married the sister he had seduced. Turton married Gen. Brown's eldest daughter first, and next the younger. Old Wakefield the fellow who ran away with the child Miss Turner, and was sent to Newgate for his impudence, is another of Lord Durham's reformers for the Canadas. So it was of old. Franklin tells us that in his time worn out debauchees and Newgate attornies were found the most fit to govern the poor colonists; and Wakefield, Turton, and the greedy convict jailor, Arthur, are the props of the hypocritical Durham in his 1000 years dependence scheme of America on England. Heaven help him! But it is quite fashionable with great men in England. Sir George Murray, the late colonial secretary, seduced a Scotch Baronet's wife, lived with her openly, and at last married her. The Duke of Wellington's wife was debauched by the Marquis of Anglesea, the Marquis of Anglesea's wife was divorced from him and she then married the Duke of Argyle, thus having two husbands alive at one. The King (George the 4th) kept the Countess of Jersey as his procuress, and several other titled strumpets, and jilted Mrs. Fitzherbert by a pretended marriage to cheat England out of a vote of money to uphold gambling and whoredom. . . .

44 LOUISIANA AND FRENCH CANADA CONTRASTED

Mackenzie's Gazette, [New York]
November 24, 1838

THE DUTY OF THE FRIENDS OF CANADA AT THE PRESENT CRISIS

. . . The Louisianase, if they became American in feeling, did so because they considered it for their happiness, and all changes since made were in conformity to that principle. But in becoming politically speaking American, they had not thereby their language destroyed, their institutions threatened, and war waged incessantly against themselves. The Laws of the State are still printed in *both* languages. Every man is free to profess whatever Religion he pleases without the fear of having an established church or established Rectories placed over his head against his will; and he is free to speak French, Spanish, or English; or to have his name terminate according to the fashion of his father's, without having, on that account, a black mark set against that name, or having "war to the knife" proclaimed against him and his race by those in power.

The great error with Britain was, that she would not "take a chapter out of the book of the Americans." The Canadians for years prayed for elective institutions, such as the people of every corner of the United States enjoy. Instead of conceding these demands, war was levied against the people – their money unlawfully seized and themselves hunted like wild beasts through the forest, whilst their habitations and the shelter of their little ones were fired and laid waste. This was not the way the Americans treated the Louisianese [*sic*]. Far different was their wise policy. It was, on the other hand, by years of insult, insolence, political degradation and political persecution that the quill drivers in Downing street have prevented the Canadians amalgamating with the British settlers. They have now their reward. They have sown in the whirlwind and are reaping in the storm, and all we pray is, that the Canadian people will never bury the hatchet until they have driven their persecutors into the Sea.

45 DISILLUSIONMENT WITH REPUBLICANISM

Mackenzie's Gazette, [Rochester] January 11, 1840

TO THE PEOPLE OF UPPER CANADA!

Since crossing the Niagara in January, 1838, I have ascertained – that the republican forms of the government of these United States serve as a mantle to conceal from the people the aristocratic machinery which, as in England more openly, moves the vessel of the state. In this great country of New York, the lawyers protect their monopoly by seven years apprenticeships, and at least as many varieties of rules of life, taken from England, her colonies, state legislation, congress statutes, foreign treaties, and British common law, as are in use among yourselves. The administration of justice is exclusively in the hands of those monopolists, the judges being often selected by the Banking influence, from among the most intolerant and exclusive of the members of the bar. Equal rights and the truths of the Declaration of Independence are not and cannot be enjoyed in the midst of a thousand city, village, clerical, manufacturing, railroad, canal, and worst of all, banking corporations, every one of them more exclusive than another. They are the props of the British monarchy beyond the sea; they are England's fortresses on the continent of America. The influence of the press upon the people here is very great; and the tongues of the lawyers and the pens of the editors move in implicit obedience to the same monied power which has prostrated the last remains of freedom in Britain. Even the President of the republic has come forward and acknowledged, that as the United States is 200 millions of dollars in debt to the English capitalists, and paying them over ten millions of specie in tribute annually, and as America clings to an anti-republican fluctuating paper currency, issued by her enemies in preference to a gold and silver one of her own, the money power of England controls this nation, causes her banks to stop payment, deranges her finances at will, and might even embarrass her government in the hour of its utmost need. England has a standing army, and the government here is quietly increasing the efficiency of a like prop of monarchy. The Church of England, in England, is richly endowed. In this state alone its priests own sixty millions value of estate. So we have an established church in right earnest, *aye, and more than one.* The State Legislature, whether whig or democrat, meets but to increase the burthen [sic] of the people, rich capitalists pass laws for poor laborers, but as to republican legislation, where is it to be found? In the Congress, a majority of prerogative made lawyers shew far more respect for English Parliamentary customs than American Institutions; and; [sic] as far as I can judge, the two great parties of ins and outs whose leaders move the people as if they were two contending armies, are the very counterparts of the British Whigs and Tories, and equally *honest* and *disinterested* in all they say and do! The ballot, of which I was much in favor when with you, would be no adequate protection to the poor voter in the present state of society in England, neither does it protect the people here. Corruption is powerful in England and with you, but beyond its influence here I should think that nothing could go....

My darling wish for twenty years was to see one great federal union of the nations of North America, by which means I expected a perpetual peace to be maintained. But the time is not yet come. The sooner we get rid of English power, the nature of which this Almanack faithfully describes, the better. While England keeps five millions of her home subjects in poor-house bastiles or for factory work, we can have nothing to hope from her sense of justice; and it would be no enviable condition to become miserable dependants of the slaveowners of the south and the usurers of the north, by exchanging the yoke of Victoria for that of Congress....

46 DECLARATION FOR THE DEMOCRATS IN 1840

Mackenzie's Gazette, [Rochester]
September 26, 1840

AMERICAN ELECTIONEERING ON THE EVE OF A GREAT STRUGGLE WITH ENGLISH MONEY POWER

TO FRIENDS IN CANADA, NATIVES OF THESE STATES, OR WHO HAVE RELATIVES AND CONNEXIONS RESIDING IN THE UNION.

You will have observed that all the British Whig and Tory papers in both Canadas are bitterly hostile to Jackson, Van Buren and Johnson, and quite in love with Harrison, Clay and Webster. The reason is, that English power, already tremendous in these States, will be greatly strengthened by an English Sub-Treasury to keep the tribute in, under the name of a National Bank, and a phalanx of national collectors of interest or tribute payable to London yearly, 450 tons of silver, under the pretence that America owes England a national debt; and if Harrison is president the country is delivered tied and bound into the hands of the most unprincipled speculators in this community and their abettors the enemies of free institutions in Europe. Jackson and Van Buren and the honest democrats in Congress and out of it have struggled since 1829 with the avaricious and greedy, the covetous and the dissolute here and beyond seas, and now comes victory if America prove true to her institutions, but if she prove false, November will give a greater blow to the cause of freedom than it has received since the adoption of the Federal Constitution.

As *you* can see clearly which is the British party here, that is, the party your tyrants desire success to, let me intreat you to write to all your friends on this side throughout the Union, urging them to support the General Government, which is opposed by about 10,000 special corporations and other unrighteous powers, the disgrace of the age in which we live....

47 THE END OF REPUBLICANISM IN NORTH AMERICA

Mackenzie's Gazette, [Rochester]
December 23, 1840

A FEDERAL EMPIRE OF NORTH AMERICA

The following letter was mailed to me at New York, post-paid, upward of two years since, but a reference to the Caroline Almanack for this year, will show the writer that I have been compelled to abandon my position, and acknowledge that a federal, republican union, of the countries composing the continent of North America, by which peace would be preserved, national disputes settled, and mankind benefitted, is at present altogether impracticable, because of the selfishness and ignorance of millions of the human family. An aristocratic, monied, grinding, sharp-biting, oppressive tyranny, by the few over the many, is a bond more likely to unite great communities on this side of the Atlantic, as it has already united a powerful empire on the other. – [EDITOR, GAZETTE.]

To the Editor of Mackenzie's Gazette:
ROCHESTER, 4th Sept., 1838.
Sir: – In your Gazette of the 1st inst., I find the following paragraph: "To speak of Canadian Independence, apart from American connection, is sheer nonsense. Canada annexed to the Union would diminish a foreign boundary held by enemies of the republic, its ancient tyrants, from 4,000 miles in length to only 1,000 yards (or the breadth of the St. Lawrence below Quebec.) Two republics, with adverse laws, institutions, and tariffs, bounded by the middle of the valley of the St. Lawrence and the line 45, would be a new thing under the sun, indeed the idea is too ridiculous for serious argument. We dismiss it."

Permit one, sir, who anxiously desires the liberation of Canada from British tyranny, to regret that you dismissed the subject so laconically. The idea of two republics may indeed seem preposterous to you, and the scheme of one vast and magnificent federal union for this great northern continent of the new world, may be practicable and probable, should future events overthrow the British power in her North American provinces. ...*

* The author of this letter was Dr. John Smyles, an English radical with Chartist political affiliations. See M. Brook, "Lawrence Pitkethly, Dr. Smyles, and Canadian Revolutionaries in the United States," *Ontario History*, LVII, (June, 1965), 79-84; and L. Gates, "A Note on Dr. John Smyles," *Ontario History*, LVII (December, 1965), 229-30.

48 CONVENTIONS AND REPEAL OF THE UNITED CANADAS

The Volunteer, [Rochester]
April 17, 1841

WHAT OUGHT TO BE DONE!

Long and earnestly have eight millions of Irishmen craved the boon from their British taskmasters, of a House of Assembly in Dublin, where patriotic men, elected by the people, could express their wishes and opinions and attend to their domestic affairs.

Suppose their requests granted – peers, spiritual and temporal, could veto their bills – every office would be in the gift of the crown – British regiments by the score would garrison Ireland – loyal mobs, and brutal partizans would disturb their elections, and spill the best blood of their country – constituencies with 75 voters, as at present, would send as many or more members than constituencies of 750 or 7500 – still, they wisely press onward for a repeal of the Union. What they ask, Canada has just obtained; a Convention, according to law, the members of which, whether returned by petty constituencies like Draper, McNab, Hale, Chesley, Killaly, Sherwood, Campbell, and Derbishire, or by such great counties as sent Raymond, Cavillier [sic] and Taschereau, containing nine times as many people as all the villages who send the eight first named, taken together, will ably discuss the great question of the day – aristocracy or democracy, which is it to be? The feudal institutions of Europe or the popular ways of America?

I consider it of primary importance that the actors in this remarkable drama, soon to meet at Kingston, should be known to the public, and for that and other reasons I have begun this work with sketches of some of them, and expect to include the eighty-three in portions of my first three numbers.

Mr. Bennett of the Herald, with a far seeing sagacity, is about to send reporters to the Kingston Parliament, and other opulent and influential editors will follow his example. The tale of Canadian wrongs will thus be spread before the children of the revolution of '76, as told by the delegates of the remaining colonies; and may Heaven grant them wisdom and prudence for the important duty they are called on to perform, so that the end may be a triumph of truth upon the earth.

49 RESPONSIBLE GOVERNMENT: A SHAM

The Volunteer, [Rochester]
May 15, 1841

RESPONSIBLE GOVERNMENT!! – A fine thing to talk about, but it means independence of foreign control, so far as it has meaning. Mr. Haliburton has been raised to a seat on the bench of the supreme court of Nova Scotia, over the heads of many older judges and lawyers; this the English Lord who rules there has done, and never even told his executive council or political, constitutional advisers, that he intended such a thing! Yet they stick to office, and Howe of the Nova Scotian has to be content with this sort of *responsible* government. It is just so in Canada; the councils, legislative and executive, share the public plunder and join the English agent in approving of any plans he may suggest, or any men he may choose, for any purpose of oppression or injustice. In the drama of Canadian slavery they are ready to take any part the Lord Thomson of the day may suggest for harrassing the people, if he will but pay them for it, or permit them to squeeze enough from the masses to pay themselves.

50 A DEMOCRATIC MANIFESTO

The Volunteer, [Rochester]
June 19, 1841

PRINCIPLES OF THE VOLUNTEER

I *Volunteer* in the cause of Temperance, Truth, Courage, Honesty; for Freedom of Thought, Speech and the Press, Equal Rights and the Law, Universal Education, National Independence, the Voluntary System in Religion, Elective Republican Institutions, Universal Suffrage, Universal Peace, after the foul evidences of Monarchy are driven from this continent, Freedom of Trade, Sabbath rest, and the heavenly law, "Thou shalt love thy neighbour as thyself."

I *Volunteer* against Falsehood, Hypocrisy, Superstition, Ignorance, Bankcraft, ORGANIZED AVARICE, or a privileged monopoly of Usurers, Priestcraft, Kingcraft, Lawcraft, or a privileged monopoly of Lawyers and Lawgivers, Judicial Landcraft, or a privileged monopoly of the soil, its products and people, by laws of Entail, Primogeniture, etc., a hereditary nobility and bench of Bishops, a National Debt, unless when voted for by the people, approved in their primary assemblies, and provision by them for its extinction, Organized Robbery as in Canadian Taxation, by the bayonet without Representation, Alien Legislation, Slavery, of whatever race or color it may be the curse, Standing Armies in time of Peace, Drunkenness, Sloth, and Sordid Selfishness, National Apathy and Cowardice, and Faction or Party, united by interest and expediency, but devoid of manly principle.

51 MACKENZIE VERSUS VAN BUREN

The New York Examiner,
October 7, 1843

"I AM NOT A CANDIDATE FOR THE OFFICE OF PRESIDENT, NOR ANY OTHER."

Upwards of a hundred newspapers have already given notices of my first number – the Plebeian, Mr. Van Buren's leading journal in New York, is evidently very uneasy about it – very abusive – and would gladly discuss the past history and present position of a "renegade," or take any other issue, rather than reply to, explain, or deny the heavy charges brought against its patron. But, I am no candidate for office. Suppose I were proved to be the ruffian, coward, renegade, cheat, murderer, hireling, profligate, &c., which the Plebeian and other journalists who praised me to the skies as it were but yesterday, have just discovered me to be, would that be any vindication of Mr. Van Buren's political sins? A friend writes me that to establish one man's purity by asserting another's impurity is an old trick of the Regency. My statements might have been anonymous, though I disdain concealment. They require no proof of mine – they refer to dates and things and places which, independent of me, all can have access to. If I have spoken falsely, however, no apology could be too humble for me to make. If I have not, Mr. Van Buren and his confederates are surely very wicked, unworthy, bad men. I am only on the threshold of my Van Buren expositions, and will not change the issue before the public by replying to continual abuse of myself, and thus diverting public attention from the conduct of Mr. Van Buren and his friends....

November 11, 1843

The Life and Adventures of M. VAN BUREN, by William L. Mackenzie.

I am preparing for publication, in four numbers, large octavo, at one shilling each, an account of the life and political adventures of Mr. Van Buren. It will be printed on fine paper, with small new type, so as to contain as much reading matter as can possibly be afforded at that price – and the object is to exhibit Mr. Van Buren's character, as shown by his conduct, in a form far more permanent than thro' the columns of a weekly newspaper. A large edition will be printed, and the usual discount, of one-third off, allowed to retailers. A work of this sort, constantly referring to documentary and other evidence and carefully confined to facts, for the truth of which I am held responsible to the legal tribunals of the country, will be much read and quoted, and cannot fail to exercise an influence on the presidential election next year. Anecdotes and sketches of the characters of prominent politicians of the Albany or Van Buren school will be interspersed throughout.

E. The Old Reformer, 1852-1860

52 MAN'S PROGRESS

Mackenzie's Weekly Message, December 25, 1852

... When we compare the past with the present it is impossible to repress a warm enthusiastic hopefulness as to the future. Since the writer was an infant in the cradle, how remarkable have been the changes, discoveries, and inventions highly favourable to human happiness! For one child that received a common school education in christendom during the eighteenth century, ten children have been well taught their rudiments within the earlier half of the nineteenth. The first Napoleon left an imperishable code of laws as a legacy to France, after sweeping away the conflicting and contradictory precepts and precedents of a thousand years. New York has united the realms of law and equity, assimilating the mode of procedure in her judicial courts. Scotland has obtained a real representation in the British House of Commons in place of a merely nominal one. England has led the way to cheap postage, begun her grand work of legislative reform, repealed ancient laws against conscientious dissent from courtly creeds and partly unshackled the periodical press. Prussia is thoroughly educating a gallant nation. The institutions of the neighbouring republic which has afforded an asylum to the homeless upon earth and increased from four to twenty-four millions of souls, have undergone very many substantial improvements. ...

France is said to be fickle, but I perceive no proof of it in her treatment of the Bonaparte family. She had struggled for liberty and been misgoverned by incapables – but rallied round the man who exhibited no trait of avarice, but a capacity fit to sway the sceptre of an empire. The French secured his victories, followed his counsels. ...

Ludwig Kossuth and Joseph Mazzini, types of revolution, are silent in London but not idle. They bide their time. Doubtless Austria and Russia, do not thank Palmerston and the whigs for harboring such dangerous persons. Germany is full of discontent. Italy's millions are ignorant, disunited, revolutionary, ill at ease. As to an inroad of the French into Great Britain, it would surely be a signal failure, try it when they might.

Political questions in the United States are assuming a dangerous, sectional, south and north aspect; and the popular English press stands powerfully out for a more thorough reform. Russell failed to stop the salutary current. Stanley is now trying his hand. The British millions are heartily sick both of whigs and tories, and these factions will undoubtedly have to succumb unless a sudden war in Europe shall put the clock of the world back ten degrees, and crush the healthful buddings of reform, as it did some sixty years ago since, when the peerage and priesthood united to compel Pitt to fight with France, though he would far rather have concluded a reciprocal commercial treaty with her.

War might help Ireland, as now situated, but it would stop internal reform in Britain, which must and will come. Fervent are my wishes for its advent. Even in my boyhood, I glowed and gladdened at the prospect, then more dimly seen, of happier and kindlier times for my countrymen. Much has since been done for the general good. ...

53 UPPER CANADIAN SECTIONALISM

*Mackenzie's Weekly Message,
June 9, 1853*

The Repeal of the Union

The more I see of the French Canadian brethren, and the measures which they compel their dependants in the government here to put forward, to empty the cash raised from us of Upper Canada into the pockets of their friends here – added to the continual thwarting of Upper Canada measures by Lower Canada majorities, – the more I think of the necessity that exists for a repeal of the Union between the Canadas, and a return to Upper Canada legislation in a free parliament of our own at Toronto. This would give us the command of our own resources – free us from a perpetual waste of time discussing tenures bills and the thousand and one other Lower Canada measures which are perpetually on the carpet here and render that legislation real which is at present only imaginary.

On the millions already voted, or to be hurriedly voted before we separate on the 10th inst. Lower Canada chisselers grasp firmly the lion's share, while a vast portion of the population of that colony scarce contribute anything to the common fund; and I fear that although some advantages will be gained by a more equalized representation in the Assembly and by an elective Senate, yet the bridle rein, as now, will remain in the hands of our Franco-Canadian friends, who, united in language, religion, and origin, will continue as heretofore to render the Union unprofitable to a large portion of the people, though beneficial to themselves.

54 INDEPENDENCE OR COLONIAL REPRESENTATION?

*Mackenzie's Weekly Message,
October 27, 1853*

A Third North American Republic

It would appear by the following despatch telegraphed last week from Halifax to the New York press, that, in addition to Mexico and the United States, there is a prospect of the establishment of a third republic on the North American continent.... Among the questions to be asked are, who would pay the military of the new Union? how would it be in case of a war, upon the expediency of declaring which, the crown and colonists might differ? what power and prerogative would remain to the crown, if the local parliaments were made elective, as they ought to be, and the governors of colonies chosen by the people? how about the duties we pay to the United States upon our exports, which are invited to their ports, by their extended system of railways and canals, by the relaxation of England's restrictions upon trade with them, and by their good markets in which to buy and sell?

Our lot in Canada is very desirably cast: we have much to be thankful for; and it is our duty as a people to canvass proposed changes.... To express an opinion upon a scheme concerning which we have only imperfect rumors, would be premature, neither is the following reference to the writer's views 20 years since at all applicable to 1853, for the colonial system has been materially changed.... We do not desire to suggest a colonial representation in the British Parliament, but much good might arise were a delegate from each of the local legislatures, where the population of any colony exceeded 200,000 souls, allowed to explain in the British House of Commons any matter in which the Colonists have an interest, but with no power to vote in any case. It would also be advantageous were a commissioner, with like privilege and authority to act in commercial matters kept constantly in London on behalf of the federal body....

55 AN OPEN LETTER TO LORD ELGIN

*Mackenzie's Weekly Message,
March 3, 1854*

... I am sure that no man in America felt more indignant at the insults you received from a pampered worthless faction here, who were struggling, in 1849, not for their country's welfare, but for the privilege of plundering their fellow men. It was little I could do; but so far as my pen might affect the English, American, and Canadian public, through the press, I was among the very humblest of your lordship's defenders; and when you stood beside the President of the United States and the magnates of the Union, I felt pleased to witness your noble and gallant bearing, while listening to your able, graceful, and most appropriate address, full of wit and humor, and unequalled in its manner by any other that day delivered before the audience of 4000, so singularly and happily convened to celebrate the triumph of science, and the arts, as enlisted in the service of the human family. You, my lord, had revived hopes which had almost died within me, that one born to rule wise in counsel, and experienced in legislation, had at length been chosen as its agent in Canada thro' the wisdom of a British cabinet, who could and would watch over and protect liberty and right, in connexion with the freemen of the lands of Sidney, Locke and Russell; of Wallace, Bruce, and Burns; of Swift, Fitzgerald, and Emmet, and Moore; that the dawn of a newer and happier era was about to dawn upon British America; and that the instrument in the hand of providence who would effect this great good and with the Queen's sanction, too was the descendant of an illustrious race, the name and noble deeds of whose great progenitor are entwined round the hearts of Scotland's sons and daughters, who glow and gladden at the sound of

"Scots wha hae wi' Wallace bled,
Ye whom Bruce hath often led."

When the Holmeses, Galts, Holtons, Roses, Johnsons, Molsons, and Redpaths, "The loyalists" par excellence of Montreal in 1837, raised the shout of "annexation" – not to procure a tardy measure of justice for the people, but to induce England to advance new loans, more treasure, the plunder of the many in both hemispheres for the advantages of the combined few here, no man denounced the selfish, sordid movement, sooner or more steadily than your humble correspondent. In 1837, I had united with others to seek liberty from cruel oppression for my countrymen – in 1849 I could not but heartily despise the men who after wading ankle deep in the innocent blood of Canadians twelve years before, were quite ready to cut the connexion they swore they loved and cherished, ready to do it PEACABLE, [sic] to save their carcasses; ready to come under the yoke of the Virginia slaveholder, united with that of the New England usurer – for self, places, and the power to plunder.

56 AMERICA'S PROMISE AND ISOLATIONISM

*Mackenzie's Weekly Message,
March 24, 1854*

True Progress! Nobility!

In nothing were we more disappointed, while residing in the United States, than in the mean, cunning, tricky character of many of their leading politicians – full of talent, but possessing a contemptible, grovelling taste.

The results have been made apparent in this, that while the aim of the national leaders has been to spread oppression, serfdom, slavery, over North America, all the honest and manly minority could effect was to offer an ineffectual opposition or compromise matters.

The tide of affairs is changing however, and free institutions and education, in the north are producing good fruit. Maine set the example of stemming the tide of drunkenness which was overspreading the land – Michigan and Massachusetts, both peopled by the descendants of the freedom loving Englishmen united in the good work – and altho' the votes of Richard and Street – and the shuffling course of slippery Rolph, threw "Temperance" into a minority last spring at Quebec, the telegraph, last Wednesday brought glad tidings, that the Maine LAW after being adopted in the Senate, had passed in the Assembly, 78 to 41, and will go into operation next May; that another prohibitory liquor law had passed the House of

Representatives of the good old German Keystone State of Pennsylvania, by a vote of 50 to 44, and that the crafty hypocrites, Cushing, Marcy, Douglas, & Co. have been foiled at Washington, and the march of Satan's kingdom, o'er the northern realms untrodden yet, by man, courageously arrested, by the VIRTUAL DEFEAT of the Nebraska Bill. O, but it is a cherishing thought, that while a desolating war is likely to bring woe, misery, and death into thousands of dwellings in Europe, young America yet affords good hope of that noble manhood which Burke, Fox, Lafayette, Washington and and [sic] the good and virtuous of many lands aimed to see! The Senate should now pass the bill for free homes in the wilderness, – and like Napoleon, cease to grasp at more widely extended empire, and govern well the patrimony they have in charge. . . .

57 THE VIRTUES OF AMERICAN SIMPLICITY

Mackenzie's Weekly Message,
January 12, 1855

. . . Our politicians should take a pattern by the Yankees in the message way. The state and federal governments begin their legislation each session by plain, clear, distinct statements of the public affairs, especially the financial. Governors and Presidents, Secretaries and Comptrollers have all to report fully how matters are – and after so doing the representatives go to work understandingly. In Canada, the legislature is assembled at anytime or place that suits the whim of a few, and not till the session is so wasted that half the member [sic] have gone home wearied, is the financial legislation begun, at midnight, and without reason, system or knowledge. . . .

58 DISSOLUTION OF THE UNION AND ELECTIVE INSTITUTIONS

Mackenzie's Weekly Message,
December 7, 1855

We are for representation – for a dissolution of the Union with Lower Canada – for a convention fairly and equally chosen by the people, in their several divisions, for the express purpose of devising checks upon the abuse of delegated power by the legislatures and executives — for an elective legislative council – for elective county offices – for short term of office, no dissolution in the midst of harvest to deceive the country, and no quorums of 20 whereby the vote of ten legislators can place ten millions of debt on the people's shoulders at midnight altho' 130 are paid $6 a day for being on hand to look after their interests. Aye, and we are for holding up to the public gaze the needy and covetous crew of office beggars, who are always ready, (MacNab-Hincks-Morin fashion) to barter whatever of principle they have on hand for lucre and place.

59 ON GOVERNOR HEAD AND FRENCH CANADIANS

Mackenzie's Weekly Message,
December 14, 1855

The Governor and our Race [*On the occasion of Governor Head's insulting remarks made on French Canada's relative poverty as compared with Upper Canada, made on a tour of the western peninsula*]

. . . Our soil, climate, municipal institutions, skill, industry, local position, education, free press, and free protestantism, the continual immigration of wealthy strangers, and good markets, are among the causes of an occasional prosperity, in Upper Canada since the union. Lower Canada prejudices, and their cold, hard country, have been drawbacks. Neither they nor us, sought a union, or were fitted for it; and had the question been put to the people – here or below in 1841 or 55 – they would have gone for "no union" with acclamation.

February 8, 1856

Are The French An Inferior Race?

If Sir Edmund Head is correct in describing the French – the Celts – as a race inferior to the English (and of course the Dutch for the language of Holland is but a dialect of the Anglo-Saxon, and the people are one race) – if he is correct, then Sir James Stephen, ex-colonial under-secretary of state, and now professor of history at Cambridge must be wrong, for he frankly admits what appears to the editor himself a true Celt, – to be the real position of France as a Celtic nation . . .

. . . REMARKS – Sir J. Stephen is the gentleman whom Sir Francis Head, whose policy Sir Edmund follows, abused and slandered so grossly in his Narrative, because he (Sir J.) was supposed to be friendly to reform here, when MacNab, Robinson, H. J. Boulton, the Sherwoods, Hagerman, and Draper, made the French of Lower Canada their constant theme – insulting themselves, their country and their religion. We were as now, opposed to political paid priesthood, and exclusive privileges, but an unpaid defender of liberty and justice both for the Celt and Anglo-Saxon.

60 AN OLD REFORMER'S MANIFESTO

Mackenzie's Weekly Message, January 11, 1856

THE PROGRESS OF FREEDOM

SHALL NORTH AMERICA BE ENSLAVED?

The Past, The Present, and the Future

For nearly forty years my daydreams have been of the future greatness and the glory of Canada.

While I have invariably spurned and cast aside as a noisome weed every prospect of ignoble gain to be made, through land-gambling, out of the toil and labour of my fellow-men – while I have held the highest honors and offices to which a Briton or Canadian may aspire, as far too dear when only to be purchased by the sacrifice of common honesty, and the abandonment of long-cherished political principle – my hope has ever been steadfast in that great and glorious future when the spread of "intelligence" among the honest and industrious people of Canada shall give our hardy sons of the soil a deservedly high and mighty name among the nations – not because of their proud barons with broad acres, surrounded by crime, vice, and beggary, – not for their pampered state-churchmen, ever ready to cover iniquity in the rich and powerful with religion's broadest mantle – not for their hordes, naval and military, invading, annexing and enslaving many lands, in order that weaver-princes and Jew usurers may wallow in wealth won by the blood and sweat of outraged humanity, and offices be created for the idle scions of the privileged – not that mercenary aristocracies of slaveholders, of place-hunting politicians, or of sharp attornies, may eat up the fruits of the soil like Egypt's locusts – No! but that elective institutions, the free and faithful instruction of youth, the spread of science; the march of unfettered intellect; the absence of numerous ills that blight the prospects of older communities, even on our borders; the richness of our soil; the healthfulness of our hardy climate; the grandeur of our young country in its scenery, lake, river, field and forest: the progress of improvement; that freedom of soul which spurns the chain be it ever so finely gilded, would combine to raise Canada to an abiding distinction in the arts, in her laws, and institutions; in her love of peace and order, in her useful discoveries, in her gifted authors, in her gigantic commerce, in her varied manufactures, in her schools and academies of every grade, and in her religion, including temperance in all things, all men having equal rights, and each man freely worshipping in the manner he might deem most acceptable to omnipotence, unpaid and unpersecuted for opinion's sake. . . .

61 A GENERAL CONVENTION IN UPPER CANADA

Toronto Weekly Message,
May 22, 1857

The Wrong and the Remedy. A Convention of the People

We are now in the midst of peace; our towns, counties and estates adjoin each other; our fates are linked together by honesty and industry; with intelligence, Canada may greatly prosper; but if we neglect our common obligations I fear the results. In the following paper which I will endeavor to place on the Assembly's journal, as a substantive proposition I have tried clearly to explain my views; and the remedy I have suggested is a Convention of Representatives in your township towns and cities at some central place in order that the mind of the people be made known with reference to those great and weighty affairs which urgently require a peaceful, prudent speedy adjustment.

In no other way to me can the public opinion be concentrated, or its decision given. In Union there is surely great strength. There is no novelty in Congresses, Conferences, Conventions; they are the most effectual remedy known in such emergencies as that in which Canada is now placed. Monarchs, republicans, nations, confederacies, religious societies, have recourse to them; and if you conclude to call a convention, and if you choose faithful, earnest, true men to attend its sittings, I may yet see the whole country going hand in hand to promote the common welfare, after concurring as to measures....

That each incorporated City in Upper Canada is hereby authorized to send not more than three delegates, each town two; each Township and village electing a Reeve, one; and those entitled to elect a Reeve and Deputy, two; that the elections shall be notified, held and presided over, and the votes taken by the person who now by law perform that duty at the annual Municipal Elections, that the same persons shall be allowed to vote as are by law entitled to vote at the Municipal Elections; that each locality shall provide for the expenses of their Delegates or Delegate, but shall not be required to choose a delegate residing in their own locality, and that any two or more localities shall be allowed to choose the same person if they think proper, that the Wardens of the several counties shall be, ex officio, delegates, and for a Preliminary Committee, and by correspondence or otherwise, agree among themselves upon the time and the place of meeting the said Convention, shall determine the rules for its own guidance, and that the result of its deliberations should be embodied in the form of a Report in the Legislature and to the Public.

62 THE INDIAN MUTINY

Toronto Weekly Message,
July 17, 1857

The Indian Situation

The immense armament of troops and warlike stores for India is as we see by the *Times* intended for the complete conquest of Hindoostan, which it estimates at a hundred and fifty millions of people. Is this right? That 25 nations and a sixth part of God's creatures should be crushed by the iron heel of despotism to enrich the influential families of one nation of 30 millions, 12,000 miles distant! Is it Christian doctrine? Or is Christianity, its mild doctrines, merely used as a cloak to cover national crimes? If India could thus conquer and enslave England by her swords, guns and pistols, would Englishmen like the doctrine of eternal submission to brute force, or the fire, the faggot, and the rifle bullet? Not likely. Who can wonder that when 200,000 Indian troopers are employed by a mercenary organization of covetous storekeepers in London to rivet the yoke on India, they sometimes rebel, and sigh for at least national independence of the stranger!

The [London] *Times* advises the blotting out every possible evidence of East Indian nationality that they may become more patient as slaves. Break every treaty!!! This is the Yankee's idea with his four millions of slaves. No reading else you may begin to think. Castes in India – color of the skin in America – Papist and Protestant in Ireland – all of them used by priests and politicians to degrade, brutify, and enslave the human race.

August 14, 1857

What Would the Independence of India Effect?

Good to the world. Great good to the United Kingdom – the land of our earlier happier, more hopeful years – the land we yet love, even more than this Canada, for whose freedom we have humbly but perseveringly struggled.

India's bondsmen, uphold England, a cold, selfish, profligate, cheerless aristocracy, a class who hate freedom and progress, and the spread of political knowledge and have ever looked upon the noblest of Britain's sons with jealousy or dislike.

All revolutions tending to ameliorate the condition of man have had their deadly enmity – all, or nearly all, the gifted sons of the soil, who proved true to their country and to their God, they have frowned down. They usurp and monopolize all the high functions of government and legislation, and rob the labourer on the banks of the Ganges, the Indus, and Hoogley, to uphold almost imperial pomp on the borders of the Thames, the Tay, the Tees, the Tweed, and the Trent. . . .

No truth is more clear to us than that British Colonies, like India, are held as a means of preserving an influence to those who are the enemies of education and true religion at home, and of liberty everywhere. Why did the deceitful, treacherous Palmerston go to war with Russia, and thus add 400 millions to England's debt and bring grief to many a home, high and humble, for those who had fallen in a strange land? To secure India? To keep down freedom in England? The Anglo-Hibernian was true to the regiment – to the aristocracy – and had it not been so he would never have been elected to fill the place of George Canning and of William Pitt.

63 THE BRITISH MONARCHY PRAISED

Toronto Weekly Message, February 19, 1858

The difference between the political conditions of France and England could not be more forcibly demonstrated than by the wide dissimilarity of the circumstances which have just brought the royal families of England and France under the special notice of their respective peoples; we may well be proud to compare the excited acclamations that greet a sovereign escaping from the hands of assassins, in his own capital, with the respectful and tender sympathy that waits upon a QUEEN bestowing her eldest child in marriage on a PRINCE worthy of the boon. The nation is comparatively happy whose Sovereign's life is undistinguished by romantic vicissitudes. *If the apex of the pyramid is seen to oscillate and tremble, we know how profound and dangerous must be the agitation of the base.*

It is as high a tribute as can be paid to the good fortune of QUEEN VICTORIA that she is never so much before her subjects, or so dear to their affections, as on the occasion of the domestic incidents which belong to the life of every wife and mother. These are the greatest and most memorable of the personal events which serve for the landmarks in her reign, and distinguish it from the coarse, vulgar, court era of her profligate relative, George IV. High as her seat is placed among the rulers of Europe, and vast as are the interests concentrated in her person, the atmosphere of the English Court is so free from the storms of dynastic faction and the poisonous breath of popular discontent, that there is nothing there to prevent royal existence from being as calm, serene, and unruffled as that of ordinary mortals. By a lot of rare felicity, it combines the most unquestionable magnificence and the loftiest state with an unimpaired capacity for the enjoyment of those simpler pleasures that have their spring in the recesses of the human heart and that constitute the true delight of existence for the highest, as well as the humblest, of the earth. . . .

64 OLD WINE AND NEW

Toronto Weekly Message,
August 30, 1859

INDEPENDENCE. Mackenzie's Weekly Message contends for,

1. A judicious and reasonable incidental protection to CANADIAN MANUFACTURES.
2. The abolition of every Custom House on the United States and Canada Frontiers, between Quebec and Lake Superior. FREE TRADE with Brother Jonathan.
3. INDEPENDENCE: the free, uncontrolled right of regulating our domestic institutions, and forming alliances abroad, where, when and with whom we please. The right now contended for by oppressed Italy.
4. Relief from that despotic and partial act which united Upper with Lower Canada under a corrupt and corrupting Legislature, to our very great injury.
5. A free Convention to frame a Republican Constitution for Upper Canada, to be submitted to the people for their approbation.
6. An efficient check upon unlimited borrowing on the credit of the public.
7. That Governors, Heads of Departments, Senators, Sheriffs, Registrars, and all County officers be elected periodically by the people; and that placement be excluded from voting in the Legislature.
8. A fixed Seat of Power, in a centrale [sic] convenient place, to be approved of by the People.
9. Simplification of the Laws; reduction of our oppressive Law Costs; an Elective Judiciary, and a uniform legal practice; also the abolition of what is called the Law Society.
10. The prohibition of Loans by the public to Railway, Canal, Banking or other incorporated Companies, or to individuals for private or local uses, unless sanctioned by the Governor and three-fourths of the Legislature, and granted without a violation of No. 6.
11. Wild Lands to be sold, in limited quantities, to actual settlers only. Land Monopoly Companies to be closed, and none such allowed in future.
12. Adequate and equal protection by law to the several religious bodies; a Common School education for our whole youth, no Separate Public Schools to increase the power of crotchety or pet sects, no monopoly of the soil to be continued to covetous priesthoods pretending to be Christian; a just provision to be made for the destitute, blind, infirm, deaf, and lunatic in our midst.
13. Patent and Copyright laws that would secure to our authors and inventors those rights over the whole of Canada West and the United States; and the same to the authors and inventors of the Union here.
14. Sweeping away legislative quorums of 10 or 20 in Houses of 65 or 130 members, and allowing no smaller number than a majority of the body the power to legislate.
15. Two year Assemblies and three year Senates, or shorter terms, to enable our countrymen to amend their choice when deceived, as any one or more persons may be.
16. The Legislature to meet annually at a fixed, convenient season of the year; the members to be paid for their services under a Statute, and the sum payable to each not to be increased nor diminished during the term for which he was elected.
17. No such sudden dissolutions of the Legislature, by Governors, as happened in 1836 and 1854 under the Colonial system.
18. A uniform letter and news postage tariff all over Canada and the United States.
19. Real Checks on City, County, and other Municipalities, as to borrowing money. The banishment of light shillings and all other base or dishonest coin now current at a pretended value.
20. The vote by secret ballot, carefully guarded; and all the Legislative Elections to be held on the same day or days.
21. Free Homesteads, and Furniture Exemptions to a just amount, so that in pressing poverty and misery there may be a humane limit, as there is now in many really free countries.
22. Burning, as a stigma upon freemen, the British Statute by which our money, the proceeds of taxation, is seized upon and appropriated to the use of strangers whether we will or not, and in violation of the statutory pledge given by Great Britain to America during the struggle for freedom.

23. Representation in any legislature that may be appointed to be fixed on the just basis of population. No pecuniary qualification to be required as a test of fitness for office.

24. The treasury to be filled with real, and not as now with the notes of pet banks, which for aught the people know may be insolvent. An immediate divorce of Bank and State. Laws against usurers and extortioners to be passed and enforced.

25. The public money to be voted in supply but for reasonable limited periods only. No appropriations to be made as now, by orders of strangers for their pew rents, or it may be for worse purposes, but in lieu of sham checks, a real final audit to be had by a really popular and efficient body.

26. The election of their officers to be in the militia, under a well considered law.

27. Divorces to be granted by the Courts of Law which the evidence shall warrant a dissolution of marriage.

28. A suitable term to be set on all appointments to public office.

65 THE REFORM CONVENTION OF 1859

Toronto Weekly Message, November 19, 1859

THE GREAT CONVENTION AT TORONTO

This was the largest popular council of delegates from the People which ever assembled in Canada. Very many of its members were among the most influential, honest, and respected inhabitants of the Upper Province – owning a vast amount of property, and who would be deeply affected by constitutional misrule.

We have long urged that such conferences are absolutely necessary. . . . I refused to attend the great Conference on Temperance street here, some years ago, because I knew that much that was to be proposed by Mr. Brown and his friends, tho' suitable, perhaps for agitation was utterly impracticable. Why seek to divide where I doubted my ability to secure a large majority? To the Great Conference in St. Lawrence Hall, recently, I was invited as an Editor, and the moment they named me on the committee to propose special committees, I stated my determination to take no part, seeing I had been the choice of no constituency, I took the place of an observer, and could only have created division had I urged my reasons for believing that nothing can be more visionary than an expectation that the spirit of the adopted resolutions can or will be acted on.

The proceedings will do vast good, however; they will make constitutional change the leading topic of discussion everywhere during the winter; and men will grow wiser and more rational as they enquire, argue, progress, reason and reflect. . . .

66 THE REFORMERS ON UNION AND ANNEXATION

Toronto Weekly Message, December 31, 1859

THE WHIGS ON ANNEXATION

. . . Upper Canada is made to consent to shoulder two-thirds of the cost of such a scheme as the above, and also to defray the expense of another governor, government, legislature, and a post of officials, or of two such sets, out of direct taxation, in order to perpetuate an alliance with a people of another language and strange manners, who are guided in a great measure by a learned and politic priesthood appointed by the mandate of an Italian Prince, the most despotic and unpopular in Christendom; who needs Austrian influence and the aid of many thousands of French bayonets to keep his crown from being trampled in the mud by his own subjects, and who publickly proclaims his abhorrence of free, elective institutions.

The Union resolutions are, in reality, Mr. Brown's: strange to tell it is but a few years since he was describing the Irish and French Canadian priesthood, of L.C. as most unworthy, during the Legislature to wrest their tythes from them, taking a stand as their most implacable enemy, and reminding society of the persecuting character of popery, and that the Roman Catholic religion was, in fact of the religion of the State.

Now however he professes to fear and hate a Union with the great Protestant, free States on our border, New England, New York, Pennsylvania and Ohio, altho' its adoption would at once sweep away every custom house or import-tax office on the St. Lawrence and great lakes, above Quebec – would reduce Canada letter postages 50 per cent – would rid the colony of a public debt – would enable us to form free constitutions and governments – open the trade of thirty millions of people to our useful industry – allow our inventors to get patents and copyrights covering nearly the whole continent – free us from the degradation of having our statute book searched for any acts which the whim of lords or dukes in the old world might desire to nullify – admit our own manufactures free with their wares to the markets of the thirty-two adjacent States – bring many thousands of wealthy and steady immigrants to settle in and give new value to our country....

Section III
Economic Ideas

THE VOLUNTEER.

VOL. I.] FOR THE WEEK ENDING SATURDAY, JUNE 19, 1841. [No. 10.

A. Agriculture, Improvements and Industry

1 THE CANADA COMPANY

The Colonial Advocate,
December 16, 1824

THE CANADIAN COMPANY

I have abstained, hitherto, from giving any opinion of this proposed incorporation, and its effects, in order that I might first learn, from the contents of other journals, in as much as possible, the nature of its designs, and the mode in which it was proposed to carry them into execution.

As well as I can judge, the company will prove of some immediate benefit to the Canadas; as causing money to be immediately expended in improvements of a general nature, and obvious utility.

I am far, however, from having a friendly feeling to the principle on which it is proposed to be incorporated. It is true, a few shares are left for Canadians to take up; but those of the farmers who have cash, will have nothing to do with such an outlandish concern; and though three or four Montreal merchants may have taken a few shares, yet *almost* all the stockholders will reside in England.

Say that the whole of the reserves are sold it at this time, at the average of wild lands in the province, that is, at about eight shillings and nine pence an acre: say that it pays over the full price to government, and that the sum so paid is laid out in that *economical* way in which the provincial administrators of the North American colonies have, hitherto, proceeded in their disbursements of public monies: say that not a whit more *favouritism* shall henceforth prevail than has hitherto been customary – there is still another question.

It is premised that, by selling these lands to a company, at a fair price, and laying the whole of the proceeds out to the best advantage, within the colony, government intend to show that they wish its prosperity. Now let us examine these premises. Does government really dispose of the *Reserves* in the most advantageous way imaginable, or is the whole an organized system to drain the country of its specie, (be the same more or less,) to enrich England? I think I can make it appear that the latter is the fact. . . .

The company, the first year, clear on a tenth, from 100 to 150 per cent., and in after years, 200, 300, or even 500 per cent; and the whole, or almost the whole, of these gains, go to England to the stockholders who reside there. One million of dollars is advanced in England to improve the country now; and, in a few years hence, *four,* or even *five* millions is repaid to England in clear gains, as interest and principal. Yes, all this goes to these stockholders, though every penny of it might be retained in the province, if government would do as is done in the United States, that is, put up the reserves at a certain fixed price per acre, and sell all that went beyond that upset price, to approved buyers, reserving the rest to another more distant period: by so doing the full value would be paid, and the proceeds placed at the disposal of the colonial legislature, in the same way as other monies raised within the province.

It is true, this foreign company would lose their anticipated profits; but it is equally true, that these profits would go into the coffers of the province without abatement, and would, probably, be laid out in improving the roads and inland navigation as judiciously as it ever can be by commissioners appointed from England, and alone responsible there.

I may have taken a wrong view of the subject; but the general opinion here seems to be – we cannot do better – let the reserves be sold, go the profit to whom it may. And they will be sold – sold to monopolists – all must be monopoly with us. In our tea trade we suffer by a monopoly: in our foreign commerce, we are made a monopoly: even in our religion, the dominant sect makes the road to heaven, by law, a monopoly. Now a company starts up, and our reserves must become a profitable monopoly to England too. . . .

2 AMERICAN AND CANADIAN CANALS

The Colonial Advocate, No. 6
September 27, 1824

ESSAY ON CANALS

There is no one subject of general interest, (if we except perhaps the steam power invention, to aid human labour,) which has engaged half the attention of our neighbouring commonwealth, to what the improvement of their inland navigation has, during the last seven years. Instead of contenting themselves with the bare theories of grand works, to be left for a future generation to bring into practice, they have wisely directed their vast resources to effect and mature those objects of national policy, which their ablest statesmen, their most intelligent legislators and mercantile men, had carefully examined, and wisely approved.

The state of New-York has given to the world a useful lesson – it has shown what a million of freemen may and can effect, in a country where their freedom is built on a solid basis, where the citizens unite talent and address with prudence and probity in commercial transactions, and who, unlike the slaves of a tyrannical government, consider their property sacred to them and their descendants after them.

... I will allow that the picture here drawn by Governor Clinton is by no means too high coloured; but might not the ruler of Canada tell the citizens of Montreal, with equal truth, that it only requires a fifth of the expense and trouble which New-York is incurring, to enable us to establish great market towns and thriving villages on the banks of the St. Lawrence? might he not inform them that this may be done by means of an uninterrupted inland navigation, extending from Montreal to lake Superiour [*sic*], affording our population a cheap and safe outlet to the Atlantic, and (if it ever be granted us) to as free a foreign market, for our surplus produce, as is now possessed by the citizens of the United States?

... Though I should rather have seen the same energy displayed at the head of the lake, as to the construction of a canal, yet, since it seems to be the desire of thousands that this canal should go on, I cannot, in my conscience, longer say a word against it. There is a probability that, if this cut be carried into execution, and it turn out a profitable speculation, in a few years there will be enterprise enough in Canada, either to widen this canal to the due dimensions for schooners, or to cut one of a proper width and depth from Burlington. ...

In conclusion I would say, that as to the propriety of continuing the present managers, or as to their being the best calculated to bring this great work to a happy and satisfactory conclusion, I cannot give an opinion, not having the least personal knowledge of any of them, nor yet heard any remarks made on the subject; but it is evident that the selecting of prudent, judicious, and well informed men, for so arduous a task as that of directing the proceedings of a canal of this size, is a matter of the utmost importance to the publick in general, and to the stockholders, in regard to the expenditure, in particular.

That Canada may flourish – that her roads and canals, her trade and commerce, her agriculture and manufactures, may make her the envy and admiration of the world – and that I may live to see her people free, prosperous, and contented, is the heart-felt wish of

THE EDITOR OF THE ADVOCATE.
Queenston, September 24th, 1824.

3 THE WELLAND CANAL & JOHN BEVERLEY ROBINSON

The Colonial Advocate,
February 21, 1825

THE WELLAND CANAL

... Even if posterity is to be burdened a little, we hope this canal scheme will be entertained. To get it made large enough for Schooners at first, would be a grand achievement. The saving of from $3 to $3 50c. per ton, on produce carried from the southern shore of Lake Erie to New York, by adopting this route in preference to the first 200 miles of the Erie canal, would, with the aid of an act of parliament bring much foreign trade through this channel, and as the country increases in population and wealth the home trade will also increase. Many articles now not dreamt of, will find their way upwards and downwards by this course, and if a judicious application of the means when raised, warrant public confidence in the undertaking, we have no doubt but that Welland Canal stock will rise in value and that very shortly. Cannot the £25,000 wanted be borrowed in London at 2½ or 3 per cent interest? That would be better than paying 5 or 6 here. As to security from the stockholders, we think it would be adviseable [sic] to get, not only the first fruits of the canal in pledge, but the faith of some ten or twelve dozen responsible stockholders into the bargain, the former as security for the principal, the latter for the interest. This, with an expenditure of £25,000 by the company, before they received the loan, would be to the public an ample safeguard. Time will tell the rest.

February 28, 1825

The following resolution passed committee of the whole house on Friday Past and a select committee was appointed to draw up a bill in pursuance of the same. The Attorney General is for the present wisely pursuing that path which leads to permanent popularity. With respect to his motives we have no right to judge – his ancient politics we never liked but when we know to a certainty that his road bill, and assessment bill have received the royal assent, when we see him come forward day after day to support measures which all allow to be beneficial to the country, our constitutional jealousy of a placeman must give way for once to the evidence of our eyes and ears, and judgement. We will therefore acknowledge once for all, that altho' we differ from him as to the mode in which the canal is to be improved – we willingly give him full credit for having acted a manly part throughout....

4 GROWING DISENCHANTMENT WITH THE WELLAND

The Colonial Advocate,
June 26, 1828

THE WELLAND CANAL – PUBLIC IMPROVEMENTS

The U. E. Loyalist insinuates that the independent part of the assembly have opposed the Welland Canal and other public improvements. This is incorrect. The independent part of the assembly wished their constituents to be happy and comfortable, & were desirous of promoting such public improvements as the Welland, by economizing in the expenses of a prodigal government. Nay, nay, said the Attorney General and his supporters, rather let us *borrow* – and it was done. Again, he proposed to mend the great highway, by appointing three commissioners to expend £25,000 thereon. Mr. Rolph asked for leave to enquire into the ways and means to meet the expense, without imposing new burthens on the people. Nay, nay, said Robinson, rather let us *borrow* the money. It was a tie. O Yes! said Speaker Willson, "the king's attorney is right. I vote with him," and he did so. Enquiry was stopt, public improvement was checked, and are the people's representatives to bear the blame? The Welland Canal may be a good thing. It is so. But is there no such thing as paying too dear for the whistle? – Would not the improvement of the St. Lawrence have been a better thing? Would it not have been better if we could have recorded that vessels of ninety tons were sailing from York U. C. to Liverpool, England? "O yes!" say the government officers. "O yes! – Where can we *borrow* half a million on the credit of the province? If that can be done, & if the job is to pass thro' our hands, it will be surprizing if we do not get a tolerable share of the cash to enrich our friends. How the money is to be repaid, the next generation can best tell. That's not our affair. The men who contracted the national debt of England, died before ways and means were required for its repayment. – ...

5 AGRICULTURAL PROTECTION AGAINST THE UNITED STATES

The Colonial Advocate,
November 24, 1831

UPPER CANADA STAPLE PRODUCTS

It is a right conceded to all nations, to impose higher duties on articles which are not, than on those which are, of domestic growth or manufacture; this is an encouragement of home productions by protecting them against foreign competition. – But the House of Assembly of this Colony, declared by their vote, on Tuesday last, that they think it inexpedient to require any encouragement to be given to the staple products of Canada against the competition of the United States; that they are satisfied that the act of last April, allowing the Americans to export their wheat, flour and other produce, duty free, from their own ports on the Atlantic to the British West Indies in British vessels; allowing them to fill Upper and Lower Canada with their live stock, pork, beef, flour, wheat and other staple commodities, free of any tax; and also to export their wheat to England as Canada produce after it has been ground by Mr. McDonell of Gananoque or Mr. Keefer of Thorold, while (by the same enactment) we dare not send any one article of the same description into any part of their territories without paying them heavy prohibitory import duties, is a good measure for the Colony!!! – The [sic] actually declare, by their vote that it is a measure calculated to increase our exports and promote a free and of course reciprocal commercial intercourse on the St. Lawrence!! But that we may not become chargeable in any respect with misrepresentation, we will at once place before the country the Attorney General's resolution, in answer to that part of the vice regal speech which referred to the trade act of last April, together with the amendments negatived by the majority.

As the law now stands, the United States have secured to themselves the supply of the British West Indies, and also the power of glutting the markets of the North American colonies at their pleasure. Wherein, gentle reader, is the agriculture of Upper Canada protected in all the operations of this system? Where are our new customers to purchase the vast quantities of United States and Colonial produce which will next year be shipped to Quebec? Yet your representatives see no necessity for protecting the British manufacturer and Canadian farmer in the enjoyment of that free exchange of commodities which has of late years happily existed between them. The officers of the local government, in the legislature, have shewn a wonderful solicitude to protect the lumber merchant, whether his operations are or are not beneficial to the empire, but for the interest of the Canadian agriculturist they manifest no anxiety. Let us not be understood, however, as censuring any party. Doubtless, all the members acted on a settled conviction that the course they were pursuing was the best for their country; and we have hastily sketched these few detached observations in order to direct attention to the important subject, while, if a remedy be required, it is yet time to provide one, against the opening of the navigation in 1832.

6 FARMERS VERSUS MERCHANTS

The Colonial Advocate,
March 1, 1832

VALUE OF PRODUCE

We incline to the opinion that wheat and flour will not fetch high prices this spring in Montreal, and warn speculators to be careful. The House of Assembly have voted in favour of the introduction of American produce into Upper and Lower Canada, duty free. Their judgments will be *enlightened,* we fear at their constituents' cost before this day twelvemonths. Our merchants appear to pride themselves more on its being noised abroad that they had severally purchased and shipped a large quantity of wheat, than on making profits. Last year, with one exception, they made a dead loss. – We don't want them to lose, for their next step is to woo the freeholders, step into the

Assembly, and become the tools of the bank, at whose mercy they then are. Last year the wheat crop was unripe, it never came to maturity, and would not grind well. The flour soured, and the cargoes of wheat exported to London and Liverpool became solid masses in the ships and had to be dug out with spades and shovels. – One house in Montreal lost by speculating in wheat alone, from £12,000 to £15,000. The buyers on the other side of the lake are giving rather higher prices than are obtained on this side. So they ought. They have two strings to their bow, the New York and Montreal markets. Our folks have only one, that is, down the St. Lawrence. But our representatives approve of that arrangement, and have also refused to improve the river. It will cost 1s. 6d., nett money, to carry wheat to Montreal from this town per bushel, this spring, storage included.

7 ST. LAWRENCE NAVIGATION: ANOTHER COMPACT JOB

The Advocate,
January 11, 1834

We have received a printed copy of certain reports and papers before the legislature relative to the improvement of the St. Lawrence Navigation by a 9 feet canal. Six or seven individuals, the majority of whom hold offices or follow occupations utterly inconsistent with such a trust, are named as Canal Commissioners, Judge Jonas Jones being their president, and to them it is proposed to give the superintendence of the uncontrolled expenditure of a work which will in all probability cost four or five millions of dollars. The acts passed require neither system nor order, they include no responsibility and seek no real security. – They have been passed by a House of Assembly illegally constituted, and are to be carried on by means which no prudent capitalists will sanction by investing their money in them. We heartily approve of canalling the St. Lawrence, after Lower Canada shall have joined in the undertaking, for without her concurrence it cannot be completed, but the present scheme is neither less nor more than a new edition of the Welland, on which nearly two millions of dollars value in money expended will not keep the canal open even for the next season, while two years' revenue of the colony would hardly finish it, that is if Wm. Hamilton Merritt and Wm. B. Robinson had the fingering of the cash and the manufacturing of the contracts. Another colonial humbug was the Shubenacadie canal in Nova Scotia, which cost £90,000, and is not worth as many brass farthings, all the specious reports to the contrary by which England was fooled out of £10,000 in aid of it notwithstanding. We would wish to wait a little to see whether Steam Boats built on Cylinders, on Borden's plan, would not render a 9 feet canal unnecessary. Indeed the faction will have to wait. The Yankees have burnt their fingers in the affair of the Welland, and enough can be stated in England to blow the concern up in that quarter. If the farmers want to keep up the price of wheat they will change the present violent race of members for more moderate men in whom England and other countries would have confidence. Then they may expect real improvement. As it now is, the violent character of the government is proverbial all over Britain and the United States, and prudent men say to each other "these men cannot stand, and the less we have to do with them the better."

8 RECIPROCITY WITH THE UNITED STATES

The Constitution,
February 1, 1837

WHEAT, FLOUR, LUMBER

To the Honorable
the House of Representatives
of the United States of America,
in Congress Assembled.
The Humble Petition of the Undersigned Freeholders and other Inhabitants of Upper Canada.
Sheweth:
That your petitioners are anxious that the oppressive and impolitic restrictions which

embarrass the trade now carried on between the Province and the United States, in Wheat, Lumber, Teas, Cottons and other articles, should be removed, so that the people on this side of the St. Lawrence . . . buy in the United States' markets such goods as are useful to them, and to pay for the same in their surplus Wheat, Flour, Lumber, or other produce, without being heavily taxed at Oswego, Buffalo, Cleveland, and the other ports on their southern frontier.

The markets of the Canadas are always open to the Citizens of the United States, duty free, to compete with the farmers, millers, and lumbermen of these colonies, in supplying our domestic consumption of Flour, Wheat and Lumber, or for exportation by the St. Lawrence. Our Lumber, Flour and Wheat, are, on the contrary, always subject to heavy taxation in the ports of the Union. When Flour is at twelve dollars a barrel in New York, Canadian Wheat is liable to about 25 cents per bushel of duty at Oswego. A great part of the country on the south shore of Lake Erie is dependent on this province for a supply of Pine Lumber, yet that indispensable article is subjected by your Government, to a heavy duty at Cleveland and the other lake ports. It appears to us that the removal of these taxes on industry would be to the advantage of all parties.

The interruption of our commerce by the channel of the St. Lawrence during half the year, and the vast and increasing trade of the Port of New York, at which purchases can be made to advantage for our domestic consumption, and forwarded to us by the Railroads and Canals of the adjoining State, induces us respectfully to represent that it might be mutually advantageous if the customs' duties now levied on Goods imported by your citizens from foreign countries, were made subject to drawback, and returned to our Merchants, on the exportation of the goods to Canada.

March 22, 1837

We have this day received a Letter from Washington, which states that an enquiry has been instituted at the proper department, whether the drawback act of 1831 cannot be applied to the frontier; but the multiplication of business at the end of the session of Congress prevented the immediate information being obtained. – Should the decision prove favorable the difficulties will be forthwith removed, but, if otherwise, the remedy will be applied by bringing the subject before Congress early in the next session. We subjoin a few remarks on the same subject from the official organ at Washington, (*the Washington Globe*,) for the information of the petitioners and the farmers of Upper Canada. – EDITOR.

9 FREE ENTERPRISE VERSUS GOVERNMENT SUBSIDIES

Mackenzie's Weekly Message,
November 17, 1853

Bytown and Prescott Railroad

The success with which this private company, unaided and rather impeded by government, has carried on its works towards completion, is a severe censure upon the executive scheme of a trunk railway, with its confusion worse confounded charter, and its disgraceful price of some $40,000 [per] mile – official aid in debentures to embarass [sic] the farmer with new taxation, &c. &c.

By the end of June next, or soon thereafter, the Bytown and Prescott Railway will, as we understand, be opened through for traffic. The cars and engines are all provided for this first class iron road, 54 miles long, with extensive grounds at both ends, and for six way stations – also good buildings. There are eight very superior engines and 132 cars. Not a penny has this road cost the government; and the whole expence [sic] cars, warehouses, grounds, engines, everything included, is but Twenty Thousand Dollars per mile, or half the price of the Quebec Parliamentary job. When will the people open their eyes?

10 RAILWAY PROGRESS: TWO VIEWS

*Mackenzie's Weekly Message,
November 24, 1853*

RAILWAY LOANS

The guarantee act of 1849 did not constitute the debentures that might be issued to certain railway companies debentures of Canada; they were not a guarantee for capital but that Canada would pay the interest of the loan secured in case the company failed to do so. The Province had a lien upon the works, of which in each case one-half was to be completed before any aid was granted – this was to be done with the company's own means – and the customs act allowed two per cent, additional taxation on the people to meet the interest in case of failure.

In 1854, Mr. Hincks and his colleagues changed this arrangement, and converted the pledge to make good a certain per centage as interest into an absolute loan of the government to the railway, but took little or no care to check waste in their expenditure – the colony is thus getting gradually hampered, and is likely to have a burthen of railways on its shoulders just as difficult to uphold, under bad management, as the old roads proved before they were sold for a song and on credit. Like the Point Levi estate. It is said that in the absence of a Governor who gets a fine house, attendance and $30,000 a year of salary, a new debt of $12,000,000 is to be incurred and that there is nothing to show for it.

December 1, 1853

CANADA WAKING UP

The great Western Railway is soon to open between Niagara Fals [*sic*] and London – 150 miles – the distance, which it took us four days to travel in a one-horse waggon in 1824, being overcome, we suppose, in five or six hours. Many rascally jobs are connected with this road – the expenditure is outrageous – but Canada can stand it all – for a finer country than the railway traverses is no where to be found. Omnibusses carry the passengers and their luggage across the Niagara on a wire bridge elevated 240 feet above the swift current of the deep and narrow channel of the romantic outlet of the surplus waters of Lakes Erie, Michigan, Huron, and Superior. Monarchy and democracy are reached upon wires, and the difference is not so striking as some would imagine – the machinery of politics, like that of railways, is very much alike.

11 A NATIVE STEEL INDUSTRY

*Toronto Weekly Message,
October 24, 1856*

Iron and Steel

Dont let Canadians lose sight of Bessemer's Iron making process for a day! Experiment upon experiment is testing the truth of his theory, and a process which in America, would reduce the prices of Iron and Steel one half, could not be too highly estimated.

Some of our Iron Masters in Canada have full faith in Bessemer's discovery. When we reflect that the more Iron is wrought under the hammer or under the rolls the more fibrous it becomes, and that heat has a wonderful tendency to enfeeble it, and cause it to return to its original chrystalized state, the results obtained by Bessemer are very gratifying; and every packet from Europe more and more confirms his theory by example or practice.

. . . What can be more conclusive than this? Those who have been prevented from entering the iron trade, as makers, thro' apprehension of the capital to be sank and the scarcity of sea Coal, will find in Bessemer a release from half their difficulties. The superior magnetic ore on the Hull estate of Randall will probably be soon wrought to great advantage. Sir W. Logan and the manager of the Marmora Works estimate the yield of the ore there at 50 to 75 per cent. We invite attention from all workers on Iron and brass to the Bessemer process: it promises much that is cheering to the patriotic Canadian, who desires fibrous Iron to be tough and cheap in price.

12 NATIVE MANUFACTURES

Toronto Weekly Message,
July 2, 1858

MANUFACTURES OF CANADA
32 YEARS SINCE

To Jacob De Witt, Esq., Montreal.

Dear Sir, – I know of no individual in Canada who has, during a series of years, shown a more ardent desire to encourage the manufactures of Canada than yourself.

It has seemed to me, however, that the Colonial Governments of this country, by whomsoever administered, have ever been reluctant, directly or indirectly, to do anything that would aid the growth of domestic manufactures among us. Our public income last year was six millions of dollars; our expenditure was nearly 11 millions; and although petitions are being presented to the Legislature asking protection, there is no probability that any well-devised system will be proposed or adopted.

More than thirty years since I urged strongly upon the people and the legislature here to cherish manufacturers as the seeds of future opulence, but was unheeded. I wanted to see the manufacturer placed beside the farmer, nor has more recent experience shown me the fallacy of my early impressions.

We have paper-makers in Toronto, but not a sheet of their writing paper do I see in the hands of any legislator. When I wintered in Washington, in 1850, Congress used home-made paper, and scarcely any other.

The movement in favour of domestic industry just now, reminds me of exertions I made in the same direction many years since. To show what was the condition of Canada manufactures 33 years since, I this day begin to reprint, from the newspaper I then conducted here, letters to friends in England, being pictures I had rudely drawn of things as they appeared to me then. – EDITOR MESSAGE....

13 IMMIGRATION AND LAND VALUES

Toronto Weekly Message,
March 6, 1857

What Raises the Value of Land?

In a wilderness, land is valueless; it yields but little to man. Give it active, orderly, thriving, industrious inhabitants; subject it to tillage; and the land becomes immediately valuable. The more numerous the inhabitants, the more valuable the land, if, as in Canada it be good, and in a good climate.

Why is it that land in Toronto or Chinguacousy townships, which 40 years ago could have been bought for 50 cents to a dollar an acre, is now worth $40, and land in York township, then worth $4, is now worth $60 to $120 per acre? It is the numbers and character of the increased population. The more numerous its orderly inhabitants the higher price will it bear; towns and villages spring up, and in them the land has a far higher price than in the country.

Why is Canada shunned by 19-20ths of the shrewd, industrious, frugal, prudent immigrants from Europe? We want them much, but here they will not come nor remain till our government and institutions become free, domestic, and representative or elective throughout. In Russia, they appoint directly or indirectly, the principal officers from St. Petersburg. Here, our system is very much Russian. We have no aristocracy like England. We can have none. To raise the worth of land – to encourage immigration – we must adopt the elective system.

14 HOMESTEADS – CANADA AND THE UNITED STATES

Toronto Weekly Message,
February 18, 1860

INALIENABLE HOMESTEADS FOR
The Humble.

A COMMITTEE of the York and Peel Council have just decided that it would be wrong to secure to poor or decayed families a spot of small value, which the sheriff or bailiff could not sell for debt in the midst of a severe winter or of sickness and no work. I blush for shame to see the names of McLEOD, the son of one of the noblest men who ever crossed the Atlantic, and JEFFERY among the NAYS. Did God make this world for sharks only? The vote, and in York country, too! was 16 nays to 8 yeas. It would be curious to enquire how many of the 16 rose from poverty to kick down the ladder by which others might avoid its dread privations. Mr. TYRRELL, it is probable, meant the move as an election hobby, but that does not affect the vote.

What harm is there if we allow a young couple to earn $800, and expend it on a house and lot, to be secured against seizure for debts afterwards to be contracted? Poverty may come – disease may come – the winters may be severe – work may be scarce – the husband may drink, he may desert his wife and her six babies. He may have gone security for a false or feeble friend. Would you turn the family out of doors? Would you place, in this as in most other things, Christianity on one side and your laws on the other?

May 5, 1860

... [The New York *Tribune*] shows that Land Monopoly, by the Galts, &c., in Canada, is well understood in the States, that of the public lands or wilderness sold or donated by the U. S. government, the part so sold or donated will cost the actual occupants, nearly 1,700 million dollars, while the net sum paid into the national treasury was only 89 millions.

With "free homes for freemen," with the rate of interest lowered permanently, and suitable penalties enforced, and with the currency upon a more equitable and sure footing – America, freed as she will be, of the curse of slavery, may expect a glorious future.

B. Money and Banking

15 BANKING, SPECULATION, AND GAMBLING

The Colonial Advocate,
August 8, 1827

BANKS IN GENERAL. THE BANK OF UPPER CANADA

... The advantages to be derived from Banking establishments in an agricultural country are perhaps more than counterbalanced by the numerous train of evils they engender. The cultivator of the soil in a country where very few pay rent ought to stand no small need of credit, and should of all things avoid banking credit. Bills to a bank at 90 days are a dangerous speculation to a farmer, who only reaps his harvest once a year, and may be tempted by the loan of money to purchase what he does not stand in need of, & unable to pay his debts from non-payments by those on whose punctuallity [*sic*] he perhaps placed too much reliance. The apparent ease with which a wealthy farmer can command money for himself or his friends by merely signing his name on the face or the back of a promissory note is real to too many of the agricultural community, and ruins the independence & breaks the peace of thousands, whose property is sacrificed and themselves transformed into humble and needy dependants upon others. If a farmer stands in need of credit, banking credit ought to be his last resource, he should borrow of a friend on interest, it would be the safest plan by far. "Village banks often prove hurtful things,– "before they were set afloat, one farmer "could loan to another on interest, after- "wards every one had to borrow, and none "was prepared to lend; – many useless things "were purchased and the day of payment "was a black one." Presidents, Cashiers, Directors, and others, by the craft and mystery of banking, make themselves rich, without adding one dollar to the wealth of the country; and although banking may be necessary in a large commercial city, yet when conducted in the country, it ought to be managed in such a way as to give aid to trade but never to encourage doubtful speculation. A province may be improved by encouraging agricultural and manufacturing inventions, but won't be saved by banking. Gambling is an evil of great magnitude, and gambling in the funds of a monied institution in order to give its notes an undue value previous to a sale, cannot be too much reprobated. We have before our eyes the fate of Jacob Barker, and others whom we could mention in New-York, Baltimore, Kingston, &c. who have risked soul and body, who have made shipwreck of honour and conscience, not from want and necessity, but that they might increase their wealth, [sic] To day the Sun Fire insurance is at 140, to-morrow it will be down to 20, and so forth – all through fraud. Who is there that heard the debates during our last session respecting the Kingston bank, and, did not feel the necessity of watching monied institutions? Who is there that has read the lengthened out details of fraud and villainy with which the New-York and London papers have been of late filled respecting chartered banks and incorporated joint stock companies, but must have felt that those concerns are too often the curse of such countries as cherish them? The public are too liable to be gulled; too willing to yield implicit confidence in their erring fellow mortals; and when the bubble bursts & ruin and misery spread their desolating mantles over the victims of air castles and money mills, it is too late to reflect on the past or hope for the future.... In the United States most of their banks are chartered without binding down the private property of the stockholders, and the consequence is that they often make failure a trade. They issue bills to a large amount, secrete the funds, spread awful reports of their own insolvency, shut their doors, make long faces, buy their own notes up through the means of active agents, at 50, 60, or 70 per cent discount, then open their doors, are ready to cash their paper and go on with their business – and are again believed! – Lotteries too, and all their train of evils, are coming fast among us. To the East, and to the West we look and their cursed effects stare us in the face. Very lately we printed 1100 tickets for a lottery now drawn & we have been called upon by three people since to set agoing in type, all the puffs and lies connected with other three lotteries. The legislature ought to prohibit the whole system. Our Welland Canal was last winter made a speculation of, not very creditable to certain persons whose knavery we shall in due time fully expose: and was not our parliament prorogued before the usual time by the influence of those, who though they hypocritically professed a wish to make the debtors of the Kingston bank pay their debts for the benefit of its numerous creditors – took effectual care to prevent any thing being done over and above the usual quantity of speeches and reports? We saw enough last session to convince us that the legislature as at present constituted is a shield & a protection rather than a terror to plunderers of this sort; and that other similar institutions who may feel hereafter a disposition to backslide have very little to fear from his excellency's government or parliament should the press be silent. The hinderance [sic] of public business, the individual loss, the shock to public credit, the costly, unpleasant and infamous disclosures, the parliamentary animosities, expenses, and costs; the disgrace, trouble, and loss to individuals, and the other numerous evils which attend the failure of a bank as exemplified in the late Kingston blow up, ought to make the country very cautious not to put their trust too implicitly in any institution the secrets of which they are unacquainted with. Gambling is a favourite study of those who have much money passing through their hands. Crockford's new gaming house in London had 700 subscribers all fashionable people, and cost in fitting up £50,000. – Fauntleroy the London banker who was hanged was very fond of speculating; and the gaming table is the resource of idleness, and ennui, to what are termed by the higher classes, "good society."

In Scotland there are no banks in which stockholders are not responsible as individuals to the full amount of their private fortunes for the debts of the bank. In Rhode Island it is so – but not in the State of New York, nor in Upper or Lower Canada. And having seen those men who professed the greatest patriotism in the house of assembly come forward to shield the debtors of the Kingston bank from making payment even at this late period – we may justly fear that there would be corruption enough on the passing breeze were another failure to occur, to prevent speedy or effectual justice from being done upon the parties. We by no means wish to insinuate that there is a probability of the failure of the York bank, we do not in this nor in an other part of these remarks question its entire solvency, nor are we in its secrets, but we feel it our duty as public men to caution the country against believing too implicitly in the trumped up reports of the profits of similar institutions, doubtful in their amount, uncertain in their reality, and which if credited without investigation may make many a credulous fool deeply repeat his infatuation. . . .

---

16 AGAINST PAPER MONEY

The Advocate,
February 20, 1834

The following extract is taken from William Cobbett's *Political Register.*

 Paper money is a monster, existing in a constant state of hostility to the ease, peace, and happiness of the world; and a government which upholds it, encourages the lazy and cunning knave in his depredations upon simple and honest industry; it encourages idleness, and discourages useful exertion; it excites a desire in young people to be impatient of all obedience to parents and masters: to aim at making fortunes at a hit, and to despise the means of acquiring a competence by labor, attention and care. This curse of all curses destroys the moral sense of a people; it habituates them to false appearances, false promises and accustoms them to consider the ruin of their creditors as a jest. It tempts fathers of families to bring destruction upon those families; it sends the paternal estates to be gambled for in the "money market" it effaces the name of families imprinted in the same spot from generation to generation. –

17 WILLIAM GOUGE ON BANKS AS CORPORATE MONOPOLIES

The Advocate,
April 10, 1834

This extract is taken from Wm. Gouge's *A Short History of Paper Money and Banking in the United States* (Philadelphia, 1833).

AMERICAN BANKING SYSTEM, OF BANKS AS CORPORATIONS

 Against corporations of every kind, the objection may be brought, that whatever power is given to them, is so much taken from either the Government or the people.

 As the object of characters is to give to members of companies power which they would not possess in their individual capacity, the very existence of monied corporations is incompatible with equality of rights.

 Corporations are unfavorable to the progress of national wealth. As the Argus eyes of private interest do not watch over their concerns, their affairs are much more carelessly and much more expensively conducted than those of individuals. What would be the condition of the merchant who should trust every thing to his clerks, or of the farmer who should trust every thing to his laborers? Corporations are obliged to trust every thing to stipendiaries, who are oftentimes less trustworthy than the clerks of the merchant or the laborers of the farmer.

 Such are the inherent defects of corporations, that they never can succeed, except when the laws or circumstances give them a monopoly, or advantages partaking of the nature of a monopoly. Sometimes they are protected by an exemption from liabilities to which individuals are subjected. – Sometimes the extent of their capital or of their credit, gives them a control of the market. They cannot, even then, work as cheap as the individual trader, but they can afford to throw away enough money in the contest, to *ruin* the individual trader, and then they have the market to themselves.

 If a poor man suffers aggression from a rich man, the disproportion of power is such, that it may be difficult for him to obtain redress; but if a man is aggrieved by a corporation, he may have all its stockholders, all its clerks, & all its proteges for parties against him. Corporations are so powerful, as frequently to bid defiance to government.

If a man is unjust, or an extortioner society is, sooner or later, relieved from the burden, by his death. But corporations never die.

What is worst of all, (if worse than what has always been stated be possible), is want of moral feeling and responsibility which characterize corporations. A celebrated English writer expressed the truth, with some roughness, but with great force, when he declared that "corporations have neither bodies to be kicked, nor souls to be damned."

All these objections apply to our American Banks.

They are protected in most of the States, by direct inhibitions on individuals engaging in the same business. –

They are exempted from liabilities to which individuals are subjected. If a poor man cannot pay his debts, his bed is, in some of the States, taken from under him. – If that will not satisfy his creditors, his body is imprisoned. The shareholders in a Bank are entitled to all the gain they can make by Banking operations; but if the undertaking chances to be unsuccessful, the loss falls on those who have trusted them. They are responsible only for the amount of stock they have subscribed.

For the old standard of value, they substitute the new standard of Bank credit. Would Government be willing to trust to corporations the fixing of our standards and measures of length, weight, and capacity? Or are our standards and measures of value of less importance than our standards & measures of other things?

They coin money out of paper. What has always been considered one of the most important prerogatives of government, has been surrendered to the Banks.

In addition to their own funds, they have the whole of the spare cash of the community to work upon. . . .

18 THE BANKS RATED

Correspondent and Advocate,
July 16, 1835

WHAT ARE THE BANKS DOING?

To the Inhabitants of the 2nd Riding of The County of York [In response to a letter appearing in the York *Courier* defending the Bank of Upper Canada against rival banks]

. . . . On seeing these assertions I thought it worthwhile to take steps for ascertaining what the practice of the Banks had been doing the last twelve months, so far as relates to proceedings in the King's Bench Court, in the District. I now lay before you the result, as far as I have obtained returns:

The Truscott, Green & Co.

During that part of the year 1834 in which Messrs. Truscott, Green & Co. were in business, they had FIFTY THREE lawsuits in the Court of King's Bench in the Home District alone, in which writs were taken out, this was over & above the mortgages, cognovits and other proceedings taken by them in cases where their debtors settled with them without further law process. How many lawsuits they had in the District Court besides for debts under £40 I have not yet ascertained. These are doubtless the "law proceedings" which Mr. Cashier Ridout, or "the Warning Voice" of the Bank of Upper Canada tells us, they have "taken out against their deluded debtors," so far as 1834 is concerned. Their law affairs in 1835 I will speak of hereafter. Baldwin & Sullivan are their Solicitors, and a glorious harvest they reap from the poverty and misery of their fellow creatures; it is not much to be wondered at that Mr. Robert Baldwin left Reform meetings and politics and subscriptions to stick to his profession. The farmer's harvest comes but once a year – the Bank Attorney's last the whole year round.

2. *The Branch of the Kingston Commercial Bank*

. . . The Branch of the Commercial, at

Toronto, brought in 1834, in the Home District alone, exactly NINETY-SIX law suits in the Court of King's Bench, over and above the confessions of judgements, mortgages, and other less costly proceedings agreed to by those of their debtors who wished to avoid having writs taken out against them; and over and above the law suits they had in the inferior courts for loans under £40. Their attornies who are enabled to build palaces and cognovit balls out of the distresses of the country and the disgraceful law tariff enforced by Judges Robinson, Sherwood, and Macaulay upon a distressed and long suffering people, from whose pockets these three judges extract £3,666 a year in salaries, paid them for giving righteous judgements for simplifying legal processes (as Mr. Macaulay said he would do when he was an attorney and forgot to do when he had the power as a judge), and for revising the tariff of low fees so that it might not become burthensome to the people – their attornies, (who with the sheriff, Jarvis, and the Clerk of the Crown, Small, and other privileged persons, get richer in proportion as other folks grow poorer,) are Messrs. Hagerman and Draper, two gentlemen who have belonged to the party of legal leeches who suck the best blood of Canada, according to law, ever since I can remember them, who have never turned their coats, nor grown lukewarm or cool in the selfish cause they early in life espoused.

3. The Bank of Upper Canada

... in the case of the Upper Canada Bank there is no need to keep any of the gold and silver paid in by the stockholders in the vault to meet demands, the specie deposits left with them by that public to whom their lawsuits are a scourge enabling them to lend out all their own money at interest. Your heartless money-loving capitalist, therefore, while he will spurn from his door the worthy, honest, industrious farmer who offers to pledge his farm in mortgage as security for a loan for two or three years at 6 per cent declaring at the same time that he would not for the world take a farthing beyond the legal interest and that he has no cash to spare – this same person will invest his means in the Upper Canada Bank scourge, and instead of 6 per cent he will net 18 one year with another, as the result of the monopolizing policy and abominable judge-made law tariff system which have obtained in Upper Canada. . . .

. . . For all this I have been anxious to uphold them (Truscott & Green) because they formed *an opposition* to the Upper Canada Bank, and thereby *mitigated* the rigour of the accursed Upper Canada paper system, of whom Doctor Strachan was *the foster father*, and Samuel Peter Jarvis, *the wet nurse*.

. . . It is bad times with us my friends when we have to trust guardians and overseers, trustees, and bank directors for relief from bad government and pecuniary difficulty. I fear however that we will have to trust them a little. . . .

19 THE FARMERS' BANK BUBBLE

Correspondent and Advocate,
July 30, 1835

One more word on New Banks and Money Dealers: one word more of caution. The Truscott bubble has burst. The *Farmers' Joint Stock Banking Company*, is, as I all along feared it would be, a clap-trap, into which, now that the spring is seen, very few more game will be caught by the leg. . . .

For relief from the terror of law costs, the heaviest that were ever inflicted on the people of the continent of North America since the days of Columbus – for relief from the baneful domination of a wicked and unfaithful Government, some of you have sought refuge in the *Farmers' Bank*, that is and is to be the bulwark of Reform! Who is its pretended President! Elmsley, the U.E. rights speculator: Elmsley, thro' whose blocks of acres the corrupt reward of power to subservience in an age gone by, hundreds of you had to level a path to the mill and the market: Elmsley, whom Sir John Colborne created a life Legislative and Executive Councillor: Elmsley, whom the pensioned Bishop MacDonnell converted from the "heresy" of the Protestant faith to the orthodoxy of the Roman creed: Elmsley, the peddler in church pews. . . .

20 THE BIBLE AND BANKING

*Correspondent and Advocate,
August 6, 1835*

What Can Wealth Do For Us?

... the *bible*, my friends, tells us, and daily experience confirms the unpalatable truth, that "the thing that hath been is *that which shall be*; and that which is done is that which shall be done; and there is no new thing under the Sun." Eccl. 1.9. And it also assures us Gen.viii, 3 that 4000 years ago, as now, "the wickedness of man was great on the earth, and that every imagination of his heart was only evil continually." Aaron, the Jewish high priest, coveted the people's wealth, and told their indignant and patriotic deliverer, who had chosen rather to suffer affliction with his oppressed and enslaved and ignorant countrymen, than to enjoy the wealth and treasures which were at his command as the adopted grandson of the Egyptian monarch that in his (Moses) absence, the people had requested him to make them Gods to go before them, that he had asked of them their gold, the ear rings which were in the ears of their women and children, and had cast them into the fire "and there came out this calf." "Thou knowest the people" added the crafty levite to the lawgiver of Israel "that they are set on mischief." Exodus XXXII. The same desire of worshipping wealth as the chief good which induced the high priest of God's chosen people, to make a proclamation before a calf of gold, "These be thy Gods, O Israel!". . .

... I have hitherto stood out in favor of a gold and silver currency in all transactions below $20, and been on the whole unfavourable to the influence of paper money. Being defeated, it is my duty to submit with such a grace as I can, and to endeavour to render the new reign as tolerable as possible. I think we can match them with paper, and beat them too. Those of my readers who may consider this letter too long will be glad to learn that they are now at the end of it, and those who think it too short will please double down the 12th chapter of Samuel and read it next Sunday by way of an appendix, that is if they live in the neighbourhood of those presbyterian, episcopalian, methodist, or catholic priests, who have thrown aside the Bible and their congregations, and placed their dependence on the ill-gotten wealth doled out by Dr. Strachan as the wages of their prostitution.

21 THE ILL-GOTTEN ROTHSCHILD FORTUNES

*The Constitution,
October 13 and November 16, 1836*

Rothschild left £20,000 sterling per annum to his widow, with his noble, (once royal) mansion, in the west end of London, with all furniture plate and jewels; £120,000 sterling to each of his daughters, (one of whom is Mrs. Josephs of New York) with other legacies; and the remainder of his immense wealth equally between his four sons, who are to continue his business as heretofore.

The Rothschild affair seems the most extraordinary thing that ever happened in the world. Here is one man, said to be only 60 years old. Thirty years ago, his credit in England was not worth one thousand dollars. Yet he dies, and has left by will 4 millions sterling; in round numbers, over $17,000,000. – Why, sir, if he had been in some useful business, a business for which he had given value in goods; the simple return of the amount of seventeen million of dollars would be a great business; it would be at the rate of $566,666 per year, $10,897 per week, or $1555 per day. Yet it appears this one man has left by will this great amount; and from what I can perceive, has never been doing any thing for the last thirty years; only dealing in government securities, and shifting and shuffling about paper money; aiding all the old governments of the world in fighting, and taxing, and tormenting each other's subjects.

What would be said, if the different governments of Europe had voted him this sum of money? All the world would have cried, shame on them! Yet where is the difference, whether a government votes this sum direct or adopts a state of things by which an individual can appropriate the same amount in an indirect manner? And where does this money come from? Why most assuredly [sic] from the labor of the people. Every honest, industrious man, in the food he eats, the clothes he wears, the house he occupies, and the things he uses, contributes to this most infamous species of plunder. Every honest, industrious man, must either labor harder, or fare worse in consequence of this paper money state of things.

22 LABOUR THEORY OF VALUE

The Constitution,
May 24, 1837

This also appeared under the pseudonym "P. Swift" in *Mackenzie's Gazette,* September 15, 1838.

... Labour is the true source of wealth.

The Farmer produces Wheat – the Miller converts it into Flour – the Labourer breaks Stones and Macadamizes Roads and these roads with the aid of Steamers and Boats convey the Flour to the place where the Foreigner will buy it at the highest price. The owner of the Flour receives his money, be it one thousand or ten thousand dollars – this is wealth, it was wealth before paper money was in existence – and I hope it will be so considered when a paper currency shall be no more.

To produce this wealth, the Farmer, the Miller, the Labourer, the Sailor, the Merchant, each contribute his share, by useful industry in an honest calling, the Weaver too, and the Tailor, and the Shoemaker, and the Hatter, and the Smith, and the Waggon Maker, the Teamster, the Ship Carpenter, the Millwright, the Sawyer, the Mason, the House Carpenter, the Cooper, the Schoolmaster, and the Government lend their beneficial aid. The Farmer is up late and early, ploughing and sowing, and fulfilling the duties of a Husbandman – the Miller carefully prepares the grain for food – the Cooper curiously fashions and hoops the barrels which are to convey this food to the consumer – the laborer prepares the highway for man's use, and toils with the Mason, the Smith and other craftsmen, powerfully assisting them by the strength of his arm and with the sweat of his brow – the Tailor, Hatter and Shoemaker clothe the body to preserve it from the inclemency of the weather or its too great heat, to keep the head from the cold of winter or the feverish excitement which might be produced by the heat of the summer's sun, and the feet comfortable under all the vicissitudes of the seasons – the steamer and schooner plough the sea or the lake to bear the food of man to the desired port – the merchant ships the produce, makes himself acquainted with the usages of other lands, their coins, their customs' duties, their most upright traders, ascertains who are the most trusty ship captains, what steamers or other vessels are the most sea worthy, and the state of the markets – and the schoolmaster by his precept and example, and opening to the view of delighted and astonished youth the history of the past, endeavors to prepare them for enacting with honour usefulness and integrity their respective parts in the work of this world, in which they are so soon to be called to take a share. Nor should I forget the Minister of Religion – he too is most useful, if he remind his fellow men at fit and convenient seasons, of the great and awful truth that they are but pilgrims and strangers here, seeking another and a better country, and looking forward to the enjoyment of happiness which this unstable world never can, never will afford.

In exhibiting the sources of wealth, I do not forget the important share of labor performed by woman. She is the nurse of infancy, a guardian in youth, a comforter in age and sickness. She prepares the food of man – she watches over his tender years – she preserves order and cleanliness thro' all her household – she smoothes down the asperities of life, and is the ornament alike of the palace and the cottage. I cheerfully admit her claim to the praises so liberally bestowed on her in the last chapter of Proverbs, beginning at the 10th verse. She deserves them all.

I have now shewn the true source of a country's wealth – labour usefully and prudently applied – the result is national riches and individual prosperity.

The description I have given of the manner in which Flour is produced and exported to another land, will equally apply to every article of commerce, that is, every product of skill and labour which one country exports to another, with the intention of exchanging it for gold and silver, or for other goods, wares and merchandise more suitable to the wants of those on whose behalf the exchange is made.

In what way are the services of a Bank, like the Bank of Upper Canada, the Kingston Bank, or any other institution issuing promises to pay gold and silver on demand in almost unlimited quantity, required to produce the wealth and prosperity I have shewn to be the result of labour and industry useful applied?

In no way whatever. The country which charters such institutions, leaving their management to a few, privileging the managers for the partners to divide whatever share of their money or means they may choose to call profits, and to enforce payment of all debts due to them with usury, while they enable these partners to set all their joint creditors at defiance, which the members of private partnerships cannot do, the country which does this tempts the managers of these Banks to act partially, interestedly and dishonestly, and will sooner or later read its crime in its punishment.

It is plain, that the Flour can be ground, carted and shipped to a foreign place without the aid of Bank notes; and it is equally plain that if we of Upper Canada want less goods from that place than the price the Flour sells for, the difference will come back to us in gold and silver, or in a bill of exchange, which is a draught by the foreign merchant on some person here in whose hands he has goods, gold and silver, or endorsed acceptances to him, payable by our fellow citizens, or who has agreed to give him a credit. If the gold and silver come from abroad in one ship, it will be at hand to send by another, in a case where we want to buy salt or any other article or articles which will come to more money than the cargo exported by the ship which is to fetch the salt, &c. If we have not the gold and silver to send, we must take credit abroad on the faith of a future cargo of the fruits of our labour, or be content with a smaller return.

Farmers of Upper Canada, depend on it you would be richer and happier, more wealthy and more contented and prosperous, were these vile Banking Associations swept from among you. They encourage and promote litigation, tax labour, cheat and defraud you out of the fruit of your industry, and are the infamous means of preventing your government from confining itself to its appropriate functions, the protection of life and property. In that way I have considered government (in the commencement of this letter) as useful, in compelling the obligation of civil contracts, preventing the strong from robbing the feeble, punishing the violent and lawless, enabling the industrious to labour in safety, and securing to him the fruit of his toil. . . .

23 GO FOR GOLD AND SILVER!

The Constitution,
May 17, 1837

EXCHANGE YOUR BANK NOTES
FOR GOLD AND SILVER.

To the People of the County of York.
YORK STREET, TORONTO.
Tuesday Evening, May 16th, 1837;

MY FRIENDS:

Although the dishonorable conduct of the executive government of this province has succeeded in erasing my name from the list of your official Representatives in the Legislature, yet I consider myself as much your servant as if I had been returned as duly elected by the officer. The tie that connects you and me is of many years standing, and founded upon the excellent basis of mutual kindness, ancient friendship, and a strong desire to promote as far as it shall please providence to enable us, the happiness and prosperity of our common country.

It becomes my duty therefore as your friend and brother, to warn you that the danger I long ago foretold, is even now about to come upon you. The Chartered Banks, and some other institutions which have for years past exchanged their promises to pay gold and silver for your wheat, provisions, and labour, are even now while *I write*, considering the question whether or not they shall declare themselves bankrupt to-day, to-morrow, or in a few days, after their friends in the secret shall have exchanged their paper promises for the few dollars that are yet remaining in their mock treasuries. I have written this letter to acquaint you with what is going on, in order that you may judge for yourselves, whether my frequent recommendations to you to get gold and silver for Bank paper had not better be acted upon with all convenient speed, lest you be too late – in which case, you who have deposited your specie in the vaults of these Banks or exchanged the produce of your labour for their rags, may find that their superb yearly statement of vaults full of wealth, and dividends of enormous profits, were but the lures of the syren to deceive the industrious portion of this community. . . .

24 MACKENZIE'S CANADIAN BANKING POLICIES REVIEWED

Mackenzie's Gazette, [*Rochester*]
September 7, 1839

THE UPPER CANADA PURSE POWER TWO YEARS AGO. THE INDEPENDENT TREASURY.

The Editor of this Gazette looks back with feelings of unmingled satisfaction at the course he pursued in Canada, as far as he was connected with its cash or money transactions, or a member of its Assemblies, or as an editor of a public journal, exercising influence over the public mind. He opposed the granting of a Charter to the Bank of Upper Canada, upon the model of the bankrupt Bank of Buffalo, and with the powers of the United States Bank, in a more limited sphere. He opposed the extension of its chartered powers afterwards, because they had proved a heavy tax upon the country, corrupted its legislation, and defrauded its people of the wages of industry. He opposed all other charters of a similar partial description, as being aristocratic, irresponsible, and calculated to injure public morals and encourage gambling and drunkenness. Many persons sent as reformers by the people to the legislature grasped at corporate powers and American system Bank Charters, and when government could not carry its other dishonest measures without such bribes, the royal assent was granted to some new extension of these infamous establishments. As Chairman of the Standing Committees on Banks and Currency, Mr. Mackenzie harrassed [*sic*] the corrupt crew who had made Banking a scourge to the community, in several legislatures, and for many years. He often overthrew their schemes, and when in England influenced the government to stop its sanction to their proceedings; at one time he carried a bill into a law to raise the standard of gold and silver to that of the United States, and it so continued till 1836, when a reformer introduced a bill at the request of the Banks, to enable them to pay their debts in silver coins intrinsically 10 per cent. below the United States standard, or in other words to shave or tax the public that amount on all foreign transactions for a time. It was carried, and is now the law. In June, 1837, after the Banks had spread ruin far and wide through the country by their swindling failure of the previous month, for such it surely was, Sir Francis Head called his mock parliament together to allow the Banks to stop payment and rob the people by law, and that legislature addressed a series of questions to individuals, in order to obtain their opinions on the condition of the currency of the colony. Among others, they requested Mr. Mackenzie's evidence, which is entered on their Journals. A few pages of their printed Journals we find among old papers saved from the wreck, containing some part of Mr. Mackenzie's view on this important question, and although they contain no new ideas, we ask our old friends on both sides of the lakes whether they have not proved correct? Upper Canada has Banks enough, but do they aid the farmer or merchant? Do they stimulate to active industry? Do they benefit the country? On the contrary, do they not prove a continual scourge to the settlers, taxing them to uphold idleness, corrupting legislation, plundering the many to enrich the few, and rendering the value of property and the wages of labor more and more uncertain? ...

25 NEW FORMS OF EXTORTION

Mackenzie's Weekly Message,
March 10, 1853

KINGSTON LOAN & TRUST COMPANY

The practice of spending the early part of the sessions of the Legislature, often idly or in the discussion of matters of comparatively small moment, and then crowding the bulk of the financial and other important business into a few days, or rather nights, near the close, when there can be no discussion, and often no knowledge of such midnight measures, as artful men may desire to push through for their private gain, cannot be too deeply reprobated. Near the close of the session of 1849, Mr. J. A. Macdonald, of Kingston introduced in Assembly an insidious, partial, and dangerous bill, having for its object the allowance of a Loan and Trust Company, incorporated at a former session, to negotiate for the shylocks of the United States, England, and all other countries out of Canada, any loans to any amount of security of property, real or personal, in Canada, and virtually at any rate of interest which they can extort from the borrower's necessities. The bill, now a law allows the company to take eight per cent on loans made by themselves, while everybody else in Canada is restricted to six. It allows them to take eight more, or 80, or any other per centage they can get, for endorsing the loans as payable in any country out of Canada, and to secure their contracts hereby taking mortgages on real and personal estate, notes of hand, or any surety they can get or agree upon with the borrowers. The unlimited usurious commission may be made payable to them from time to time, as if it were interest, and the agreement, for loans may contain any conditions which the parties can agree upon, the usury laws affecting everybody else notwithstanding. This bill constitutes whoever may be the company, into a board of licensed usurers, to whose operations there is no limit, and gives them a close monopoly of the crime of fleecing those whom necessity may drag in their spider's web, the court of chancery to have the office of executioner and grave digger for a consideration.

26 FREE BANKING LAWS IN THE UNITED STATES

Mackenzie's Weekly Message,
November 24, 1853

Bases of Banking in the United States

Fourteen banks in Ohio are chartered under the free banking law. Their notes are secured by the pledge of State Stocks with the Government. Forty banks in Ohio are branches of one State Bank, the strength of which lies in the liability of each branch to receive the notes of all the others in payment of debts. A sinking fund of 10 per cent, secured by bond and mortgage, is provided to redeem the notes of any branch which through mismanagement may fail; and which, if not fully sufficient, the balance to be paid by each branch in ratio of the circulation to which it is entitled.

There are also twelve banks secured by the State of Ohio and U.S. Stocks, deposited with the Treasurer of State to the full amount of their capital – and five old banks upon our Canada system, one of which, the Bank of Massillon, has just failed.

Kentucky banks are on a specie basis, as are the old Virginia Banks. Virginia passed a free banking law in 1851, making it imperative thence forward that all chartered banks should secure the public by pledging public stocks to the amount of their issue.

27 MACKENZIE AND THE PUBLIC ACCOUNTS

Toronto Weekly Message,
January 25, 1858

The Books Shut

"It will be seen by the report of what took place in the [Accounts] Committee Room that Mr. Anderson, a witness empowered by the Committee to examine the books of the Receiver General's department, has been refused an opportunity of so doing. It is certainly a most high-handed proceeding of the officers of this department to interfere with the right of a Committee of the House to enquire into the Public Accounts. Mr. Cayley at first appeared to desire that Mr. Anderson should have access to the books, but afterwards recommended that a memorandum should be left with Mr. Patrick, a way of giving the go-by to the enquiry. We trust that every opportunity will be given for the most ample and minute investigation." – *Globe, June 22.*

REMARKS – When I got to be chairman of the above committee in 1854 every book was open to me; but the moment I began to tell what I had seen, Tache [sic] and Cayley agreed together to allow no member of the finance committee to see any book or paper. "Ask for extracts" was the reply. When I told that the Receiver General had not once balanced his books in six years; that money had been twice drawn by warrant for same payment; that many thousands of interest had been forgiven by mere office clerks; that the Board of Works' books would not balance, and were a mass of confusion; that in the Crown Lands the agents were far in arrear, probably heavy defaulters, and the books not brought up, any more than the Receiver General's for many months although his clerks worked all the Sundays – and when I sent these and similar facts to the governor and the public the books were shut to us all, I was deposed, the guilty were encouraged, and in 1857, Macdonald, Cartier, Morrison, Cayley & Co. never once allowed the Committee to assemble at all. It seems, however, that they could now order the Receiver General's officers to attend them with the Journal or other books and examine for themselves. – ED. MESSAGE.

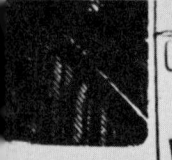

OPENING OF THE "30TH ANNUAL SESSION OF THE RIGHT WORSHIPFUL THE GRAND LODGE OF THE LOYAL ORANGE INSTITUTION OF BRITISH NORTH AMERICA"

IT is advertised that this remarkable body, with its queer title, is to meet up at Hamilton next Tuesday; and that (duly to encourage Orangeism,) now become the Jackal of Popery, the GRAND TRUNK, NORTHERN, PRESCOTT AND OTTAWA, and BROCKVILLE and OTTAWA RAILWAYS, which have been built chiefly on the credit of Canada, will convey the orange delegates back and forth at half the price charged to the Queen's other subjects, during ten days. Religious discord is thus converted into a State Institution, in which the wily Popes of Belleville and Brockville, with Geat-Grands Attorney General Macdonald, and Postmaster General Smith, and Grand Tyler Carkeek, direct the ceremonies.

In the United States, Orangemen, by their name, were long since put down both by law and public sentiment; but a party whom Archbishop Hughes, and others, who play the game of the despots of Europe against free schools, had called into existence as "Native Americans," in 1836, formed themselves into a secret society of Orange Lodges, with pledge, grip and password, in 1852, under the quaint name of "KNOW NOTHINGS." The haters of Roman Catholics joined it from principle, many others did so from curiosity, while crafty politicians took prominent parts, to enable them to turn the rank and file of the order to profit as political machinery, saleable in Albany and Washington for place and plunder. Some editors called them Hindoos, others "the Dark Lantern," but they elected congressmen and assemblymen, and became, like the orangemen and papist bishops here, a power in the State, at the expence of public tranquility. We dislike all secret societies in a land where political associations are free: in Italy the only excuse for their existence is the treacherous character of the local governments. Our Canada Orangemen contain their full share of such Wolves as we sought to pourtray last week; but from that picture we readily exclude Grand-Master ALLEN, whose jolly figure and joyous physiognomy are surely the antipodes of all things lupinus.

The picture exhibits a secret meeting of Orange or Know Nothing leaders, in masks, to consider how best to turn their disciples to private account. Bishop Lett preached to the Orangemen on the fair green here not long since "DOWN WITH Dissenters!"

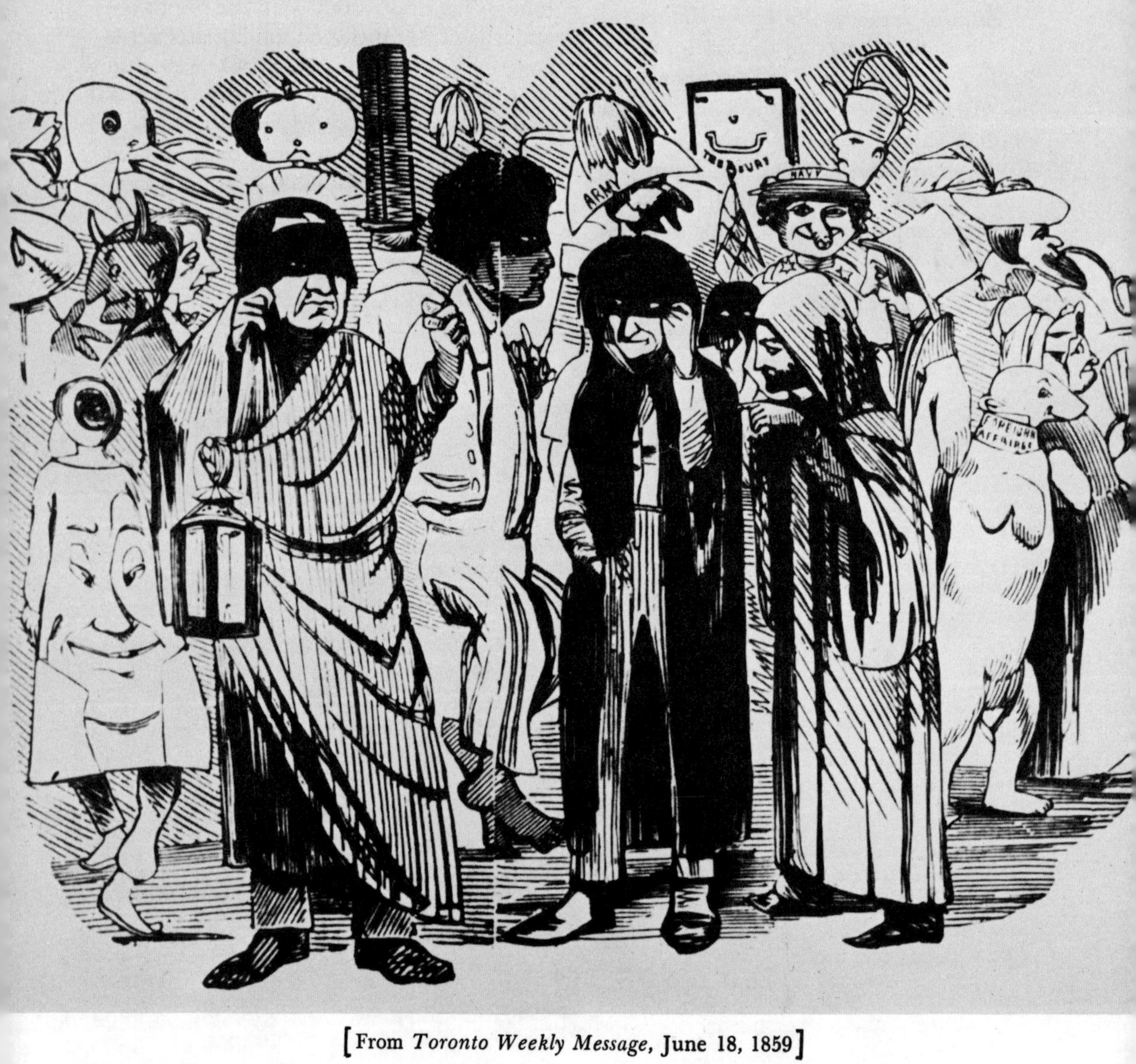

[From *Toronto Weekly Message*, June 18, 1859]

Section IV
Social Attitudes

A. Labourers, Slaves and the Poor

1 ANTI-SLAVERY

*The Colonial Advocate,
November 25, 1830*

ABOLITION OF SLAVERY

If it should so happen, and we think it probable, that the present parliament of England will take effectual measures for the abolition of slavery in the colonies of Great Britain, the government of the United States, and the several states themselves, will have to follow the humane example of their parent state, instead of which they ought to have taken the lead. Their surplus revenue is abundant, and would, if properly applied, instruct the coloured population of the southern states in the duties of freemen, and gradually afford the means for the entire abolition of slavery, and the compensation of the slave-owners.

2 POVERTY IN GREAT BRITAIN

*The Colonial Advocate,
July 27, 1833*

Letter from W. L. Mackenzie to Randal Wixson, dated Dundee, Scotland, April 15, 1833.

... To return to matters here. There are too many people in this country – far too many – they are like the trees in a nursery which soon choke each others [sic] growth unless transplanted and placed at due distances. If there is a farm to be let for 14 or 19 years, half a dozen of persons are ready to embark their capital on the improvement of the bare walls of the house and the acres that surround it, and to offer a rent which all experience tells them must be ruinous or at least unproductive to themselves. Is there a house to be built? The contractors are ready to under-bid each other, and he who succeeds is generally in a worse state than his idle competitors. Is there any work to be done, in whatever branch of business or trade it may be, there are so many persons unemployed and ready to do it that they ruin each other, and become the slaves of a capitalist's interest, toiling without even the hope of better days either for themselves or their children. The farm servant works for a miserable pittance and fears to marry the woman of his choice, least the blackest poverty should be their lot and the lot of their offspring. The weaver or other mechanic toils in hopeless poverty and neglect, and all the professions dependant [sic] on the working classes become equally precarious. Bankruptcy stares the most prudent in the face, and while a comparatively few riot in luxury the many are in despair. Poor laws appear to be the only remedy, and they are at best an inefficient one. The Scotch poor laws leave the poor to starve – the Irish have no poor laws. It is a melancholy fact, that in proportion as a nation becomes very rich and very full of people, with the wealth produced by its industry placed in the hands of a few, the very poor become more and more wretched: hospitality diminishes, the sight of the wretched becomes more hateful, and the habit of giving is less fixed. Such a state of things cannot exist in America for centuries to come, and to obviate its effects here, benevolence must be compulsory. Mr. Gourlay* was no visionary when he spoke of the advantages of removing 200,000 a year annually from Britain to the Colonies; they would be unspeakably great. It is said that there are 800,000 paupers in Ireland, and I believe that there are not less than 200,000 in Scotland, the latter, very little better off than the former. Dr. McCulloch** gives fearful testimony of the present condition of the poor of Scotland, and is borne out by the evidence of others. There is not a more cruel species of animals in existence than your very rich people. The Scotch and Irish absentee peers and landed gentlemen screw the last shilling out of their miserable tenantry, leaving the poor to die in ditches or starve by inches. ...

* A Scottish agronomist and radical who visited Upper Canada in 1817-18. He was driven from the province because of his political agitation among the farmers of the colony, and on his

return to England wrote *A Statistical Account of Upper Canada*, 3 vols. (London, 1822). [ed.]

** Probably John Ramsay McCulloch, a Scottish economist and statistician. A friend and disciple of David Ricardo, he published a popularized version of Ricardo's ideas in 1825. [ed.]

3 MACKENZIE AND HIS PRINTERS

The Constitution,
October 26, 1836

THE PRINTERS' UNION

Sometime in 1832, certain Journeyman Printers of this City associated themselves as a Society "for the interest of the employers as well as of the employed." In 1834, their rules were revised and printed. Some of them were as follows: ... I asked them if it was fair to the employer, to combine in the midst of existing contracts to demand wages which would be ruinous, without giving several months notice, seeing themselves had fixed the rate of wages. They replied that it was my own fault, that I had taken the contract too low, and that they would have $8 immediately. On this I instantly discharged six of them, and sent notice to the office of the House of Assembly that if the strike continued I could do no more work.

Journeymen printers need never lose an hour in a year. They walk into a warm and comfortable room at eight in the morning, are attended to by the apprentices, and their tools all furnished by their employers. After 10 hours work, at a species of labour so light and easy that women could perform it better than men, they have their evenings to themselves and seven dollars in cash punctually at the week's end. Yet with this they are so discontented, that they hesitate not to use their utmost efforts to ruin and injure their employers. I told my foreman that if he preferred remaining in a society, combined to injure his employer, and to prevent the young and rising generation from learning the trade, I must dispense with his services also, but he disapproved of their unkind proceedings, and instantly abandoned the association. But for him and my apprentices this paper would have been of the size of a seven by nine pane of glass. This explanation will, I think, satisfy the public that the combination whose rules and conduct I have described are unworthy of public sympathy, and will plead my excuse for depriving the readers of *The Constitution* of the usual quantity of news. The workmen in all the other offices followed the example set them by mine. So there is a general turnout.

Had there been a combination among the employers suddenly to lengthen the hours of labour or to reduce the rate of wages beyond that which the associated journeymen themselves had fixed, the public would have condemned the employers – for the upholding of a fair price for labour is necessary to the well being of a state. It would be well for these journeymen if they would employ their evenings in studying the true principles of economy which govern the rate of wages. Had they so done previous to their present ungrateful movement, it never would have been made. They would have seen that combinations among workmen, intended solely to keep up the rate of wages, are of precisely the nature of combinations among masters to keep up the rate of profits. They are both confederacies against the public, liable to the same objection as monopolies, in which the interest of individuals is sought to be supported at the expence of the interests of the community. Competition is restrained 1st, in the supply of labour, and 2nd, in the supply of capital.

Combinations, like that of the printers, are useful when not carried too far. But, when they begin to foment divisions and animosities in society, when they array classes against each other who would otherwise be united by a common interest, when they attempt to deprive the youth of a city (Toronto for instance) of the privilege of choosing the trade they would desire to pursue, when they attempt to establish a monopoly in the rate of labour instead of leaving it to be regulated by the supply and demand, they become injurious to society; and were all trades and professions to combine like our printers, the effect would be to split up the community into so many selfish and mischievious [sic] monopolies, like the guilds and incorporated trades of the 14th, 15th and 16th centuries.

Upon the principle the journeymen assert, every machine by which their labour is curtailed ought to be interfered with, because it cheapens labour. Yet it must be evident that such a rule generally followed would carry us, (as a Glasgow weaver said to a Committee of the House of Commons,) so far that we "could never stop till we came to *our teeth and nails.*"

The works printed by our journeymen are for home consumption. Were they *for exportation*, like ashes, flour, staves, &c., such a combination as the journeymen printers have gone into would go far to ruin employers and employed, because the province would have to compete with the products of countries where no such combinations existed. Fluctuations in employment, with high wages to-day and low to-morrow are not so good as stationary fair rates. Seven dollars to a printer are as good as eight or nine to a carpenter – for the latter has his tools to furnish and often wet days to take off. Not so the printer; he never loses a day.

In this City, within the week, threats and intimidation have been held out to journeymen. This is provided against in England by a special statute, by which workmen are made independent of any combination, and allowed to contract to labour where, when and with whomsoever they see fit.

Refusing to work with non-associated workmen by virtue of a concerted act of resistance, seems to me unjust – the lawyers say it is illegal. Waiving that view of the case, however, the employers have resolved to employ no member of the obnoxious association until he abandon it, and I am sure that in this instance the public will approve of their decision.

Labour sometimes needs protection – witness the horrible treatment of the factory children in England. There, cruelty and injustice, required to be met by combinations – but it is not so here.

If our journeymen could but change situations with their employers for a few short months and contrast the difficulties of the latter with the ease and comfort the former enjoy, we should never again hear of such an ungrateful and censurable proceeding as has occasioned this article.

4 NEGROES, REFORMERS AND BOND HEAD

The Constitution,
September 26, 1837

The Coloured People – Consistency

After advocating unweariedly the Emancipation, of the Catholics, and their restoration to equal rights, that body in Toronto, in March 1832, rewarded our zeal by hanging and (we believe) burning us in effigy, attacking our person, and tendering it necessary for scores of our fellow citizens to guard our premises with swords and firearms. Again, at the 2nd riding election last July, they joined (with few exceptions) their orange neighbours to hoot and hiss us, voted us down, triumphed in our defeat, and left us as much as ever a friend to the glorious principle of catholic emancipation.

Since the dawn of manhood we have hated slavery, and rejoiced in every change which brought light and freedom and peace, to the oppressed and tortured and benighted African or coloured race. As a magistrate we created their rights to equal protection with ourself – as a public journalist we have never failed to espouse, and delight in advocating the heaven-born principle of abolition of slavery, of every race of which it may be the curse. The *Colonial Advocate* and the columns of the *Constitution* are witnesses for us. But the coloured men of Toronto were ready to a man, in 1832, to join our enemies; and in 1837 it would have taken but little of coaxing to induce hundreds of them to follow the beat of tyranny's drum, in order that the oppressor's collar might be more firmly rivetted on the necks of the patient and cruelly treated people of Lower Canada. When the writer of these remarks ceased to be the chief magistrate of this city, the joy of the coloured people was manifested in a very unequivocal manner; we will not readily forget the hearty cheers they gave because reformers had been put down in the city. For all this we adhere to principle, and as heretofore desire to be numbered among the most uncompromising abolitionists of this continent. We delight to look at the children of the coloured people, as we pass their school from time to time, receiving that education the cruel slaveholder would deny them. Good will surely follow it. . . . These remarks, made in justification of our application of the code of political morality, will serve as a preface to the case of

Moseby the Slave and Sir F. B. Head.

Moseby was doomed by law to perpetual slavery in Kentucky – his master might buy and sell and torture him, not because he was a criminal, but because his complexion was dark! Moseby sighed after liberty, and they say he mounted his tyrant's horse, and sought a home and freedom in Upper Canada. This is his crime with Sir Francis!!

> Bred in a cage, far from the feathr'd throng,
> The bird repays his keeper with a song;
> But if some playful child sets wide the door,
> Abroad he flies, and thinks of home no more;
> With love of liberty begins to burn,
> And RATHER STARVES than to his cage return.

Moseby's master sought him here, applied to a kindred spirit in Sir F. B. Head, for authority to take him back. The benevolent people of Niagara prayed that he might not be sent back to meet, no doubt, a terrible fate, an example to others the sons of African misery. Sir Francis received both applications, ordered the slave back to Kentucky, and returned the following answer to the Niagarian philanthropists: . . .*

* Moseby or Mosely escaped from jail during a riot staged by the Negroes of the area. He was later allowed to return and was never extradited. See R. Winks, *The Blacks in Canada*, (New Haven: Yale University Press, 1971), p. 170.

5 RICH VERSUS POOR

The Constitution,
November 1, 1837

"THE OLD WORLD AND THE NEW," is the title of an eloquent and entertaining work, in two volumes, by the Rev. Orville Dewey, published by the Harpers, in New York, *and for which orders will be received at our Book Store*. It is a series of notes on a tour in Europe, interspersed with reflections by the author, who is an able writer, on the subject of the differences between the social and political condition of Europe and the United States. Admiring, as we do, his confidence in the honesty of the people, and believing that free and enlightened government will yet be admitted in these colonies to be the safest and best, both for the rich and for the poor – we intend to copy an article from his second volume, upon the interesting question, whether it would be safe for the rich to trust the poor, or whether it would not be better that the few should combine (as they do in Canada) to keep the poor, ignorant, debased and enslaved. Moderate men of all parties will read such articles with attention, they are generally desirous of ascertaining what can be said by those who differ from them, although men of strong prejudices and violent party feelings will refuse to listen to reasonings which they do not wish to believe. We often hear the wealthy portion of this community talk about the *stake* they have in its prosperity, *their* lands, *their* money, *their* merchandize, and then speak of the poorer or more industrious classes with contempt. Two questions from a poor man would, in many cases, silence them: – "What keeps me poor? What has made you rich? – Have you not changed your creed, sacrificed your principles, betrayed those who trusted in you, flattered those who had offices or gifts to bestow upon you, been cruel to your debtors, unjust to your creditors, in short been guilty of every meanness in order to acquire wealth and power?" "Have not I, by disdaining to climb your step-ladder, remained one of that despised class whom you, and such as you, would trample in the dust?" Ah, turncoat!!

6 WHITE SLAVES AND BLACK

Mackenzie's Gazette, [Rochester]
May 11, 1839

Mechanics Listen!
Modern Pharisees Unmasked – Negro
Slavery – The Emancipator,
British Freedom

I understand that my letter in no. 57 to Mr. Wallace, wherein I denounced what I sincerely believed to be base hypocrisy in the agents of the English Manufacturers in New York who continually cry out against the Slavery of men with black faces, in their *Emancipator*, but have not one word to say in condemnation of the far more cruel bondage in which Englishmen, Irishmen, Scotchmen, Canadians, and Bengalese are involved, gave offence to some friends of Canada. I am opposed to slavery, of whatever race it may be the curse – I have been so – I trust I ever will be. But who imposed and forced negro slavery on the Southern States? The aristocracy of England! How did they raise the money? By screwing the last dollar out of their domestic cream coloured serfs, the most miserable wretches in all God's creation. Why did they give a pretended freedom to the West India negroes? Out of envy, malice and hatred to the prosperity of the United States, and in the hope that by conciliating their own negroes and adding to the discontent of those they had forced upon the Americans while their colonists, they would in the event of a future war be able to succeed better if they landed in the Southern states than they did at New Orleans with Andrew Jackson. The English aristocracy tried to dissolve the Union, through John Henry, Governor Craig, and the importers of Boston before the last war – they are at it yet – and those presses in the north which go the length of stirring up the south against the north in order to force on an immediate abolition by Congress in violation of the Constitution, are chiefly upheld and fostered by the agents of the aristocracy of England, whose credit rests on English capital and English silks and calicoes. . . . I should be sorry to be thought a friend to slavery, sorry to see the amelioration of the condition of the ill-used African race abandoned, but when I behold the word "abolition" used as a political brand of discord to stir up the most bitter animosity between the north and the south, mar useful legislation in Congress, and endanger the stability of a Union in which the generous and the good all the world over, confidently trust under providence, as the strong tower of human freedom I ought not to withhold my views. Some say this is not your sphere of action, yet it cannot be denied that in the result the people of Canada are deeply interested. Was it to extend the empire of Liberty on earth that England organized, armed and paid the black slaves of the north last winter for shooting, burning, plundering, imprisoning, and banishing the reformers of the Canadas!!!

I am for no interference with the municipal laws of the south except where through acts of kindness and friendship, and generous offers to aid the men of the south in their efforts to remove the yoke. When I see the purse-proud rag-barons of Rochester, who are grinding the mechanics of the state to the very dust, bawling with the whigs and tories of England for anti-slavery petitions, and yet behold these rag-barons bitterly inimical to freedom for England, Ireland, or Canada, I begin to suspect that their *liberal* feelings squint awfully at upsetting of this democratic form of government. . . .

7 ABOLITION WITH COMPENSATION

Mackenzie's Gazette, [Rochester]
September 7, 1839

SLAVERY IN THE U.S. – How is it to be got rid of? When slavery was about to be abolished in the north, many persons went and sold their slaves to planters in the south. These persons are ready to abolish slavery. How would they do it? By *forcing* the southern states to emancipate their slaves? That would be the signal for a dissolution of this happy union, an event which England earnestly seeks to bring about, and which would be fraught with misery and woe to mankind.

Does the abolitionist believe that by filling the minds of the blacks with sentiments of hatred and revenge against their masters, and putting the latter in continual fear of assassination, this great good is to be brought about? No sincere follower of Christ will say so. England has given more personal liberty to her West India slaves of late. Why has she done this? Is her motive benevolent? Had it been so she would have refused to deliver over the Lower Canadians, whom she acknowledges to be the most peaceful, moral, and kindly peasantry in the world, to slavery, murder, rapine, robbery, burning, banishment, and utter destitution. They were free. She forced them into slavery because they earnestly prayed for justice! — for leave to educate their children!! To the millions in Britain and Ireland, too, the cruelty of the English Government is proverbial—so too in India. A number are emancipated in the West Indies, because it is hoped thereby to weaken and divide the southern States, and break up the first federal union of popular sovereignties in America. What then would you propose? Let these sincere philanthropists who desire to better the condition of the slave, and remove this great blot from the escutcheon of America consult the Saviour's golden rule, and do unto the southern planters as they would wish to be done by, were they situated as their southern brethren now are. Obtain the consent of the slaves states to the following proposition: — That a law be passed in Congress authorizing the purchase of the freedom of the whole colored race, upon any fair principle of valuation; let the nation give its bonds to the several slave-owners for the amount; and let the interest, and gradually the principal, be paid, by a direct or other tax, fairly and equally laid on the whole union, of all races and colors. Let slaves be admitted to the elective franchise, according as the several states may decide, but only when they can read and write, and are shewn to be qualified to perform the duties of freemen. Any attempt to remove slavery, exclusively at the expense of the slave-owners, will be likely to cause difficulties yet more formidable than even slavery itself. Slavery is recognized by the federal constitution, and slave-owners give hundreds of thousands of votes for federal officers *because they are slave owners.* But let the whole union put its shoulder to the wheel and slavery will soon cease to exist....

8 RELIEF FOR DEBTORS IN NEW YORK

The Volunteer, [*Rochester*]
May 1, 1841

THE POOR MAN'S FURNITURE

Mr. Weed, of the Albany Evening Journal, humanely proposes to the Legislature there to put the household furniture of the poor of this State beyond the grasp of avarice and vindictiveness in a creditor, as has been already done in Ohio and some other liberal and enlightened States. This would be true christianity—an enactment on which the historian and moralist would delight to dwell in future and brighter days. The laws of New York for placing credit on the basis of character, rather than fear and compulsion, and for protecting the person and dwelling of the industrious laborer and mechanic from the grasp of creditors whose god is their gold and whose feelings are blunted towards human misery, display in bold relief the nobility of soul to be met with in a republic, as compared with the grinding, heartless, despotisms which afflict Canada and the old world. The worst charge brought against the legislators of America, and the best founded, is, that while they have labored unweariedly to make the rich richer by gainful monopoly, they have most unwillingly added to the privileges and comforts of the poor.

9 WAGE-SLAVERY ON THE RAILWAYS

Mackenzie's Weekly Message,
February 10, 1853

A correspondent who dates from Vaughan, asks us, how it is, here in America, that while mechanics work ten hours, and while ten hours was held to be a day's work by the Board of Works, when here, the workmen and day laborers on the Northern and other Canadian Railways, are compelled to work from six to twelve, and from one to seven, twelve working hours! If this is so, it is a shame, and steps should be taken to stop the like in the future. What leisure for rest, comfort, family conversation, and the cultivation of the mind, can that man have, who is kept at hard labour twelve hours in each day? Talk of Sunday to such a man, worn down as he is with labour slavery, a pittance of pay, and his mind and body seeking rest – what use is it? Our pious people who abhor the practice of keeping a post office open for an hour, for such persons on Sunday to get their letters, should go to the root of the evil.

10 LABOUR AND THE HIGH COST OF LIVING

Mackenzie's Weekly Message,
September 22, 1853

The mechanic is entitled to higher wages, or to a higher price for the articles he manufactures, for the price of everything he buys is far higher. Add these prices to the unjust charges made for groceries, through the union of Lower Canadian attorneys with our lawyer tribe here, and the higher tariff they exact, and then the heavy house rent, and if the farmer who profits by high prices, do not pay honestly and punctually, his gain is the mechanics' loss, he and the place-hunting lawyer who lives on the product of the taxes, are benefited while the mechanic is impoverished. House-building costs far more than it did a few years ago and mechanics are twice as scarce, they move to places where it is easier to live than here.

11 WORKERS VERSUS CAPITALISTS

Mackenzie's Weekly Message,
August 25, 1854

THE WORKMAN'S STRIKE

Come, Working Brothers, round me rest,
    And ponder o'er our course to-day.
If life's a battle at the best,
    Why, let us fight in reason's ray;
Content to live our troubles down,
    Content in honest work are we,
For honest labour is the crown
    Of man's supremest dignity;
And though upon life's varied soil
    The Taskman plucks the richest dowers,
        And hoards the spoil –
        The sweat, the toil,
    The hand that yields it him is ours.

Now Summer makes the heart rejoice,
    For Summer still with plenty pours;
Now rings our happy children's voice,
    In play, beside our peaceful doors;
Now roll the days a merry chime –
    When Work's rewarded, Comfort's won
But ah! in bitter Winter time,
    The harvest of our hands is gone
And little do the masters guess
    The woe that with the Winter lowers
        When idleness,
        And sharp distress,
    Want, misery, and death are ours.

What is the workman's just demand?
    The recompense his labour brings;
His only wealth springs from his hand,
    His life is sacred as a king's.
And past the time when one might keep
    The harvest of a thousand's toil,
For now the hand that sows must reap
    A certain blessing from the soil;
Slaves to their selfishness, no more
    The toiler to the taskman cowers.
        If from them pour
        The golden store,
    The hand that makes them rich is ours.

Hard is the lot of working men;
    The power of riches harder still,
Yet, who should dread the battle when
    The right is theirs, and theirs the will?
If monied masters, hand in hand,
    Are marshall'd in the worldly strife,
The WORKERS, too, must shape their band
    And strugle [sic] for THEIR right to life
In numbers strong, in reason bold,
    Let justice equalise the powers
        If theirs the gold,
        Let them be told
    The work that yields it them is ours.

THE MONEY KING

His kingdom vast extends o'er every land,
And nations bow before his high command.
The weakest tremble, and his power obey
The strongest honor and confess his sway.
He rules the rulers! – e'en the tyrant Czar
Asks *his* permission ere he goes to war;
The Turk, submissive to his royal might,
By his consent has gracious leave to fight;
While e'en Britannia makes her humblest
  bow
Before her "Barings," – not her *barons* now
Or on the Rothschild suppliantly calls,
Her affluent "uncle" with the golden balls,
Begs of the Jew that he will kindly spare
Enough to put her trident in repair
And pawns her diamonds, while she humbly
  craves
Leave of the *Money King* to "rule the
  waves!"...

12 THE POOR AND THE DEPRESSION OF 1858

*Toronto Weekly Message,
March 5, 1858*

RELIEF OF THE POOR

Last Saturday, a meeting was held in St. Lawrence Hall, to consider how best to alleviate the wide spread distress caused in Toronto by cold weather, sickness, poverty, want of work, and the monstrous taxations by the city and provincial governments. Clerk Daly forgot to advertise the meeting in the papers, and very few attended. Mr. Cameron had only found one placard in the western parts of the city.

Mayor Boulton presided; and Sheriff Jarvis (candidate for the Legislative Council), J. Hilliard Cameron (would be candidate for the Assembly), Bishop Strachan, several other preachers, and Messr. John Duggan, Heward, &c, were present.

It appears that there is no poor rate, but that, out of the enormous income of the city, $2000 were voted to the poor, to be expended by an Association called the House of Industry. Six hundred to eight hundred respectable mechanics have nothing to do, and many of them families to support, while a stranger from Europe, a mere transient person, demands nearly thirty-two thousand dollars and a palace, tax free, for propping up misrule. Henry John Boulton boasts that he has acquired a greater influence over *His* Excellency than even Madame Killaly exercises with *Her* Excellency. Dr. Strachan's income is enormous; R. Baldwin wallows in wealth; the Robinsons, Boultons, Cawthras, &c, are very rich. Dr. Green proposed to levy a tax upon the citizens for the poor, to whom, he said, soup had been dealt out liberally from the poor-house, also 2,000 loaves of bread. A penny in the £ would produce $8000 a year, as some thought. Mr. Williams, the undertaker, stated that extortionate fees are levied from the poor at the city cemeteries, and suggested that the poor be employed at preparing a new burial place free of these oppressive charges. The Governor, Chief Justices, and Judges, were absent; nor do they give much to help poverty in distress. Cameron made up some capital for next election, aided by the bishop.

Dreadful Distress in Toronto

JOHN A. MACDONALD and the official and judicial upstart tribe dont feel it; they get double the value of their services, while our citizens starve. At the meeting last Monday, in St. Lawrence Hall, Rev. Mr. Kennedy gave a graphic sketch of the distress of the city. So late as Saturday, he visited a poor family where the father lay dying. The mother and daughter were ready and willing to work, but could get no employment; and for two days they had been without a mouthful to eat, or a stick of wood to make a fire. That was but one instance out of many. The mechanics of the city were, he knew, suffering an amount of misery hardly conceivable. Some of them had sold almost everything in the house to procure the means of subsistence, and lay sick on the floor, with hardly a rag to cover them. This was especially the case in small houses outside the city.

13 FREE TRADE IN OCCUPATIONS

Toronto Weekly Message,
April 30, 1858

THE RECOMPENSE OF USEFUL INDUSTRY

We received last Friday from New York, a number of a weekly, put forth by an association of working men, in which they complain that, between the banker, or usurer, the merchant, jobber, importer, country retailer, and the employer and landlord, or owner, of the soil and the buildings, they do not obtain their fair share of the fruit of their industry.

They allege that, supposing the product of a hundred days' labour of 25 of their number is worth $200, the 25 workmen get but $100, while the employer, merchant, landlord, banker, &c., monopolize the other $100 for their trouble in exchanging.

But occupations are free. No man is compelled to remain a labourer; he may become an employer if he avoids the tavern, &c., he may turn banker, or take shares in a bank, if he has surplus funds – he may buy a lot and rent the dwellings if he has saved anything to purchase with – he may carry his labor to whatever market on earth it is most likely to be better recompensed than where he is, just as the employer, or merchant, can carry his products elsewhere – he may turn pedlar or country merchant, risking returns, bad seasons, and poor prices of grain, where he credits all round – he may sustain heavy losses and fail, as thousands of bankers and merchants do, instead of getting 25 per cent of profits, and if an employer in England, he may be induced by bad markets at home, by markets glutted with the products of Labour, to sell in New York at auction vast qantities [sic] of his manufactures at half their cost....

B. Religious Toleration and Minorities

14 A PLEA FOR RELIGIOUS TOLERANCE

The Colonial Advocate,
April 7, 1825

IRELAND

The dispute between the British government and the Irish catholics, is simply this: Whether the religion of the church of Rome, as professed by four-fifths of the people of Ireland, would or would not become dangerous to the constitution, should its followers be admitted to like privileges and rights in the state, as are enjoyed by their fellow countrymen professing to adhere to the faith established by law? Viewing the matter in this light, and with all the knowledge which we possess of the Roman catholics in Italy, France, England, Canada, the U. States, and Germany, as well their creed as the uses to which it is applied; and comparing the articles of faith adhered to by the church of England, as well as by protestant dissenters of various denominations, therewith, we cannot refrain from lifting up our voice in favour, not only of catholic emancipation, but also in behalf of that wise and salutary policy among an enlightened people, of leaving religion and man's duty to his Maker to the dictates of his own conscience and the laws of God, and of enacting judicious laws and statutes to protect and regulate all dealings between man and man. Legislation in religion may confirm apprentices in hypocrisy; but it will scarcely ever bring within the pale one true convert. Our bodies may be maimed and tortured; but the inquisition of the papist, or the disabilitating law of the protestant, never will, never can curry conviction to the soul, in favour of the polemical dogmas of either church. Away, therefore, we would say, with all religious persecution, and either render Ireland independent or admit her sons to a free participation of those rights and immunities which in times of trouble they are called on to defend, at the risk of their properties and lives. Invest the ministers of all denominations with the "armour of faith, and the sword of the spirit;" "Allow them to teach, allow them to preach;" but do not annoy, or distract by civil disability, the followers of him who said while on earth, "my kingdom is not of this world.". . . .

15 QUAKER SOCIETY

The Colonial Advocate,
February 22, 1827

A few miles from Lake Erie, in the township of Bertie, in a quiet and retired spot, near by a concession road, stands the plain and unadorned place of worship of the society of friends; and at a little distance beyond, their school.

On entering the latter, I recognized in the teacher my old friend, Mr. William Wilson. He had from twenty to thirty boys and girls round him, the children of the neighbouring quaker families. The healthy, happy, cheerful, and placid countenances of these young innocents it was delightful to look upon. How happy is youth when placed at a distance from the snares of vice, and far away from the cotton or lace factory: – here is the native abode of innocence and peace. These children never see their parents contending and quarrelling about dogmatical points in religion or politics, for their parents refuse to adopt creeds, and are loyal and true to the government which protects them; willingly obedient to the law, enemies of oppression, the friends of all mankind, charitable and humane. This is the character of a true professor of the religion of Fox, Barclay, and Penn. . . .

16 MOSES SWARTZ, THE WANDERING JEW

The Colonial Advocate,
October 9, 1828

THE THREE JEWS, or the Children of Israel in Upper Canada!

There are now in the prison of this city, three descendants of Abraham; two of whom, Barnet, of Baltimore, and Isaacs, of London, are charged we believe with stealing a horse from Moses Swartz, the third Jew, who is also confined as prosecutor, being unable to find security to carry on the prosecution at the assizes.

The chin of Moses Swartz is adorned with a beard which for length and breadth would have rendered venerable the countenance of a Judge of Israel, or a successor of Aaron, the Levitical high priest of antiquity. Moses himself is a man of great bulk, but uncouth appearance; possessing a number of high attestations of character; the first by the Rev. M. Reilly, of York Pa. and the other apparently founded thereon. The certificates set forth that said Moses came down from *Jerusalem* in Judea to Baltimore in America, and there was defrauded of much valuable property by his brother Israelites, by which he came to great poverty. Governors Shultz and Heister of Pennsylvania are among the attestators and the documents so far are perfectly genuine. Moses also exhibits a Baltimore daily newspaper, of August 1827, containing an official narrative of the trial, conviction, and sentence of Anker and Barnet for conspiracy to defraud him out of said valuable property, among which was a gold snuff box of $650 value (see advertisement).

The three circumcised Jews travelled lately together from Cincinnati on the Ohio, till they came to Waterloo, in the Gore District, and the history of their recent quarrel we have not now room for. Swartz says he was chasing them, and they aver that they were in search of him. They all seem to tell a cock and bull story, and next week our readers may come to court where legal sentences and Jewish cunning will be set in array against each other for a pitched battle.

The late companions of this modern Moses, exhibit a States paper in which he is represented as a magician and necromancer of no mean grade; and as we find the same story related in the Montreal Courant of last July 23d, with a coment, [sic] we have copied it for the amusement of our readers. Moses tells that he has seven silk dresses, and a gold repeating watch, in possession of a dutch innkeeper at Waterloo – he appears to us to have plenty of cash, and yet it seems to be borrowed on the way: altogether he is a puzzle for the curious. Constantine who acted as interpreter at the police office, believes him to be a Polish Jew, as they probably all are, and if banished we trust they will be sent, not to New York but rather to Judge Noah's dominions on Grand Island, for a term of seven years, to wage war with the smugglers and squatters who now usurp dominion in and over that chosen land. . . .

17 IN DEFENCE OF YORK'S CATHOLICS

*The Colonial Advocate,
January 1, 1829*

Christmas. – Not being of that denomination of protestants who consider *Yule* a religious festival, we went, perhaps from motives of curiosity, to the Roman Catholic Chapel, to hear the Christmas sermon, a novelty to us, who had never before been within the walls of a church of that persuasion in the province. The congregation was large and respectable, and very decorous and attentive throughout the service. The music was slow and solemn, and might assist some other churches *that we could name* in improving their psalmody, as far as tunes go. The Reverend Mr. McDonell, nephew of the Bishop of Rhesina, went thro' the ritual of services appointed for the day, with much devotional solemnity in his manner, but we must confess we took very little interest in the ceremonial. Not so with the sermon. An excellent and impressive discourse was delivered by a minister (whom we afterwards understood to be Mr. O'Grady) who is evidently a superior scholar, and no mean divine. He quoted the bible in many instances & applied apposite citations to his subject; he seemed to have the classics at his fingers' ends; he spoke with ease and fluency, without notes or memoranda of any sort before him, lashing the most prevailing vices of all classes with an unsparing hand, and in elegant and chaste language. He is undoubtedly a whig in religion whatever may be his politics, and speaks truth fearless whom it may offend. In kind and affectionate terms he warned his flock to shun vice, and demonstrated to them the inestimable advantages of a well spent life, both to their temporal and eternal welfare. In all this we heard very little of the peculiar tenets of the church of Rome, and had it not been for the clerical parepharnalia [sic] of the altar, we might have fancied ourselves listening to a sound orthodox protestant divine of the old school. The catholics of York have built a handsome brick church, by far the best and most beautiful house devoted to religious worship in the country, and in concluding this short notice of their progress, we would bid our protestant readers remember, that if the church of Rome persecuted and was intolerant when armed in Europe with temporal power, so did other denominations in like circumstances. In America the Roman Catholics were the first to unfurl the standard of religious liberty, and we trust it will be remembered to their honor.

18 BRUTALIZATION OF INDIANS

*The Constitution,
October 19, 1836*

An Indian in the Augusta district, had a reservation of land – it was an old homestead. He had been repeatedly applied to by white men but would not sell. His claim, by some oversight, was not marked on the maps in the land office, or, if marked, had been erased. This homestead was entered by a speculator. A short while back the man who entered it went to the place, and told the Indian the land was entered, and he must leave it. After the man had retired, the Indian called his wife, and told her of another instance of the white man's oppression. He told her that he was too old to hunt for their support – too old to go west; that they had better die. It was agreed to. He arranged his wife and three children in a row, and called in his brother-in-law, (a white man) and told him of his designs, and wished him to witness their execution, and to tell, afterward, what he witnessed, and the cause that led to it. He then, with a tomahawk, split the heads successively, of his wife and children, and stabbed himself. These are facts. The poor devils have been much wronged; not by the government, but by speculators. They have dared to violate every principle of humanity and honest dealing, and have made large fortunes. Will the Great Spirit suffer it to benefit them. A rascal ventured to hint to me how advantageous it might be to me if I would aid and abet him in his fraudulent schemes.

19 THE NEW TESTAMENT VERSUS CHURCH ESTABLISHMENT

*The Colonial Advocate,
November 8, 1832*

CHURCH AND STATE

... We proposed a train of queries in our last, calculated to lead our readers to reflect on the nature of the system of tyranny and oppression practised by the Church of England. On more mature reflection we find that the New Testament has nothing to do with the Church of England in any shape whatever. The New Testament simply describes the Church of Christ which is an entirely different Church from that of England; – different in origin, different in government, different in laws, different in principles and hence totally different in practice.

The parallel betwixt the two seems in short to run thus, the Church of Christ has Christ himself for her head. "For Christ is the head of his body the Church;" and having such a pure and holy head, the church itself partakes of his pure and holy nature, "he hath given unto us this spirit," by which we are made partakers of the divine nature, "if any man have not the spirit of Christ he is none of his."

The Church of England acknowledges the temporal King of England, (whatever Royal whoremongers may chance to sway the sceptre,) to be her head; and from such an impure head we may expect the body to partake of its pollution and impurity, "the head is sick and the whole heart is pained." Does not corruption, impiety, impurity, profanation and presumption obtain to a wonderful degree in that body.

The Church of Christ originated in his free choice, "ye have not chosen me, but I have chosen you." Moreover the Church of Christ is supported by his Royal munificence so strongly that "the gates of Hell cannot prevail against it."

The church of England originated in the dark ages of nominal christianity, and is suppored [sic] by the munificence of earthly Kings, who have given her licence to plunder the poor and needy with impunity and licence her magnificent appearance so widely differing from the humility of the Church of Christ.

The Church of Christ is a distinct thing in government from all worldly establishments, 'my kingdom is not of this world,' says Christ, and being not of this world it needs no support from human institutions and human laws.

The Church of England is mixed in an indiscriminate jumble as part and parcel of a kingdom of this world and supported entirely by worldly institutions of human invention.

The Church of Christ as a "kingdom not of this world" is under a system of laws and regulations, not of a worldly nature, but his word is the law of her heart "I will put my laws in their hearts and write them in their minds."

The Church of England is governed by a creed of a totally different origin backed by a liturgy of cunningly devised nonsense. . . .

20 CLERGYMEN DENOUNCED

*Mackenzie's Gazette, [New York]
December 8, 1838*

State-paid Priests. – The whole race of them are a curse to any people. The strumpet that takes the wages of whoredom, the thief that cuts your purse off, the murderer who stabs you in the dark, are less an injury to society than the clerical spy whom it nourishes in its bosom to sting it into misery and death. A foreign power holds possession of Canada by the means of its slaves in red-coats, and its wealth obtained from every clime. A state-paid priesthood are the organized spies of that foreign power. Jesus, poverty, humility, and benevolence in their mouths – avarice, malevolence, mischief in their minds. The people struggle to get free from bondage in Lower Canada, and the French Catholic priests of the Montreal Seminary spread their ill-gotten gold before their tyrants to strengthen the hands of Sir John Colborne, and enable him to hold out a better bait to the scum of the population called volunteers – while in Upper Canada every state-paid priest, Catholic and Protestant, is prowling through the land, seizing, informing against and obtaining the arrest of every honest reformer whose firmness may have made him obnoxious to them ...

21 RELIGION IN AMERICAN POLITICS

*Mackenzie's Gazette, [Rochester]
September 26, 1840*

INFIDEL LECTURERS. – A few days since Benjamin Offen, an Englishman, who has lectured every Sunday at Tammany Hall and other public places in favor of infidelity and against revealed religion and deity, was haranguing the whigs of New York in the log-cabin, he having joined that party. I saw the Evening Journal recently attempt to call the Democrats atheists because Abner Kneeland had spoken in their behalf. Is this manly? Are all modern whigs infidels because Offen spoke in their Log Cabin? By no means. If I go to hear Mrs. Frances Wright deliver a political lecture, is that evidence that I approve her views on religion? Because Maj. Noah the Jew goes in his Star for the whigs does that affect their religious belief? There is something very unmanly in the Journal's reasoning; it appeals to prejudices, and encourages hypocrisy, by denouncing every man who holds unpopular religious principles and avows them. I never attended an infidel or free-thinking lecture in my whole life – I never uttered a sentence against revealed religion. But I despise the policy which would denounce a whole party, because persons of a peculiar belief or religion might belong to it. Is this a free country? If so will you fetter thought? Is opinion free? If so, will you denounce a whole party, because one man in it may not, like Offen, believe in Christianity?

22 THE GAVAZZI RIOTS IN QUEBEC

*Mackenzie's Weekly Message,
June 16, 1853*

Alessandro Gavazzi, formerly an Italian monk had broken with the Papacy over the Italian Revolution in 1848. In 1853, he toured North America for the patriot cause and denounced popery resoundingly from Protestant pulpits.

... If a sectarian mob can successfully overawe a peaceful congregation in a Presbyterian Church at Quebec, shed blood, and glory in violence, in the ancient capital of Canada, may they not also deprive of freedom of speech and in voting, any member of the Legislature whom their leaders dislike. May they not destroy the utility of the Legislature altogether? From intimidation there is but a short step to Louis Napoleon's coup d'etat.

A majority of the assailants were Irishmen – belonging to that impulsive race, who are capable of the noblest efforts in favor of human rights, which any people ever made – but who, under peculiar circumstances, have, in their own country, suffered sadly through religious discord. What is the difference in the position of the courageous Gavazzi and Mazzini, and the noble O'Brien, Meagher, Martin, and Mitchell. Did not Gavazzi and Mazzini struggle like true patriots for Roman freedom? Did they not compel Austrian and Bonapartean tyranny to send to Rome hosts of armed mercenaries to put down the Roman citizens, and coerce a gallant people at the point of foreign bayonets?

Irishmen who are forced to pay tithes to a priesthood whose doctrines they dissent from and whose ministrations they do not desire, should remember that the brave Italian whose life has been endangered here is, like Meagher, and O'Donohue, an exile because he has been faithful to his country. They should never forget that America is the land of freedom from dominant creeds – that if men are allowed freely to write and to preach for or against contending doctrines, truth must prevail – that if one may choose to leave protestantism and another popery and if the new converts shall see fit to try to convert others, it is their right. . . . For thirty years I have equally denounced all outrages, by whomsoever perpetrated. Had a Roman Catholic at Toronto been treated as Gavazzi has been I would have been the first man to denounce it.

23 CIVIL MARRIAGES

Toronto Weekly Message,
February 13, 1857

Marriage Laws of Canada

I brought into the Assembly of Canada, in 1852-3, bills for equality in solemnizing marriage, and for registration of births, deaths, marriages, &c. The French leaders, mean and obsequious toward their priests, thwarted me at every step. Others have fared no better since. The union of the French priests and the Strachan regiment, for church and state, and the spoils, has since then made bad worse. A very able article on the subject appears in the *Christian Guardian,* where it is stated, that, while the marriage laws authorise ordained ministers of every church to solemnize marriage, upon condition that they appear before the County Registrar, file a certificate of their ordination and take the oath of allegiance; and though the law contains no notice that any are excepted from this condition, yet the ministers of the Episcopal Church of Scotland and the Church of Rome do not observe this legal requirement, to obtain a recognition of their authority to solemnize matrimony. Why is this the case, when law declares that there is no state church or churches in Canada, and that all are placed upon a civil equality of rights and privileges?

In England, Ireland, Scotland, France, and the most of the United States, the law looks upon marriage as a civil contract. The rules in these countries as to the marriage ceremony, registration, &c., should be enforced here, and some influential member should take the matter up.

24 POPES, PRIESTS AND CANADIAN POLITICS

Toronto Weekly Message,
February 12, 1858

NEVER, till England's aristocracy bargained with the Pope, was a Roman Catholic bishop allowed to exercise his functions in French Canada. Now, some of the bishops are pensioned, and all of them are under contract to play the political tool to the government of the day. Though Papists, they busily interfered on behalf of Strachan and the Scotch and English churches in the matter of the Reserves, and were deadly enemies to Papineau and the Reformers of 1834, who gave them no special privileges. They are now working their own downfall, and will in the end destroy their own tythes, as by statute tythes are put an end to in Upper Canada. The Pope is poor, borrows heavily of England, is a political pageant propped by French bayonets, and the tool of the powers that thus prop him. As constituted, the dignified political priesthood of Rome are the most deadly enemies of all that is free in the Canadian constitution. . . .

C. Moral and Social Reform

25 SUICIDE AND SOCIAL DISINTEGRATION IN UPPER CANADA

The Colonial Advocate,
July 29, 1829

Self Murder. – On the morning of Friday last, an inquest was held in the new jail, over the body of Margaret Tripp, who had that morning been found dead in one of the cells of the prison. The jurors, by Mr. Charles Baker, their foreman, found, that being of sound mind, she had feloniously put an end to her own existence by swallowing poison. The following particulars of her previous life may prove a salutary warning to others....

We shall not here take occasion to speak at length of the laxity of morals so prevalent among us; the evil and pernicious examples afforded by some of those whose high stations in society make their gross improprieties so much the more deserving of reprobation; the inefficient state of our police and local magistracy; the latter entirely removed from all responsibility, save and except the daily duty of shouting out "loyalty! loyalty!" – the utter neglect in which education is held, and the want of encouragement which teachers of youth experience, unless, their political and religious creeds are held to be orthodox by Doctor Strachan. The regulations of taverns and houses of entertainment, obliging their proprietors and occupiers to shut up at proper hours and neither to harbour worthless characters nor allow them near their premises, are an old story; and gambling, drinking to excess, and other vices akin to these, receive no effectual check. The government of the colony have not appointed, we believe, one justice of the peace, either in Scarboro' or Pickering, a tract of country nearly thirty miles in length, and if the adjoining part of Markham is added, containing 4000 inhabitants!! Is it because there are none among the people worthy of the trust?

26 THE SOCIAL SOURCES OF INSANITY

The Colonial Advocate,
September 10, 1829

Insanity. – Dr. Esquirol, the first authority in France upon the subject of insanity, states that in no country is it so frequent as in England, which he attributes to irregular habits of life; excesses attending an advanced state of civilization; marriages contracted solely from motives of ambition or interest; anxieties attending speculations; the idleness of riches; and the abuse of spirituous liquors. The changes of manners in France within the last thirty years, he says, have been more productive of insanity than all the political turmoils. – He remarks:

"Religion no longer intervenes, but as a mere form, in the most solemn transactions of life; she is no longer a source of consolation and hope to the unfortunate; her principles have ceased to direct the understanding in the narrow and difficult path of life: every source of kindly feeling has been dried up by cold egotism; the domestic affections, respect, love, authority, and the consequent mutual dependence on each other, have lost their influence; every one lives entirely for self. Marriage is only regarded in the light of formal unimportant ceremony; education has become vitiated, cultivating the mind but neglecting the heart. If the habits of life of the women in France, their almost exclusive devotion to the study of the art of pleasing, their immoderate taste for novel reading, for dress, and curiosities of every description, are added to the above causes, there will be no longer reason to wonder at the perverted state of our morals, both in public, and private life; nor shall we have any right to complain of nervous diseases and especially insanity, are rapidly increasing; so indubitably true is it, that whatever appertains to man's moral good, has the most intimate connexion with his corporeal well being and the preservation of his health. It is therefore of the greatest importance to avoid matrimonial union between individuals born of insane parents; to adopt a system of education more religious in its character; children must be trained to bear opposition to their caprices; their moral and intellectual feelings should not be excited and over excited by the too early application of their faculties to study; errors of diet must be strictly avoided; and their passions should be controlled and judiciously directed."

27 ON RAISING INDUSTRIOUS DAUGHTERS

The Colonial Advocate,
April 21, 1831

The following extract is taken from the *Journal of Health.*

RULES FOR A YOUNG LADY

1. Let her go to bed at ten o'clock – nine, if she pleases. She must not grumble, or be disheartened because she may not sleep the first night or two, and thus lay ruminating on the pleasures from which she has cut herself off; but persist steadily for a few nights; when she will find that habit will produce a far more pleasant repose than that which follows a late ball, a route or assembly. She will, also, rise in the morning more refreshed – with better spirits, and a more blooming complexion.

2. Let her rise about six o'clock in summer, and about eight in winter – immediately wash her face and hands with pure water – cool, or tepid, according to the season of the year; and if she could by any means be induced to sweep her rooms, or bustle about some other domestic concerns for about an hour, she would be the gainer, as well in health as in beauty, by the practice.

3. Her breakfast should be something more substantial than a cup of slops, whether denominated tea or coffee, and a thin slice of bread and butter. She should take a soft boiled egg or two, a little cold meat, a draught of milk or a cup or two of pure chocolate.

4. She should not lounge all day by the fire, reading novels, nor indulge herself in thinking of the perfidy of false swains, or the despair of a pining damsel; but bustle about – walk or ride in the open air, rub the furniture or make puddings – and when she feels hungry eat a custard or something equally light, in place of the fashionoble [*sic*] morning treat of a slice of pound cake and a glass of wine or cordial.

5. Let her dine upon mutton or beef plainly cooked, and not too fat – but she need not turn away occasionally from a fowl or any thing equally good; let her only observe to partake of it in moderation, and so drink sparingly of water during the repast.

6. In place of three or four cups of strong tea for supper, she may eat a custard – a bowl of bread and milk – or similar articles, and in a few hours afterwards let her retire to bed.

7. At other periods of the day which are unoccupied by business or exercise, let her read – no sickly love tales, but good humoured and instructive works; calculated, while they keep the mind unincumbered with heavy thoughts, to augment its store of ideas, and to guard it against the injury which will ever result from false perceptions of mankind and of the concerns of life.

28 FREEDOM TO BREATHE

The Colonial Advocate,
June 14, 1832

Communications.

For the Colonial Advocate.

ON TIGHT LACING

Mr. Editor. – Permit me thro' the medium of your useful paper to make some remarks upon the fashions of the day. Among other vile and sinful habits which mankind have fallen into, there is one practiced by the female part of our species, which I consider to be truly ridiculous. – Upon this subject, I should have remained forever silent, could I have preserved a clear conscience in doing so. I have long beheld, with a mournful silence, the folly to which I allude; and have often asked myself is there no remedy? I have wondered why physicians did not offer a salutary warning, but, also, perhaps they think that they get more employment by preserving a silence upon this subject, and no doubt they do. But, Sir, ought they to be silent from such selfish motives, when they well know that such a vile practice is destroying its thousands of females annually? The vice to which I refer is tight lacing, or in other words, what the vulgar people call wearing b***y-b****s; those machines of death, Mr. Editor, formed of different materials, according to the quality of the wearer; the higher classes, I am told, having them made of whale-bone, the middle classes of steel while the poor girls have to content themselves with a supply from the wood pile to lash about their bodies. By this time I think I perceive a sneer and hear a laugh, the readers exclaims what old fashioned bigot is now undertaking to lecture us upon dress? They will say, your correspondent is surely some silly old fool, to be meddling with the girl's stays . . .

. . . Societies on a very extensive scale have been formed in order to prevent the destruction of the male part of our species by intemperance, and why not use a little exertion for the preservation of our females.

In conclusion, I have only to beg pardon for so long an intrusion, and to remark, that if my pen in this broken essay, should be the means of awakening the pen of some more capable writer on this subject, I should feel myself richly paid for my trouble in writing this.

I AM AN OLD FASHIONED COUNTRYMAN.

Fashion Town, May 26th, 1832
Note by the Editor. – We are inclined to think notwithstanding the advantageous post for the best information upon his subject, which our correspondent seems to occupy, by his residence in Fashion Town, – that he has not been a very attentive observer – otherwise he would have learned that there are a great many effeminate dandy fops of young gentlemen, who are following the ridiculous practice which he so severely and so justly condemns in those dear creatures which are destined by nature to become their better halves. I barely mention this contemptible in our young dandies in order to enable our correspondent to keep an eye on them.

29 SOBRIETY AND HONEST GOVERNMENT

The Advocate,
June 26, 1834

. . . The vice of drunkenness, both in man and woman, obtains in this province to an almost incredible degree – a careful observation enables us to say that it appears to be on the increase. In this disgusting practice we recognize another formidable obstacle to political reform. The tippler and the sot may bawl for "Liberty," but they are unworthy of its blessings; we can expect but little permanent advantage from their support. The lazy also, and the idle, the gay and the dissipated, the hunter for office and the hunter for aggrandizement, these will in all ages oppose real reform in the municipal institutions of their country. We care no longer to conceal the opinion which very recent events have forced us to entertain, namely, that unless the really virtuous and honest part of the community shall so far overcome national prejudices as to act together in choosing and supporting faithful candidates, the next four years of Upper Canada legislation will be likely to prove much more inimical to the happiness and comfort of the settled population than were the four that have passed away.

30 TEMPERANCE FOR THE WORKING CLASS

The Constitution,
September 21, 1836

TEMPERANCE CONVENTION. – We again call our readers' attention to this important meeting, and are glad that other presses have done so. Tradesmen and mechanics who employ from 6 to 12 workmen weekly, pay them ample wages regularly every Saturday, depend on their honorable fulfilment of their engagements, and find them lying about the filthiest and vilest of our licensed taverns, in a state not fit to be named, on the Mondays or Tuesdays thereafter, will wish the convention every success.

31 PROHIBITION VS. LICENSING

The Volunteer, [*Rochester*]
April 25, 1842

The Friends of Temperance may be interested to learn that in consonance with what appears to be the prevalent sentiment in Boston, the Corporation of that city lately resolved to license no person to sell spirituous liquors for the ensuing year.

We trust that the progress of common sense will soon explode the practice of "*licensing*" the sale of liquors anywhere. Public opinion, all-powerfully manifested in the Temperance Reformation, is better than all *legal* restrictions on the traffic or use of liquor. At any rate, government should not undertake to "LICENSE" such traffic. Let those who choose, sell rum as they would opium or arsenic.

32 FEMINISM: A SATIRICAL AFFIRMATIVE

Mackenzie's Weekly Message,
July 28, 1853

Woman's Rights in New York. Reverend Girls

The whole World's Temperance Convention, down at New York, was a scene of as much intolerance as that at Quebec last June where the patriot convert Gavazzi was assailed; and on the Sunday thereafter the Reverend Miss Brown (doesn't it sound droll?) preached a sermon in the Metropolitan Hall, where the rent is $100 per Sunday, and yet no contribution money was taken. Five thousand persons attended, and the services, says the *Tribune*, were quiet and orderly. Mr. Greeley finds in Matt. xxviii, 7, a command by angels to women to "go quickly" and announce the resurrection of the Saviour of Mankind; repeated (v. 10) by the risen Saviour himself; and we have heard Quaker ladies of high respectability travel thro' England preaching; nor do we see an impropriety in a woman diffusing useful knowledge by speaking any more than by writing, as Hannah More, Mrs. Sherwood, &c have done. The idea of "Reverend Miss Brown" is a comical one, because the phrase and the association are unusual and at variance with custom. Many protestant clergymen, instead of teaching the christian virtues, and rebuking known vices, expend their Sunday hours in railing at popery with all the variations, while parson Cahill the eloquent Irish papist scold, rails back again at protestantism, backed by a thousand priests. Other preachers, of all creeds, discuss some relatively uninteresting, unimportant but very abstruse, passage of scriptures, with their hearers fast asleep. From such dullness and bigotry, it is possible that a lively sermon pithily delivered, by sweet sixteen with a "reverend" prefix, may afford seasonable relief, altho' the New York *Evangelist* quotes Saint Paul to prove that girls are inadmissable to the clerical office . . .

It is said of the Reverend Miss Brown that she dresses splendidly, with a rich gold chain, has fine teeth, a pious and pretty face, and excellent elocutionary abilities – and is young and handsome. Where so many women are set like steel traps to entice men the wrong way, we see no harm in an angel or two like Miss Stone and her reverend sister setting their wits to keep 'em right . . .

33 SABBATARIANISM

Mackenzie's Weekly Message,
October 6, 1854

Brown's Sunday Labor Bill

Our clever neighbor, Mr. George Brown, of the *Globe*, evidently scandalizes Messrs. Cayley, Macnab, Spence, Hincks, *et al.,* for their Sunday Cabinet making. It is lawful to do good on the Sabbath day, and *good* Sunday work of necessity and mercy are proper under the strictest phase of puritan rule; but the Macnab [*sic*] cabinet is a very bad one, and therefore Mr. Brown brings in his bill, &c. &c.

The bill provides that no post-office shall be opened nor any mail despatched or made up between Saturday and Monday – and if a mail start on a Saturday night, it shall stop over Sunday, – but it is made lawful for the mail if it leave Montreal on a Saturday evening to keep on till it reach Quebec – and if it leave Toronto it may proceed till it reach Kingston. So the bill reads.

The canals are to be closed from midnight of Saturday till ditto on Sunday.

Nothing is said about telegraphic despatches by the wires on Sunday, nor is political cabinet making on that day specially condemned.

We are for the bill, and for Sunday as a day of rest; the idea is sublime, and the bill a humane one.

34 THE MAINE LAW AND PROHIBITION

Mackenzie's Weekly Message,
November 3, 1854

THE MAINE LAW ADOPTED NINETEEN TO ONE
(A Letter from the Editor)
Quebec, Oct. 26, 1854

After getting 29 votes for the ballot this afternoon, where we got only 8, fifteen months since, a discussion of the Maine Law came on, and the question was, will the House adopt the principle, that *"It shall not be lawful for any person to manufacture, barter or sell, any alcoholic liquor, except for a medicinal, chemical, or manufacturing purposes"* – In other words to add a general prohibition to moral suasion. . . . Nothing ought to be licensed. If right and proper in itself there should be no prohibition. Equality of rights does not license one and punish another. If bad and injurious, there should be no licence. The welfare of the human race required the suppression of the liquor traffic. That New York, with its three millions of well educated, intelligent people, was warmly for the Maine law, and that altho' one bad Governor (Seymour) had thwarted the well understood wishes of the people, tho' frequently expressed, directly and indirectly, in favor of total prohibition, yet it was hoped he would be got rid of next November. Connecticut rejoices in the law – Massachusets [*sic*] anxiously watches for its success – Maine triumphs in its operation – and even in New Brunswick, tho' Governor Head was opposed, the law favored temperance. Murders, blood-shed, cruelty, robbery, crime, misery, disease and wrong were the results of licensed taverns and grog shops, those pitfalls where weak men and women, mentally blind, are tempted to their ruin. In many murders tried before the law courts, rum, gin and whisky, are the remote or direct causes. Abolition of the drinking house, as a vile nuisance is the grand reform of the age, even to the Indians had the selling of the liquor been made a crime and why not to whites also? Look at the noble minds whom indulgence in liquor has crushed and destroyed! Look at the immensely large class whom no moral suasion can reach, whom prohibition alone can save. It would not do to have half measures. If the distiller in Kingston is to be stopt, dont allow the schooner that arrives there to land whisky by the hundred barrels. Intemperance in eating is not like intemperance in drinking – the former vice affects but the individual – the latter sends a madman out into the streets, to knock down his peaceful neighbours, to commit murder, to quarrel and to disturb society – aye, to apply the incendiary's torch or his match to a peaceful dwelling. We should not only guard society against fire, but also against fire-water. We seize improper butchers' meat, because it is a poison – why not seize also and destroy the vile alcoholic poison that paralyzes the energies of millions! Thousands of our laws interfere with individual freedom. Our land laws do this. Even the Pre-Adamites may cry out that we interfere with their natural rights to run about naked – but they will remain unheeded. . . .

35 THE LUNATICS: WHO WILL PAY?

Mackenzie's Weekly Message,
February 10, 1854

THE LUNATIC ASYLUM

York township was taxed $556, under

Hincks and Ross's Lunatic Asylum bill, last year. Vaughan was mulcted in another $456. What an enormous sum Upper Canada pays, while Lower Canada gives not a cent! Hincks & Co. would draw people's teeth out, in taxation, if they could turn them into dollars. They are the keenest, greediest of all the locusts that have alighted in Canada. It is not to the Asylum only the cash goes – and while this tax is persisted in, millions of gold are lent to pet banks to be by them lent to favorites to corrupt the colony. – Bad mode this to promote loyalty. . . .

April 16, 1858

LUNATIC ASYLUM

This humane institution, according to the report of its superintendent, is terribly crowded, much against its efficiency as a place for curing disease. Year after year, the unfeeling Governor and his council put off the extension of this asylum, although ample means are in their hands. In like manner do they prevent the asylum for the deaf and dumb from being commenced. We find it only in the Statute Book. Sir E. Head's expenditure for his own and family's use of public money and means would almost endow an asylum . . .

36 THE EVILS OF GAMBLING

*Toronto Weekly Message,
January 4, 1858*

LOTTERIES

Why is it that no government will bring in a bill to annihilate all lotteries, foreign, and domestic? These lotteries are generally cheats, and whether or not, they induce silly people to strive to live by gambling instead of honest, useful industry. A scheme of all the lotteries in Maryland, was put into every box in the Post Office, Toronto, on 2nd. inst. When shall such nuisances be abated? England has annihilated them – so has New York and New England. Why not Canada also?

37 PROSTITUTION AND ITS REMEDY

*Toronto Weekly Message,
February 18, 1858*

This extract is taken from the New York *Herald*.

PROSTITUTION IN GREAT CITIES

"For two thousand years good and sensible men have been studying the question of prostitution, with results which have varied in everything but their uniform failure. Every student and every legislator has started from the principle that the abandonment by a woman of her chastity and modesty for hire was an evil; but no one has ever devised a method of preventing that evil. There have been laws under which prostitutes have been buried alive, thrust into cages and drowned, whipped naked through the public streets, pilloried and mutilated; there are laws under which the single fact of prostitution exposes a female to imprisonment; every penalty, every form of punishment, in short, has been or is inflicted in the view of prohibiting public prostitution; and yet there never was a time when public prostitutes did not infest all large cities.

"There has been a meeting held in London to devise measures to rid some of the larger thoroughfares of women of the town. A speaker proposed to license prostitutes, and the question was laid over. The license system, in force in France, Prussia, and other countries, has never been adopted in England or the United States. In the former countries prostitutes and prostitution are recognized by the laws; the women are not subject to punishment, but subject to compulsory attendance at a public dispensary, and to various disabilities. Each woman is ticketed, and can be identified or followed by the description of her person, taken when she is entered on the books of the police. The advantages of this method are, *greater security for health*; less likelihood of robbery; greater police control over a class naturally turbulent. The disadvantage is the seeming wrong in recognizing and licensing an evil which nobody pretends to be able to put down.

"From the names of the persons who are identified with the reform movement in England it may be anticipated that the subject will receive a thorough handling...."

REMARKS – No one can read the *Globe*, *Leader*, and *Colonist*, and their excellent police reports, without seeing that Toronto is full of houses of prostitution; that these houses are often the haunt of the thief, the gambler, and the cheat; that health is ruined there; property lost, female character degraded, and life often endangered.

All experience shows that prostitution cannot be put down; and the London press therefore discussing the question of public safety, as in France, Prussia, and part of Germany. It is objected on the one hand that you license sin, as in the case in theatres, circuses, &c.; on the other hand, it is argued that every consideration of public safety, health, and morals demand a speedy and practical change.

38 LIQUOR DISTILLING FOR EXPORT

Toronto Weekly Message,
May 5, 1860

MANUFACTURE OF GRAIN AND ALCOHOL

At Good's Extensive Foundry are to be seen the Machinery, Wheels, Heavy Castings and Millstones of a very Extensive Establishment, now in progress on the Don, the cost of which will exceed $140,000, and which is intended as we understand, for grinding grain, and distilling extensively, including Alcohol for the European Market.

Among the Machinery are two Wrought Iron Shafts of great length, each capable of driving four run of Stones. When used for grain they can grind (8 tun) say 300 barrels a day or more.

Messrs. GOODERHAM & WORTS, the proprietors of the new concern are prudent, cautious, enterprising gentlemen, possessing all the qualities essential to success. We have sometimes thought they had struck upon a gold mine down at the Don, but perhaps it's their skill and tact that ensures much success.

D. Education and Science

39 A UNIVERSITY FOR UPPER CANADA

The Colonial Advocate,
May 18, 1824

We coincide with Mr. Strachan, in opinion respecting the very urgent necessity which exists in Canada for the establishment of a university, and transcribe from his tour a few remarks on the subject.

"The liberal professions now demand the establishment of a university. The church requires a long course of study, which cannot at present be obtained. Young men designed for the bar, have not the necessary opportunities for preparing themselves for that important profession. The students of medicine, the sons of liberal merchants and of the more opulent landholders, would certainly attend a seminary on an extensive scale; and it is very certain that, in a few years after its establishment, more than one hundred students would be found at the university of Upper Canada."*

The number of students found at the university, if it be established, will very much depend upon circumstances. If it is to be an arm of our hierarchy; if students are to be tied down by tests and oaths to support particular dogmas, as is the case in Oxford, the institution will answer here no good purpose.

Arts and science, manufactures and commerce, have greatly progressed thro'out Europe and America during the last fifty years. The invention of the steam engine, and the useful application of steam pressure, has placed us centuries in advance of even the last generation, in point of power. The whole world is indebted to Great Britain, for many a banquet rich with mental luxury. Let us, therefore, lose no time, but free from party spirit and narrow sectarian motives in our institutions, endeavor to benefit by this general diffusion of knowledge. Let us remember Lord Bacon's wise and laconic saying, "Knowledge is power."

We ought to enrich the minds of our youth, by giving them such instruction and conformation of character as may enable them to serve their country, by the practical application of a systematic education, and like William Pitt, to blend the wisdom of age, with the complexion of youth.

We very much want men in Canada, who have received a liberal education; men untainted by the enjoyment of power and place, who, if called on, would not hesitate to sacrifice their personal interests for the good of their country; and who, if elected to our house of assembly, would return to their homes at the end of a fourth or fifth session, as free from the enthralments of patronage and place, of honors and pensions, as when they were first placed in the honourable situation of guardians of their country's rights.

We want barristers who would at all times prefer, on principle, to plead the cause of a poor man oppressed, rather than of a rich oppressor; who would rather *physic pomp* than pamper it – rather *despise* arrogance, clothed with a little brief authority, than cringe to and flatter it ...

* Strachan's *Canada,* 132. [Mackenzie's note – ed.]

40 ON AMERICAN COLLEGES FOR CANADIAN YOUTH

The Colonial Advocate,
May 27, 1824

Let our Canadian readers think of the benefits received at these colleges; let them consider the genius that they have encouraged and the talents which they have caused to shine forth – their Adamses, their Websters, and a host of others, who perhaps but for the education they obtained at these schools would never attained the foremost rank among their countrymen. We have read the travels of Americans, but who has ever heard of the travels of a Canadian? No one; though we have learned that our *ambassador* is to favour the world with his remarks *en passant*; he having received two subscriptions from the province, amounting to ten or twelve thousand dollars *to account*.

Let our readers compare these very moderate charges with the expenses of a common, or of a district school in this country.

We do not presume here to give advice; but we would ourself *far rather* send our sons to Harvard or Yale, than to any district school now in Canada. In the British Senate Lord Nugent most appropriately terms the U. S. Americans *our brothers in origin and in feeling*; and adds, "*I shall always think of them as I think of them now – with the warmest interest and admiration.*" Such language from such a quarter is most useful in removing and dispelling the mist of prejudices that has so long and so injuriously operated against our own interests. In old times our Scottish youths went often to Utrecht and Haarlem to finish their studies: yet their fathers had no fears lest their children's minds should receive among the Dutch republicans, anti-monarchical prejudices; nor were our Scottish legislators ever so foolish as to enact statutes prohibiting their youth from benefiting by titles so conferred, whether in Divinity, Law or Physic. How would the great Doctor Pitcairn, have liked, on his return from taking his degrees at Leyden, after shewing his diplomas, and before he could either have bled purged or blistered to have been catechised by Horne, Sampson, Powell & co. as to his abilities.

If then our children return among us impressed with ideas unfavourable to our institutions, it must be from some defect or defects in these institutions; some unpleasant feeling like that which a West Indian youth is sensible of when, after receiving a liberal British education, he returns to his native island, and hears the crack of the modern Egyptian task-master's whip. Is it at all wonderful that he abhors to behold Negro slavery; that his soul revolts at sight of the brutal system of cream-coloured tyranny? No; for to him the *past* and the *present* present too well-marked, too striking a contrast. If then, it is found impossible to establish in Upper Canada an University as free from *test-oaths* as are Harvard and Yale; if government chooses to have an established church University, as well as an established church, it is well: let them have it. We, in such a case, would certainly prefer to be unconnected with the pile of intolerance.

It is true, on coming home from an American seminary, our sons would be apt to entertain unfavourable notions of arbitrary and absolute power, as also of national churches; but we believe there are few parents who would love their children the less for entertaining such sentiments.

41 THE NATURAL HISTORY SOCIETY OF MONTREAL

The Colonial Advocate,
July 23, 1829

[Inserted by request of the Recording Secretary.]

NATURAL HISTORY SOCIETY.

Notice is hereby given that the NATURAL HISTORY SOCIETY of Montreal, anxious to encourage a spirit of research, and to create a taste for scientific pursuits, have resolved upon offering FOUR SILVER MEDALS for Essays on scientific subjects, thereby endeavouring to rouse the dormant talent of the Province by exciting a praiseworthy emulation.

For THREE of these Medals, the competition will be open to the public generally, and ONE only will be exclusively confined to the competition of the several classes of Members.

The Medals offered are as follows: –

1. *A Silver Medal* for the best Essay descriptive of the QUADRUPEDS of British North America, their generic and specific characters, their modes of life and the uses to which they can be applied. This essay to be open to general competition.

2. *A Silver Medal* for the best Essay descriptive of the PLANTS indigenous to the Canadas, their generic and specific characters, their habits and their uses, medical and economical. This essay to be open to the competition of the Honorary, Corresponding and Ordinary Members of the Society, resident in the British North American Provinces, *only*.

3. *A Silver Medal* for the best Essay on any branch of general Literature, the particular subject thereof to be chosen by the respective authors. This essay to be open to general competition.

4. *A Silver Medal* for the best Essay on any branch of philosophy or science other than Natural History, the particular subject thereof to be chosen by the respective authors. This essay to be open to general competition . . .

42 MIND, MORALS AND EDUCATION

The Colonial Advocate,
November 19, 1829

The following is taken from Joseph Hume's *Essay on Education.*

Extracts From the Catechism of Education.

SECTION I

INTRODUCTION

1. *Q. What is Education?*

A. The best employment of all the means which can be made use of by man, for rendering the *human mind* to the greatest possible degree the cause of human happiness.

2. *Q. On what does Happiness depend?*

A. Happiness depends upon the condition of the body, either immediately, as where the bodily powers are exerted for the attainment of some good; or mediately, through the mind, as where the condition of the body affects the qualities of the mind.

3. *Q. What is required as the foundation of a good Education?*

A. Good practice; *which can, in no case,*

have any solid foundation but in sound theory.

4. Q. *What is theory?*

A. The *whole* of the knowledge which we possess upon any subject, put into that order and form in which it is most easy to draw from it good practical rules.

5. Q. *In what does the character of the human mind consist?*

A. In the sequence of its ideas.

6. Q. *What are the grand instruments or powers, by the use of which the purposes of education are to be attained?*

A. Custom; and Pain, and Pleasure.

7. Q. *To what points is Custom to be directed?*

A. First, to form those sequences which make the component parts of a good train of ideas; and secondly, to join those sequences together, so as to constitute the trains.

8. Q. *Does every operation of the senses imply judgment or belief, as well as simple apprehension, notion or imagination?*

A. Yes.

9. Q. *Whence are all our trains of ideas?*

A. They start from a sensation, or some impression upon the external or internal nerves.

10. Q. *Which are those sensations, or aggregates of sensations, which are of the most frequent occurrence?*

A. Those which occur in the ordinary business of life.

11. Q. *Is it not of the greatest importance that beneficial trains of ideas should commence from those sensations?*

A. It surely is.

12. Q. *Which are the aggregates of sensations of the most frequent occurrence?*

A. Rising up in the morning, and going to bed at night; also, the commencement and termination of meals.

13. Q. *Did not the practical sagacity of priests, even in the rudest ages of the world, perceive the importance, for giving religious trains an ascendancy in the mind, of uniting them, by early and steady custom, with those perpetually recurring sensations?*

A. It did. The morning and evening prayers, and the grace before and after meals, have something correspondent to them in the religion of, perhaps, all nations.

14. Q. *What effect will be produced by skilfully selecting the trains of ideas which lead most surely to the happiness, first of the individual himself, and next of his fellow creatures, and effectually uniting with them by custom the sensations which are most apt to give commencement to trains of ideas?*

A. A provision of unspeakable importance will be made for the happiness of the human race.

15. Q. *What is appetite?*

A. It is the feeling towards pleasure or pain in prospect, and has great power over the mental trains of ideas.

16. Q. *What are the best means of applying the prospect of pleasure and pain to render beneficent trains of ideas perpetual in the mind?*

A. We must first ascertain, what are the really ultimate objects of human desire; Next, what are the most beneficent means of attaining these objects; and lastly, accustom the mind to fill up the intermediate space between the present sensation and the ultimate object, with nothing but the ideas of those beneficent means.

17. Q. *As a train commences in some present sensation, and may be conceived as terminating in the idea of some future pleasure or pain, what description of ideas intervene between the commencement and the end?*

A. Either beneficent or hurtful.

SECTION II

QUALITIES OF MIND, TO THE PRODUCTION OF WHICH THE BUSINESS OF EDUCATION SHOULD BE DIRECTED.

18. Q. *What are the qualities with which it is of most importance that the mind of the individual should be endowed?*

A. Intelligence, Temperance, Justice, and Generosity.

19. Q. *What are the ingredients of Intelligence?*

A. Knowledge and Sagacity.

20. Q. *What effects are produced by an union of these qualities?*

A. The one afford the materials upon which the other is to be exerted; knowledge, shewing what exists; sagacity, converting it to the greatest use; knowledge, bringing within our ken what is capable, and what is not capable of being used as means; sagacity, seizing and combining, at the proper moment, whatever is fittest as means to each particular end.

21. Q. *What is Temperance?*

A. A perfect command over a man's appetites and desires; the power of restraining them whenever they lead in a hurtful direction; that possession of himself which insures his judgement against the illusions of the passion, and enables him to pursue constantly what he deliberately approves.

22. Q. *Is Temperance indispensably requisite to enable mankind to produce the greatest possible quantity of Happiness?*

A. It is.

23. Q. *What is Fortitude?*

A. The power of resisting Pain.

24. Q. *In how far are these two qualities, the* intelligence *which can always choose the best possible means, and the* strength *which overcomes the misguiding propensities, sufficient for the happiness of the human race?*

A. They appear to be sufficient for the happiness only of the individual who possesses them.

25. Q. *What, then, are the qualities with which an individual ought to be endowed, to make him produce the greatest possible quantity of Happiness to others?*

A. A man can affect the happiness of others, either by abstaining from doing them harm, or by doing them positive good: To abstain from doing them harm, receives the name of Justice; to do positive good receives that of Generosity.

26. Q. *Do the four cardinal virtues of the ancients, Intelligence, Temperance, Justice, and Generosity, include all the qualities, to the possession of which the human mind should be trained?*

A. The description is far too general. What is wanting is, that the incidents of human life should be skilfully classified; both those on the occasion of which they who are the objects of the good acts are pointed out for the receipt of them, and those on the occasion of *which* they who are to be the instrument are called upon for the performance. The science of Ethics, as well as the science of Intellectuals, must be carried to perfection, before the best foundation is obtained for the science of Education . . .

43 ANTI-SCIENTIFIC TORYISM

The Colonial Advocate,
July 9, 1831

Hints to the York Tories.

The following article is suitable for Sir John Colborne's friends, Messrs. Strachan, Boulton, Robinson, and the rest of the tories, who would confine Education to the few in order that they might long trample on the liberties of the many.

[From the Edinburgh Scotsman.]

Antipathy between Science and Toryism.

A correspondent says – "I was much amused the other day, with a leading article in the Morning Post, in which the writer seriously argued the *political* dangers to be apprehended from the rapid increase of Mechanics' Institutions because their principal promoters were Liberals. *This sagacious journalist, seeing such men as Lansdown, Brougham, Mackintosh, &c, very active in extending to the humbler classes the means of procuring education and acquiring scientific knowledge,* thinks it very *suspicious*: he cannot exactly see the end of it, but he is sure nothing good came out of what is encouraged by Whigs and Reformers! He is afraid that sedition will be insinuated in electricity, blasphemy combined with mathematics, and that the free use of a library of historical and standard books must inevitably lead to the subversion of social order! It is impossible to avoid being pleased with the compliment here paid to the enlightened Liberals referred to, or with the indirect, but not less pointed, reflection upon this wiseacre's own rotten cause, and the phalanx of rank, wealth, and power, by which it is supported. If there be any thing in his argument, all the writers on the side of loyalty, religion, and legitimacy, all the clergy, the bible and tract societies, &c. are no match, in regard to talent or influence, for their literary adversaries, notwithstanding the slight matters of Libel, Law, Fines, and Prison, thrown into the scale against the latter!"

44 THE INDUSTRIAL REVOLUTION IN UPPER CANADA

*The Colonial Advocate,
July 4, 1833*

Steam Engines.

The various purposes to which these useful and powerful pieces of mechanism may be applied are so obvious that any recommendation we could bestow upon them would be perfectly superfluous. The generation of steam for various manufacturing purposes appears to be increasingly appreciated in the vicinity of this town. So much has this subject excited our capitalists, that a laudable competition has been entered in the building of the numerous steamboats with which our navigable waters are daily becoming more splendidly supplied, for the convenience and comfort of the traveller and the accommodation of commercial interests, by facilitating our numerous exports and imports, – but also for the purposes of domestic manufactures.

For instance, there are now two excellent Cupola Furnaces propelled by Steam Engines in this town, which were but a few months ago propelled by horse power, in which castings of every description are made with the greatest expedition, inferior to none in America.

There are also, two Steam Engine manufactories in successful operation in the town, viz. Sheldon, Dutcher & Co's and Charles Perry's; the latter of which we lately visited and was particularly struck with the superiority of the workmanship of a Steam Engine now preparing for Messrs. Worts and Gooderham's Windmill near this town. It strikes us very forcibly that we never saw anything of the kind wear the appearance of a more superior finish. From Mr. Perry's superior Steam Engine Factory we took a turn down to a Steam Saw Mill, recently erected near the Windmill for the purpose of examining its Engine recently manufactured by Mr. Perry, and to say the least of it we are decidedly of opinion that very few such pieces of workmanship are to be met with in North America.

The rage for Steam Saw Mills may be said to have commenced in right earnest in this neighborhood. Mr. Bickett has lately erected one in the pine woods east of the Don in this immediate vicinity, the Engine of which was manufactured by Mr. Perry.

We should not be at all surprised if the Steam Engine should supercede water power for the use of mills, not being subject to the casualties of broken dams, stoppages by drought and frost, to say nothing of the unhealthiness of Large ponds of stagnant water generating pestilential *miasma* and causing thereby an unhealthy state of atmospheric air throughout the surrounding neighbourhoods where such mills are situated, and the total waste of perhaps 50 to 100 acres of excellent meadow lands ...

45 COLONIAL IGNORANCE

*The Constitution,
December 19, 1836*

Education.

What is the Legislature, and what are the different Religious denominations doing to promote Education among the people? Let no man trust in empty Despatches from the English Colonial Office. They are a pack of plausible lies. How can those who do their utmost to prevent the English people from being educated, in order that an Aristocracy may be necessary to control them, desire for us that moral, religious and educated population which would render the existence of an aristocracy in the Government unnecessary? One thing is certain – no free popular Government can exist unless the people are informed. An ignorant Republic would surely degenerate into a most corrupt and hateful Government. – The patriots (we have seen that) need watching by their constituents.

46 A GEOLOGICAL SURVEY OF UPPER CANADA

The Constitution,
July 19, 1837

Mackenzie claims to have initiated this survey in 1836. Cf. *Mackenzie's Weekly Message*, June 4, 1858. [ed.]

Report of the Committee on Geological Surveys.
To The Honorable The House of Assembly.
The Committee appointed to consider and report a plan for the Geological Survey of this Province, beg leave to Report to your Honorable House what they conceive to be some of the strongest reasons in favor of a Geological Survey of the same.

Of the resources of a new country, manufactures are necessarily out of the question. Old countries where labour is reduced to the lowest possible amount which will sustain human life, must always possess a superiority in the manipulation of commodities over a country where labour is both scarce and dear. Agriculture and Mines are the only things which a new country can cope with an old. The former on account of the low price of land and the absence of taxation, and the latter, from the superior facility of procuring the property in them in fee simple, and as the case may be, the superiority in the productiveness of the mine itself.

The first advantage to be derived from productive mines in a country such as ours is, that those who work them consume the produce of the agriculturist within our own bounds, and thus convert a commodity which is bulky, expensive in transport, and liable to damage, into one which is small in proportion to its value, cheap in transport, and which, if it be not totally lost in the passage, can suffer no injury from wind and waves.

Thus: suppose a copper mine was discovered on the Huron, and that the copper could be worked at a rate that would repay the miners when sold in England, the persons engaged in the mining, cleaning, and smelting of this copper, must consume agricultural produce, in the shape of provisions, to perhaps one-half of its price in England, and a considerable portion of the remaining moiety must come from England in the shape of British manufactures.

Again, when time has equalized everything, the farmers of the western parts of this Province cannot expect to get the present prices for their wheat – this wheat has to be converted into money in England by a tedious process of transmission; but let it be used on the spot by those who mine and manipulate the copper, and we will obtain a higher price for it; because, what we cannot supply on the spot must be brought at the risque and charges from a distance, and, by consequence, our profits must be theirs *plus the charge and risque of bringing it from a greater distance,* which is of itself a great addition to the profit. Again, the charge upon the transmission of goods comes out of the pocket of the farmer. Wheat at Montreal sells for, say five shilling, per bushel, whether it is grown at La Prairie or on the Huron; but the La Prairie farmer can put his wheat into his canoe and run it across the rapid to his market; whereas the western farmer must pay for agency, storage, and freight and shipping; incur the risque of wind and waves; pay for bags, agency, and storage when it arrives; all which is necessarily deducted from his profit, even if he ships on his own account; but if, as it is most probable he does so, through country store-keepers, he has their profits and those of their Montreal agents (or principals, as the case may be) to pay in addition ...

R. G. Dunlop, Chairman

47 FREETHINKING DEFENDED

Mackenzie's Gazette, [New York]
September 22, 1838

Mrs. [Frances Wright] Darusmont's Lecture.

There never was a greater error than to judge people's worth by the resemblance of their profession of religion and politics to ours, and to esteem them according as that profession approached our standard. We have never said a word against the Christian religion in our lives, but we feel friendly alike to those who profess one faith and those who adhere to another, judging all by their conduct. Go to a school or college and you will find the reverend presbyterian or methodist professor teaching history, latin, or Greek out of Cicero, Seneca, Horace, Homer, Eschylus, Herodotus, Plutarch, Virgil, Ovid, and so forth, persons who never believed a syllable of the Bible, old testament or new, when in life, but had gods and goddesses by the dozen, gross, or score, which were of wood and stone. Let one of these presbyterians or methodists hear that a modern sceptic, like Mrs. Darusmont, intends to deliver a lecture on history, morals or government, science or literature, (not meddling with divinity;) up he starts, ascends the sacred desk, denounces her and all her works, and then returns to his cloister or college to teach youth from Hume or Homer, Horace or Herodotus, men who thought as he thinks, and doubted as he doubts. The cry of "Mad Dog" once fairly got up in the congregation his reverence is quite safe. But his conduct is unchristian, uncharitable, and unjust, and deserves strong censures. We never heard Mrs. Darusmont speak, but she has been thought worthy of so much abuse from the loyalists of Canada, the federal presses here, and the corporation of Philadelphia, that as she is a natural orator, we intend to attend a lecture, gratify curiosity, listen with attention, and state candidly the impression made upon our minds by what we hear and see, next Saturday, more especially as the Canada question is to be considered, a matter in which we feel deeply interested.

48 AMERICAN EDUCATION APPRAISED

The Volunteer, [Rochester]
May 10, 1842

The Rochester Collegiate Institute

A good Education, physical, moral, *and* intellectual, was, in the opinion of that early friend of our country, General Lafayette, "the best inheritance that parents could transmit to their children." The view he took was eminently scriptural. "Take fast hold of *Instruction* (saith an inspired writer), let her not go, keep her, for she is thy life – Poverty and Shame shall be to him that refuseth *Instruction* – *Understanding* is a wellspring of life to him that hath it."

On the intelligence and virtue of the people this republican system of government is based – the mechanic or farmer of to-day may be the magistrate, juror, or legislator of to-morrow. Yet out of fourteen millions of freeborn Americans in the states, there are by the last census, not less than 549,693 entirely destitute of the rudiments of a common education – while there is reason to fear that in many cases those who are taught are neither taught well nor wisely. In some seminaries, the history of human ambition and grandeur, of wars against freedom and the free, and of Greeks and Romans "stained with outrages on the superior faculties of man," is held up to admiration while the study of the Creator's glorious name and character is neglected, and our Saviour's great rule, that *we should love our neighbour as ourselves* (the whole family of man being here included), ridiculed as unfashionable and obsolete.

There is reason to believe, however, that our common or district schools "are on the gain." Like the colleges on the European continent, and the excellent seminary of which in these essays, I am to give a brief account, the district school places on a perfect level children of all circumstances and conditions, before the pride of wealth or family has taken root in the youthful heart. There they are taught there is no royal road to learning, – superior diligence, good conduct, with improvement, carry off the prizes; and on the tender minds of the pupils are early implanted these great principles of equal rights, equal duties and equal advantages, on which our people and moral government was intended to rest ...

49 THE NATURE OF DISEASE AND ITS CURE

Mackenzie's Weekly Message, February 10, 1853

Doctors Upon Doctoring

A number of regularly educated physicians in New York have issued a manifesto and formed themselves into a medical society. They reason thus:

"Disease, we affirm to consist in disturbances of functions, which if prolonged or not specifically arrested, induced permanent derangement, destruction of structure, and ultimately extinction of being or death. But maladies cannot arise without vital energy being impaired or lessened. Hence debility ever precedes distemper, for if vital forces are in a normal state disease can make no inroad. The phenomena of life are characterized by periodic or tidal alteration of attractive and repulsive movement in the various organs of the body – these when manifested in an orderly manner, constitute healthy life, while their correspondence with inverted order, is accompanied by disease; and the only true and legitimate function of the physician in the treatment of the sick hath this extent, the restoration of the ordinary periodicity of health, by the judicious use of these healing medicines, and other appliances, which it has pleased a beneficent Providence to bestow upon his creatures."

The Allopathic or the old medical practice is thus spoken of:

"Adam Smith, author of the 'Wealth of Nations' affirms that 'the cause of the quackery *out* of the profession is the *real quackery* in the Profession.'"

50 EDUCATION AND CIVILIZATION

Mackenzie's Weekly Message, September 29, 1853

Clergy Reserves. Education

England has been a powerful nation for many ages – her monarchy spend their five millions of dollars yearly – her bishops grumble at $30,000 and a charity purse – her nobility boast of incomes of $20,000 to a million per annum – her merchants and manufacturers die, leaving their tons, aye hundreds of tons of silver each to aristocratic descendants – but the people are left in comparative ignorance – drunkenness prevails greatly in Scotland, where education is on the decrease, while in England the average intelligence of the people is far behind that of Upper Canada. With the great fact before us, proclaimed by Solomon and echoed by Bacon, that Knowledge is Power, shall we longer hesitate in giving the people that education which the Clergy Reserves could amply confer? Shall we consent to be longer trifled with by profligates, parasites, and buck parsons? If we leave lands and lawyers to our children, with ignorance, the lawyers and the bankers and the bureaucrats will, as in Britain and Ireland, soon own fifty times their fair share of the country, while our boys and girls will suffer and emigrate as their ancestors had to do before them. Uphold a free press, farmers, but take care that it is a free one. In Spain, Austria, France, Russia and Poland, now, (and five years since in Ireland) no truths can be told that rulers do not like to hear – else the truth-teller goes to the dungeon.

England is the richest country in the world, yet so mean and sordid are her rulers that out of every hundred men married there in 1850 only 65 could write their own names, the other 33 made their mark, while of the woman they were married to 46 out of every hundred had to make a cross, being unable to read and write. While this is going on, covetous wretches like Lord Guilford make the laws, seize the revenues, and keep from education even those special funds which good men in past ages had devoted to the improvement of our nation and of our race.

I write thus, not because I am captious and censorious, but as a lover of my native land, anxious to shame her oppressors. Last session has assuredly given us an earnest of real reform, which I am glad, very glad, to witness in England ... Education is a mine of wealth compared to which all the gold and silver mines in the world are but as dust. One educated man, thro' the steam engine, another thro' the telegraph, a third thro' the steamboat, and a fourth thro' the railway scheme have done more for mankind, than all the ignorance of Europe could have achieved in centuries of European darkness...

51 THE TECHNOLOGY OF PRINT

Mackenzie's Weekly Message,
October 20, 1853

Progress of Papermaking and Printing

It is but 90 years since cotton was first planted in America – but 223 since the first newspaper was struck off – but 86 since Watt's improvement in the steam engine, and scarcely twelve years since the lightning telegraph came into general use. Napier's press, which revolutionized printing, is a very recent improvement and we are now called upon to chronicle the invention of excellent writing paper from straw, and a press that will print 30,000 copies of the London *Times* or New York *Tribune*, ready for the carriers, within one hour!

If instead of becoming the dupes of political priesthoods and mean politicians, and making earth a Tophet with our quarrels about the way to heaven, mankind would imitate inventors and compete as to who could confer the greatest booms upon the world, what a paradise earth would become! Stereotype printing was invented 68 years since, and its benefits are incalculable. Last week we had the pleasure of recording a most desirable improvement upon it.

It is now nearly thirty years since the Editor of the *Message* called a public meeting by handbills in Toronto, for the encouragement of the paper manufacture. He moved in that meeting resolutions asking the legislature to grant $500, or some higher bounty, to the first manufacturer of paper in Canada – drafted a petition, got it well signed in town and country – the small boon was given – and Hon. James Crooks, near Dundas, got the $500 as our first Canadian paper maker. We printed a newspaper for many months on paper of his make, and collected rags at our office for his paper mill.

The *Tribune* states that the great feature of the Crystal Palace, N. Y., as regards paper is the specimen's strong construct [?], of good color and cheap, of writing paper made of straw by a French house, who are building a mill in Pennsylvania...

...The French patent does not extend to Canada – that is one advantage of our colonial condition – and we advise our paper makers to ascertain the mode of using straw instead of rags, and thus lower their prices and increase their sales. Straw is cheap enough in Canada...

[There follows a description of the Hoe cylindrical press which will print 30,000 sheets on both sides in an hour. (ed.)]

52 AN INTERVIEW WITH WILLIAM LOGAN

Mackenzie's Weekly Message,
June 23, 1854

Montreal, Donegani's Hotel.
Monday, June 13.

I hastened to pay a visit to the bureau of Mr. Logan, the Provincial Geologist, this forenoon, and came away loaded with so much useful information, communicated orally, that it will fill two of three letters when put upon paper.

The bureau is a very large house opposite the Place d'Armes here: and I was glad to learn that the public will speedily be admitted daily, without charge, to view its scientific treasures, which are nearly all arranged. There is no end of metallic, mineralogical, and other geological specimens – all of them Canadian. It will gradually become a museum on the excellent principle of the British Museum, London.

COAL

The first question I asked of Mr. Logan was about coal: "Had he seen what was said in the *Owen Sound Lever*, about it?" He had: – but he adheres to his former opinion: that there is no coal in Canada: that the

Canadian rocks are of those kinds *below* which no coal has ever been found; that the bituminous shale seen at Owen Sound and elsewhere, (as designated by him on a large map which I examined,) is almost always associated with coal, but that the coal is invariably above the shale not under it . . .

. . . Many brief enquiries were made as to stone, and was shown specimens of the dressed granite (gneiss) used to build the Quebec Water Reservoir. Mr. Logan affirms that Canada abounds with better granite than the celebrated Aberdeen kind, so much in use in London. I think he said he had met with the best in the Eastern Townships. Thorold stone, Guelph stone, marble, slate, &c., are represented in the Museum, also excellent Lithographic stone from Marmora,— none better! It does good work.

Among the specimens of Marble I saw a beautiful one from the Eastern Townships, very like the Sienna – Serpentine marble equal to the *verde antique* of Italy, which admits of a very superior polish.

While examining the fossils, a class I have probably entered without knowing it, Mr. L. affirmed that they change very gradually to solid rock; and lose their character for illustrating the progress of matter. In opposition to received theories, he said he had never seen anything of what are called primary formations of rock; he had found all sorts of rock in a state of transition.

"Look Nature through – 'tis revolution all."

53 ELECTRICAL CURES FOR CHOLERA

Mackenzie's Weekly Message,
August 18, 1854

Lightning Rods. Platinum Points. Cholera.

. . . Mr. EDITOR – I received from your office the *Albany Evening Journal*, containing a story headed, "The Lightning Rod Man." I do not know whether I am the individual referred to or not, but one thing I do know, the arguments used by the author has about as much weight as a feather and that a very small one. None but an Old School Presbyterian would introduce foreordination as an offset against the use of lightning rods. As well might the man in the cholera say to the doctor, "away with your drugs; I will have none of them for God has numbered the hairs of my head, as well as my days, and if your drugs can save me you make the Author of Truth a liar!" God made the thunder and the lightning. We cannot live without electricity. Yet too much of it will destroy life. In my humble opinion cholera is caused by an excess of electricity in the atmosphere. On days in which the cholera has raged the worst this season the atmosphere has been so heavily charged with electricity, that it was with difficulty that the telegraph wire would work, and this state of the atmosphere has been proved time and again by many terrific thunder storms taking place between four and nine p.m. during July. This month the thunder storms have abated and the cholera has almost entirely disappeared. I have not heard of a death by Asiatic cholera in any house thoroughly protected with lightning rods that possess our magnetic platinum points, properly erected and well connected with the ground. Lightning rods erected on our principle are a protection to life and property and conducive to health . . .

Yours respectfully,
THE TRUE LIGHTNING ROD MAN
Yonge Street, Toronto
Aug. 14, 1854.

54 AMERICAN EDUCATIONAL REFORMS FOR CANADA

Mackenzie's Weekly Message,
February 1, 1856

Free Schools.

While Charbonell and Strachan, the priestly nominees of the British authorities in England denounce Free Schools, Governor Clark, freely elected by a hundred and fifty thousand votes across the lines, is for entire freedom. Except the intolerant priests wish their name and memory to send forth the odious flavor of the apothecaries' ointment named in Scripture, they should cease to interrupt the public peace.

I would also suggest the expediency of making the schools of the State entirely free. Twice when this question has been submitted to the people, their verdict has been rendered by a large majority in favor of it.

There is evidently a growing repugnance to the rate-bill system, and it is now time that the subject of its final abolishing was fully discussed. The imposition of an additional tax for the maintenance of public schools for a given time, not less than eight months, to be assessed upon the several towns in comformity with the recommendation of their respective Boards of Education, would supply all the means requisite for schools during each year. If instead of school districts as now organized, it should be left discretionary with the educational officers of each town to establish schools whenever necessary in different localities in the town, it would be far easier to disburse the school moneys equitably than under the present arrangement, where districts are formed of different sizes, and with no general regulation as to population or available resources. This policy has been adopted in several States with decided advantage. The interminable controversies between school districts, the adjudication of which occupies so large a proportion of the attention of the State Superintendent, and which seem every year to become more numerous, more bitter, and more mischievous, would be obviated. A more equitable division of the school moneys, greater economy in their application and the convenience of the public would be effected.

55 AGRICULTURAL EDUCATION

Mackenzie's Weekly Message,
February 22, 1856

Mr. David Christie, M. P. for Brant, is one of the largest practical farmers in Western Canada, in which he has resided twenty-three years, and was last year President of the Provincial Agricultural Association.

While attending the Annual Exhibition at Cobourg last October, we listened with real pleasure to his official address, ably delivered to an attentive audience of thousands; and although it was published at the time, we are sure that our country subscribers will find no more useful or interesting passages in this week's issue than such as are selected from Mr. Christie's sound and eminently practical advice to his brother cultivators.

We desire especially to direct attention to those passages where Mr. Christie reminds the agriculturist that without more improved farming Canada must shortly fall behind as a grain-exporting country – where he demonstrates that without combining scientific instruction with practical labour on the farm, you cannot educate thoroughly the tiller of the soil – and where he contends for the dignity and usefulness of agricultural pursuits, and rebukes the folly of those who seek seemingly easier modes of getting independent.

. . . That a few terms at the University here, under competent teachers and at the lowest possible rates at which state-salaried officials could thoroughly instruct agricultural pupils, would be invaluable to the Cincinnati of Canada, Mr. Christie's essay has very clearly proved. – ED. MESSAGE.

56 DISENCHANTMENT WITH LOGAN

Toronto Weekly Message,
June 4, 1858

Logan, Chapman, and the Bowmanville Coal.

Twenty two years since, in Assembly, this writer moved for a special committee to take measures for a geological survey of Canada. We wrote to General Dix, at Albany; got from the Secretary of State's Office the printed records of what had been done across the lines; laid them before the Committee which reported favorably. After the mists of 1837-8 had cleared up Mr. Logan was chosen as geologist, and altho' we had no power to check his proceedings, we have watched them carefully.

Like the most of the sly and smooth saints (some would bluntly say vampires or sinners) who suck the life's blood of Canada, this man, Logan, himself the very picture of avarice, has converted his survey into a permanent job of trying "how not to do it."

First, he and his men bled Canada at the rate of $2,000 a year, then at $20,000 a year; and now they add $30,000 a year to the $20,000 for contingencies. A book of maps, of which two would have served for the 23, was foisted by Logan upon the printing committee last March without contract, and turned up at some $24,000, binding included. Logan managed to get that thro'. What his share of the spoils may be, if any, we may know if Matthews, the mapman, gets into a crooked humor.

By means of the rascally trick of ordering the public chest to be emptied now and then of 50,000 dollars at a haul, to pay jobs like Logan's, the legislature evades all real control of them; and Derbishire, Logan and others are looked at with envy by a nest of like parasites, who would all be ready to play the very same game.

Logan has been a costly pet to the country. Whether his reports, be they secret or public, have enabled official knavery to fatten on good things it wouldn't otherwise have discovered we say not.

It was poor laborers who first found gold in California – it was not the hirelings of real or pretended science who met with it first in Australia. Logan & Co. have issued their declaration that in all Canada, 1,800 miles long, there is no coal; just as England's manufacturers, a hundred years ago, resolved that in America not even a hobnail could or should be manufactured. An English miner, however, says he has found excellent bituminous coal at Bowmanville. It looks like coal, feels like coal, burns like coal, is bituminous like coal, has every essential element of coal; and yet learning and genius, taking the form of Prof. Chapman, hesitate to analyze it, but dictatorially proceed to show why it cannot be coal, because it is found in the wrong place, as if a guinea couldn't be gold, even if found in the till of a Scotch or Michigan wildcat banker.

The miners of Mr. Bates's farm have bored down 60 feet, 6 inches wide, and other 30 feet 3 inches wide – they affirm there is a seam of coal six feet thick: we have seen the coal they brought up; the water is black and like ink, and yet the university professor neither analyzes it nor views the locality, but gives us a specimen of logic without investigation.

We quite agree with the Bowmanville Statesman, and with Mr. Balsdon, the English miner, that these lazy, costly drones, the Logan staff, should be set to work to disprove their own theories by opening up the shaft. They certainly cost enough to the country upon which they are unfortunately quartered, and at least some visible benefits should result to the public. Dousterswivel, in the *Antiquary,* pretended that there were mines where there were none. Logan and Co. deny their existence where there are!

The learned Lardner decided that steam boats could not cross the Atlantic, and instantly, they crossed it. The wise of France and London hooted Fulton's proposition of steam navigation, but the steamboat is a fact, the pope and his cardinals punished Galileo for affirming that the earth was a revolving sphere, but it moves. Logan, Chapman & Co. are about as infallible as the pope, but not more so.

57 HIGHER EDUCATION

Toronto Weekly Message,
December 24, 1858

The University of Toronto

Much is it to be desired that one vast school or seat of learning, which would afford the best and most extensive description of physical, moral, and intellectual education to be had in America, to all who might seek it, as an inheritance, may be established in Toronto, where instruction in the highest branches of human knowledge would be attainable! What a vast improvement for Ireland would be the affiliation of Maynooth with Trinity College, Dublin! We wish we could hope, even yet, to see the old Bishop's name once more connected with the Toronto University; posterity will allow him a higher degree of credit than he now receives. His great error lay in not distinguishing between a national or a provincial institution, upheld by and for all, in which no exclusive sectarian lest should permit a monopoly; and a college, like that of the Free Church in Scotland, which, as it was endowed and upheld by a sect, might provide, if it chose, that the teachers should hold Free Church doctrines. The Bishop has done so in Trinity, but we doubt his success . . .

The new buildings for the University are having quite a European air of grandeur and permanence about them; the location is a choice one; there is a 15,000 volume library, too, in which the public may read; and undergraduates are thoroughly instructed, free of cost, by a staff of professors of whom any seminary of learning might well be proud . . .

Let us have a college in which not only ideas and principles, but also the application of Chemistry, Botany, Mineralogy, &c to the arts and the Agriculture, for efficiency in industrial pursuits, will be taught. Why cannot girls be there as well as boys? Why exclude Flora Nightingale? Let us have a class of well-instructed, clever artisans, clever artisan-millwrights, machinists, architects. – Teachers in every department and subdivisions of useful science and learning, leaving it to the scholars to choose their branch of study . . .

As there is "no royal road to learning," everything possible should be done to render University College popular, and to induce families from a distance to avail themselves of its privileges. If first class professors can continue to be provided, and the patronage not be prostituted, Toronto may become famous as a great seat of learing.

The results of a former enquiry into the management of the finances of the University was exceedingly discreditable to all concerned. What it would be now we really cannot tell. In the Legislature, such seemed to be the avidity for wealth, that this writer shrunk from even asking for a Committee. Exposures of carelessness or fraud in Canada are only useful to teach clever knaves how to cheat more scientifically. *Foi est tout* is now often rendered, "dollars are every thing.". . .

Guide to Mackenzie's Newspapers

Information on Mackenzie's printing career is scattered. Further detail than that given below might be found in the Lindsey and Kilbourn biographies, in J. J. Talman, "The Printing Presses of William Lyon Mackenzie, prior to 1837," *Canadian Historical Review*, XVIII, 4 (December, 1937), 414-18; and E. Firth, *Early Toronto Newspapers, 1793-1867*, (Toronto, 1961). Invaluable for the American years are Lillian Gates' articles on *Mackenzie's Gazette*, and the *Volunteer*. See bibliography.

The Colonial Advocate (1824-34)

Originally published in Queenston, Upper Canada on May 18, 1824, and reputedly printed across the border by the Lewiston *Sentinel*. Late in 1824, Mackenzie moved to York and within a short time had his presses destroyed by the outraged tories on June 6, 1826. After resuming publication in December, the *Colonial Advocate* remained relatively unchanged in format until the eighteen thirties. In December of 1833, the paper underwent a minor change when the title was shortened to *The Advocate*, and Mackenzie's brother-in-law, Peter Baxter, took an active role in the proprietorship and publication of the newspaper. The last issue apappeared on November 4, 1834. Circulation figures for the *Advocate* are uncertain, but before 1830, Mackenzie often claimed between 400 and 500 subscriptions. Its terms remained static throughout the ten years, £1 per annum, whether delivered in town or sent by mail to rural areas.

The Correspondent and Advocate (1834-36)

Formerly *The Correspondent*, it was published by a fellow Reformer, Rev. William J. O'Grady. Its first issue November 13, 1834 announced that Mackenzie's extreme preoccupation with provincial politics and municipal government had forced him to withdraw

147

from the *Advocate*, but that his name "has a magic in it that strikes terror into toryism . . . and shall find an asylum, though humble, in the columns of this journal." Mackenzie submitted editorials to the newspaper on an irregular basis until mid-1836. At that time he announced that he was never concerned "either directly or indirectly in the establishment of the *Correspondent and Advocate*."

The Welland Canal (1835)

Only three numbers of this journal were ever printed, from December 16-30, 1835. A result of Mackenzie's appointment as a Director of the Welland Canal Company in 1835, this newspaper attempted to expose the Compact's misuse of public funds. Its sensational headline disclosed, "If the Welland Canal now gives a return of £4,000, to doubt whether in a few years it will pay £25,000, is no more reasonable than to doubt whether a Calf, if it lives can ever become a Cow. Extract of a letter by Chief Justice Robinson to Mr. President Merritt, December 18, 1834." A libel suit resulted, with a token fine assessed against Mackenzie for two shillings.

The Constitution (1836-37)

This radical journal began publication on the auspicious date, July 4, 1836. Mackenzie's son, James, was advertised as the publisher, with himself as editor. Printed on an expanded format with new presses and types imported from New York, the paper sold at $4 per annum. Its last complete issue was printed on November 29, 1837, and its type was being set on the 6th of December when it was brought to an abrupt end by the loyalist forces who invaded Mackenzie's printing office. His later estimates of his assets at this point were considerable: – "the finest, largest, newest printing establishment in the colonies, 20,000 volumes of books in my store, with a bindery, and the bible and testament in stereotype, plates, much stationery, &c, value $13,000 to $15,000, while on my books were $9,000 to $10,000 in debts, many of them of course, not good."

Mackenzie's Gazette
(1838-40)

Mackenzie's first newspaper in exile, the *Gazette* was published in New York on May 12, 1838 with a projected subscription list of 4,000. The nominal proprietor was his brother-in-law, Peter Baxter, and the terms of the newspaper much the same as his earlier weeklies. Gradually subscriptions dwindled, and the paper was moved to Rochester where it began publication on February 23, 1839. Within a few short months it was again in financial trouble, and Mackenzie himself was jailed for fomenting revolution against Canada in June of 1839. He continued to edit the paper from the Rochester jail until his release in the spring of 1840. Then, for a short time in the summer of 1840 it ceased publication briefly, then revived and finally died on December 23, 1840. In deep financial distress, Mackenzie simply stated, "I am unable to continue without such a weekly loss as would soon turn my family out of doors."

The Volunteer
(1841-42)

The first issue was printed in Rochester on April 17, 1841. Shifting in emphasis from American to Canadian politics, it concentrated upon the Canadian parliament and the ministry of Lord Sydenham. But it was published on a shoestring, and only lasted a year. During the last month of publication from April to May 10, 1842, Mackenzie announced that he had not secured a dollar through the mails. Its particular earmark as a journal was its use of arresting graphics to catch the attention of the few readers it could command.

The New York Examiner
(1843)

This publication had a very brief run of five issues from September 30, 1843 to November 11, 1843. Initially it seemed a much larger operation than the *Volunteer,* announcing as it did a much larger format, and a circulation of 3,000 copies. The editorial policy was blatantly anti-Van Buren, whom it considered "a weed more dangerous than the Canada Thistle or Deadly Nightshade." The purpose of this short-lived paper may well have been to promote Mackenzie's forthcoming publications on Van Buren and on the lives of famous Irishmen.

Mackenzie's Weekly Message
(1852-56)
Toronto Weekly Message
(1856-60)

On its first masthead, dated Christmas Day, 1852, the *Message* carried the city of Toronto coat of arms, and the motto, "Industry, Integrity, Intelligence." The terms of the paper were $2 per annum with no orders taken on credit outside of the city limits, or 2½ d. per issue at three locations within the city. Beginning with a professed circulation of under 1,000 in 1852, Mackenzie estimated by 1854 that subscriptions could be boosted easily to 5,000 or 6,000. Such expansion he however considered unwarranted because of his small share of government patronage and advertising contracts, and the difficulties of recovering outstanding accounts. In 1856, the newspaper changed its title to the *Toronto Weekly Message* as further acknowledgement of its metropolitan character. The paper ceased publication on September 15, 1860, almost one year before his death.

For Further Reading

Books-General

Blau, Joseph (ed). *Social Theories of Jacksonian Democracy.* Indianapolis: Bobbs-Merrill, 1954.

Clark, S. D. *Movements of Political Protest in Canada, 1640-1840.* Toronto: University of Toronto Press, 1959.

Craig, Gerald. *Upper Canada: The Formative Years, 1784-1841.* Toronto: McClelland and Stewart, 1963.

Cole, G. D. H. *Chartist Portraits.* London: Macmillan, 1965, 2nd ed.

Dent, J. C. *The Story of the Upper Canadian Rebellion.* 2 vols. Toronto: C. B. Robinson, 1885.

Dunham, Aileen. *Political Unrest in Upper Canada, 1815-36.* London: Published for the Royal Colonial Institute by Longmans, Green and Co., 1927.

Firth, Edith. *The Town of York 1815-34.* Vol. 2. Toronto: Champlain Society, 1966.

Guillet, E. C. *The Lives and Times of the Patriots.* Don Mills: Ont. Publishing Company, 1938.

Halévy, Elie. *The Growth of Philosophical Radicalism.* Boston: Beacon Press, 1960.

Hobsbawm, Eric. *Primitive Rebels: Studies in Archaic Forms of Social Movement in the 19th and 20th Centuries.* Manchester: University Press, 1959.

Kesterton, W. H. *A History of Journalism in Canada.* Toronto: McClelland and Stewart, 1967.

Kelley, Robert L. — *The Transatlantic Persuasion: The Liberal-Democratic Mind in the Age of Gladstone.* New York: A Knopf, 1969.

Meyers, Marvin. — *The Jacksonian Persuasion: Politics and Belief.* New York: Vintage Books, 1960.

Mott, F. L. — *American Journalism, A History, 1690-1960.* New York: Macmillan, 1962.

Read, D.B. — *The Canadian Rebellion of 1837.* Toronto: C. B. Robinson, 1896.

Schenk, H. G. — *The Mind of the European Romantics: An Essay in Cultural History.* London: Constable, 1966.

Smout, T. C. — *A History of the Scottish People, 1560-1830.* New York: Scribner's, 1969.

Thompson, E. P. — *The Making of the English Working Class.* New York: A. Knopf, 1963.

Books-Biographical

Colombo, John (ed.). — *The Mackenzie Poems by W. L. Mackenzie and J.R. Colombo.* Toronto: Swan Publishing Co., 1966.

Fairley, Margaret (ed.). — *The Selected Writings of William Lyon Mackenzie.* Toronto: Oxford University Press, 1960.

Flint, David. — *William Lyon Mackenzie: Rebel Against Authority.* Toronto: Oxford University Press, 1971.

Kilbourn, William. — *The Firebrand: William Lyon Mackenzie and the Rebellion in Upper Canada.* Toronto: Clarke Irwin, 1956.

Lindsey, Charles. — *The Life and Times of William Lyon Mackenzie.* Toronto: P. Randall, 1862, 2 vols. (Coles Canadiana Reprint edition, 1971).

| | *William Lyon Mackenzie.* Toronto: Morang & Co., 1912, vol. IX of *The Makers of Canada* Series, edited by G. G. S. Lindsey. |
| Smith, William. | *Political Leaders of Upper Canada.* Toronto: Thomas Nelson, 1931. |

Articles

Armstrong, F. H.	"The York Riots of March 23, 1832," *Ontario History*, LV (June, 1963), 61-72.
————.	"The Reformer as Capitalist: William Lyon Mackenzie and the Printers' Strike of 1836," *Ontario History* (September, 1967), 187-96.
————.	"William Lyon Mackenzie, First Mayor of Toronto: A Study of a Critic in Power," *Canadian Historical Review*, XLVIII (December, 1967), 309-31.
————.	"William Lyon Mackenzie: the persistent hero," *Journal of Canadian Studies* (August, 1971), 21-36.
Gates, Lillian F.	"The Decided Policy of William Lyon Mackenzie," *Canadian Historical Review*, XL (September, 1959), 185-208.
————.	"*Mackenzie's Gazette:* An Aspect of the American Years," *Canadian Historical Review*, XLVI (December, 1965), 323-45.
————.	"W. L. Mackenzie's *Volunteer* and the First Parliament of United Canada," *Ontario History*, LIX (September, 1967), 163-83.
Mackay, R. A.	"The Political Ideas of William Lyon Mackenzie," *Canadian Journal of Economics and Political Science*, II (February, 1937), 1-22.

Moir, J. S.   "Mr. Mackenzie's Secret Reporter," *Ontario History*, LV (December, 1963), 205-13.

Rea, J. E.   "William Lyon Mackenzie – Jacksonian?" *Mid-America*, L (July, 1968), 223-35.

Mackenzie's Publications

Essay on Canals and Inland Navigation. Queenston: *Colonial Advocate*, 1824.
The Catechism of Education. York: *Colonial Advocate*, 1830.
Sketches of Canada and the United States. London: E. Wilson, 1833.
A New Almanack for the Canadian True Blues, by Pat Swift. Toronto: *Colonial Advocate*, 1834.
The Seventh Report from the Select Committee on Grievances, Upper Canada, House of Assembly. Toronto: M. Reynolds, Printer to the Hon. The House of Assembly, 1835.
Mackenzie's Own Narrative of the Late Rebellion. Toronto: Palladium Office, 1838.
The Productions of the Evangelists and Apostles: A Faithful and True Translation of the Scripture of the New Testament. Toronto: W. L. Mackenzie, 1837.
The Caroline Almanack, and American Freeman's Chronicle for 1840. Rochester: *Mackenzie's Gazette*, 1839.
The Lives and Opinions of Benjamin Franklin Butler, U. S. District Attorney for the Southern District of New York, and Jesse Hoyt, Counsellor at Law, formerly Collector of Customs for the Port of New York. Boston: Cooke and Co., 1845.
The Sons of Emerald Isle, or Lives of One Thousand Remarkable Irishmen. New York: Burgess and Stringer, 1845.
The Life and Times of Martin Van Buren. Boston: Cooke and Co., 1846.
Head's Flag of Truce. Toronto: *Mackenzie's Weekly Message*, n.d.
The Canadian Repealer's Almanac for the Year 1856. Toronto: *Weekly Message Office*, December, 1855.
Almanac of Freedom and Independence for 1860. Toronto: *Weekly Message Office*, December, 1859.